MW00809054

Given by:

Nancy Potter

In Memory of:

Angeline Whitford Douglas Potter

*Down by*

*the Old Mill Stream*

# Down by the Old Mill Stream

*Edited by*

*Linda Welters &*

*Margaret T. Ordoñez*

*The Kent State*

*University Press*

*Kent, Ohio,*

*& London*

# QUILTS IN RHODE ISLAND

© 2000 by

The Kent State University Press

Kent, Ohio 44242

ALL RIGHTS RESERVED

Library of Congress Catalog Card

Number 99-21671

ISBN 0-87338-627-2

Manufactured in China

05  04  03  02  01  00    5  4  3  2  1

Designed & composed in Monotype
Fournier by Will Underwood at The Kent
State University Press.
Printed & bound by Kings Time Printing
Press Ltd., Hong Kong.

Frontispiece: Engraving, "The Old Slater Mill," Pawtucket, Rhode Island, *Ballou's Pictorial,* 1855. Rhode Island Historical Society, Providence. Background: Fig. 39, Star, 1830s.

*Library of Congress Cataloging-in-Publication Data*

Down by the old mill stream : quilts in Rhode Island /
edited by Linda Welters and Margaret T. Ordoñez.

p.     cm.

Includes bibliographical references and index.

ISBN 0-87338-627-2 (alk. paper) ∞

1. Quilts—Rhode Island.  2. Textile industry—United States—
History—19th century.  I. Welters, Linda.  II. Ordoñez, Margaret T.

NK9112.D68      1999

746.46'09745—dc21      99-21671

British Library Cataloging-in-Publication data are available.

# Contents

# Foreword

IN THE 1970S AND 1980S QUILTS BECAME VALUED AS WORKS OF ART AND as material culture documents helping bring to light the untold but worthy stories of American quiltmakers. In the 1990s quilts are increasingly valued as textile scrapbooks which preserve the fabrics that graphically record the history of textiles in the United States. People interested in American history as told through quilts and extant textiles have eagerly awaited the published results of the Rhode Island Quilt Documentation Project. They will not be disappointed.

Just as every American schoolchild learns that Rhode Island is the smallest state in the union, everyone who ventures to understand textiles in the United States soon learns that Rhode Island is one of the most influential states. This tiny state made giant contributions to the textile industry. Cotton fabrics produced, dyed, and printed in Rhode Island undoubtedly appeared in quilts made in every state of the union.

Rhode Island played an important part in developing my own interests in textile history. A speaking engagement in the 1960s at a stitchery symposium held in the historic Slater Mill in Pawtucket, Rhode Island, fueled my own interest in studying the American textile industry. Impressed by a tour of the restored mill, I returned home, then in Connecticut, to read about Samuel Slater and his work. I soon discovered that the floor I had just walked on held the eighteenth-century spinning equipment that had launched the textile industry in this country. I learned about William and Amasas Sprague, who owned one of the largest cotton mills in the world in the nineteenth century, and discovered that their firm continued in business as the Cranston Print Works.

Several years later, when I decided to develop a textile unit for my ninth-grade home economics students, I remembered the Cranston Print Works in Rhode Island. In the 1960s Cranston offered a wonderful little swatched booklet that clearly illustrated the transformation of cotton greige goods into beautiful printed fabrics that could even be napped and embossed. This excellent teaching aid further raised my respect for this tiny New England state and its printed fabrics. I became and remained a fan of Rhode Island.

In the early 1980s when my interests turned to Victorian silk template quilts, Rhode Island again came to the fore. I learned about the Adeline Harris Sears signature quilt, acquired by the Metropolitan Museum of Art in 1996 (Fig. 1). This quilt is a strong candidate for the masterpiece of American silk template work. It includes the signatures of six presidents and numerous other mid-nineteenth-century worthies. Sarah Hale, editor of the leading nineteenth-century periodical for women, introduced this quilt in the April 1864 issue of *Godey's Lady's Book*. She noted that the then-anonymous "young lady from Rhode Island" was recording history in "an original and very womanly way."

*Down by the Old Mill Stream* reveals the stories of numerous other women and men from Rhode Island who worked in the remarkable tradition of Slater, the Spragues, and Sears. Truly, one cannot study quilts and textiles in depth without meeting Rhode Island. We are fortunate that the Rhode Island Quilt Documentation Project attracted notable scholars to write chapters for this book. The book has double value, because the editors, Linda Welters and Margaret Ordoñez, decided to pursue two distinct, but complementary, themes.

First of all, the book includes valuable analysis and interpretation of the numerous quilts documented by the project. The presentation flows clearly and reveals both unique and universal characteristics of Rhode Island quilts. The results add significantly to the wealth of data generated by all state project reports and will allow us to make further comparisons between the New England region and other areas of the country. Linda Welters and Catherine Cerny expertly handle the historical, cultural, and social analysis. Their essays are enriched by small historic vignettes that highlight special Rhode Island quilts. The variety of professionals and students who contributed these important blocks of information clearly attests to the depth of interest in quilt history research and documentation in Rhode Island.

The second theme of the book is textile science and technology. Gail Mohanty, Martin Bide, and Margaret Ordoñez provide rich and reliable reports on fabric production, textile dyes and colors, and printed fabrics. Their essays will help the reader understand the fabrics that were sold to quiltmakers across the country during the nineteenth century. I have always been fascinated by advertisements such as the one George P. Smith, wholesale dealer in dry goods in Pittsburgh, Pennsylvania, placed in the Wooster, Ohio, *Wayne County Democrat* newspaper on September 23, 1852.

FIG. 1. (*Opposite*) Signature quilt, 1857–64. Silk, 77 x 80 in. Made by Adeline Harris Sears (1839–1931). The Metropolitan Museum of Art, Purchase, William Cullen Bryant Fellows Gift, 1996 (1996.4). Photograph © 1996 The Metropolitan Museum of Art.

In 1864 the editors of *Godey's Lady's Book* published the pattern and a description for this quilt, attributing it to a "young lady from Rhode Island." The young woman was Adeline Sears of Providence, daughter of a mill owner. The quilt, in the Tumbling Blocks pattern, includes the signatures of 356 prominent men and women, including six U.S. presidents.

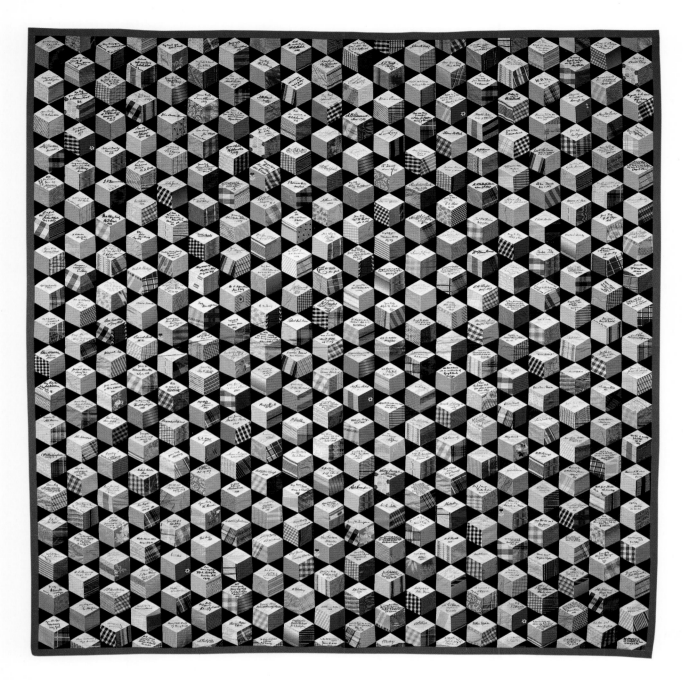

He advertised a mind-numbing variety of prints: "New Fall styles of Spragues, Unions, Perkins; Globe; Merrimack; Allen's, Dunnell's, Manchester; American; Ripkas; Garrets; and generally of other styles in Madder, Chintz, and steam work." Reading this book will help people facing similar lists truly understand the textiles offered by Rhode Island and other New England textile manufacturers to Americans from coast to coast.

Amos Bronson Alcott, a noted nineteenth-century New England teacher and philosopher, defined a good book as one "which is opened with expectation, and closed with profit." Such is the case with *Down by the Old Mill Stream: Quilts in Rhode Island*. Read it with pleasure—to understand the contributions of the state of Rhode Island to American quiltmaking and to the American textile industry. Then keep it handy on your reference shelves. If you love quilts and textiles, chances are good that you will want to revisit it often.

Virginia Gunn

# Preface

NEW ENGLAND LAGGED BEHIND IN THE GRASSROOTS EFFORT TO DOCU-
ment the nation's quilt history despite the early origins of quiltmaking in
this region. The state-by-state effort to record America's quilt heritage began in Kentucky in 1981 and quickly spread to other states.[1] When the Rhode
Island project began documenting quilts in 1992, in New England only Vermont Quilt Search had completed enough work to publish a book.[2] Now, at
the turn of the century, each New England state has a project in progress.

The Rhode Island Quilt Documentation Project (RIQDP) held its organizational meeting on December 19, 1990, at the University of Rhode Island's Kingston campus. Spearheaded by faculty and staff in the Textiles,
Fashion Merchandising and Design Department, the project aimed to survey quilts in private and public collections made in or used in Rhode Island
before 1949. Because women's history and social history had been well re-
searched in earlier projects, we chose to emphasize an underexplored topic,
production and consumption of fabrics found in quilts. This theme is particularly well suited to Rhode Island, the birthplace of the American textile
industry.

RIQDP was a collaborative project from the very beginning, involving
faculty, staff, and students at URI; consultants; newspaper reporters; volunteers from local quilters' organizations; staff of public libraries, historical houses, and museums; and the general public. Like other state projects,
RIQDP had three phases. Phase I consisted of project personnel and trained
volunteers registering, examining, and photographing 886 quilts (Figs. 2 &
3). Volunteers recorded the history of each quilt and elicited information
about the quiltmaker's background. Phase II involved exhibition at museums and historical societies and through other educational forums. Phase

III included presentation and publication of the project's findings through lectures, articles, and this book.[3]

RIQDP held sixteen public documentation days from 1992 to 1997. The public came with quilts, photographs of makers and their houses, genealogical records, and stories about the quiltmakers and quilts. We visited eighteen textile collections housed in institutions such as art museums, historical societies, or historical houses. Figure 4 shows locations of documentation days. The information gathered during the documentation days has been assembled into an archive that is housed in the Special Collections Department of the URI Library where it is accessible to quilters, students, and scholars. With the help of students, we compiled information into a computerized database for research purposes.

Quilts from the project have been exhibited numerous times as listed below:

*Selections from the Rhode Island Quilt Documentation Project.* Quilt Market, Boston, Massachusetts, May 22–24, 1993.

*The First Five Years: New England Documents Its Quilts.* New England Quilt Museum, Lowell, Massachusetts, October 2–November 11, 1993.

*Stitches in Time: Rhode Island Quilts.* Rhode Island Historical Society, Providence, Rhode Island, February 3–June 30, 1994.

*Nineteenth-Century Patchwork in Rhode Island.* Vermont Quilt Festival, Northfield, Vermont, July 8–10, 1994.[4]

*Pieced and Patched: Rhode Island Quilts and the Textile Industry.* Slater Mill
  Historic Site, Pawtucket, Rhode Island, September 15–December 20, 1994
*Selections from the Permanent Collection.* Smith's Castle, Wickford, Rhode
  Island, June 17–18, 1995.
*Home from the Mill: French-Canadian Quiltmakers in Rhode Island.* Musée
  Marsil, Saint-Lambert, Quebec, May 8–August 25, 1996; Musée Beaulne,
  Coaticook, Quebec, October 23–December 18, 1996; Slater Mill Historic
  Site, March 1–June 1, 1997.[5]

This project could never have been done without collaboration among
faculty, staff, and students at the University of Rhode Island; volunteers
from quilters' organizations; the public who brought quilts to documentation days and loaned them for exhibition and photography; staff at libraries, community centers, museums, historical societies, and historic houses

Fig. 3. RIQDP volunteer photographing a
detail of a quilt. RIQDP Archives.

FIG. 4. Map of Rhode Island with locations of documentation days.

Woonsocket •

Pawtucket •

Providence •

North Scituate •    Cranston •

• Barrington

Warwick •

Coventry •

East Greenwich •

• Portsmouth

Wickford •

North Kingstown •    • Middletown

• Little Compton

• Newport

Kingston •

• Ashaway

• Narragansett

• Westerly

• Block Island

who opened their doors to us; and newspapers and publishers who expressed interest in Rhode Island's quilt history. We are pleased and grateful to have worked with so many generous and talented individuals.

Projects like this one do not happen without financial support. For this we thank the Rhode Island Committee for the Humanities (RICH) for their unfailing enthusiasm for this project. RICH funded RIQDP through all phases—documentation, exhibition, and publication. We are especially grateful to Jane Civens and Thomas Roberts. RIQDP also received contributions from

Cranston Print Works, Eastern Color and Chemical Corporation, Linda Hilliard, Rita Hindle, Evelyn Siefert Kennedy, New England Quilters Guild, Ninigret Quilters, Seville Dyeing, the University of Rhode Island Foundation, VF Corporation through an International Textile and Apparel Association Grant, Westerly Community Credit Union, and Zeneca Corporation (now BASF).

Volunteers from Rhode Island's quilting groups—Narragansett Bay Quilters, Quilters by the Sea, and Ninigret Quilters—gave up many Saturdays to document quilts. Volunteers from these groups and other individuals included Christine Bagley, Barbara Barber, Caroline Barlow, Anne Beebe, Edna Bide, Jeffrey Butterworth, Kathy Cabrera, Joan Clarke, Patricia Cole, Karin Conopask, Patricia Coughlin, Pauline deLaar, Laura DeLuca, Veronica DeLuca, Gloria DePaola, Dorothy Depointe, Marie DeRoy, Susan DiPippo, Kathleen Donahue, Cynthia Drescher, Elizabeth Dubrovsky, Margaret Earle, Linda Eppich, Denise Fenick, Louanne Fox, Tess Fredette, Jean Fujio, Mary-Joyce Grinsel, Audrey Della Grotta, Linda Hilliard, Linda Hufnagel, Claudia Iannuccilli, Dorothy Keach, Irene King, Susan Kirby, Rose Koretski, Loretta Krebel, Agnes Krueger, Marie Lanzi, Dorothy LeClair, Kathy Lemay, Kathleen McAreavey, Elizabeth McClung, Susan McGreevy, Milly McLean, Diane Montenegro, Josephine Moore, Sandra Munsey, Peggie Narcizo, Drew Ordoñez, Libby Ordoñez, Elaine Papa, Fran Pedersen, Susan Perrine, Linda Perry, Elvia Purnell, Gail Putnam, Catherine Ramella, Arlene Reynolds, Joyce Reynolds, Joanne Rodgers, Carolyn Skaggs, Patricia Soares, Tora Sterregaard, Tracy Stilwell, Allison Stilwell-Cyr, Polly Swanson, and Marsha Wiencke.

Thanks are due to the many libraries, community centers, and museums that opened their doors to RIQDP. Sites for public documentation days included Barrington Public Library, Block Island Historical Society, Cranston Public Library, East Greenwich Preservation Society, University of Rhode Island (Kingston), Middletown Library, Newport Public Library, North Kingstown Free Library, North Scituate Community House, Portsmouth Public Library, Rhode Island Historical Society, Slater Mill Historic Site, Warwick Police Station, Westerly Library, and Woonsocket Public Library.

The following institutions permitted us to add quilts in their collections to the database: Ashaway Public Library, Babcock-Smith House (Westerly), Block Island Historical Society, Cranston Historical Society, Little Compton Historical Society, New England Quilt Museum, Newport Historical Society, Paine House (Coventry), Rhode Island Historical Society (Providence), Rhode Island School of Design Museum of Art (Providence), Slater Mill Historic Site (Pawtucket), Smith's Castle (Wickford), South

County Museum (Narragansett), URI Historic Textile and Costume Collection (Kingston), Varnum House (East Greenwich), Warwick Historical Society, and Watson House (Kingston).

Many thanks to Sally Neeld for her excellent color photography. She spent long days photographing quilts. Thanks to Linda Eppich at the Rhode Island Historical Society and Gail Fowler Mohanty at Slater Mill Historic Site for making space available for photography.

Appreciation is extended to the RICH scholars and evaluators for their insights. These include Jan Armstrong, Maury Klein, and Hetty Startup.

RIQDP received enthusiastic support from the University of Rhode Island. Special thanks go to Barbara Brittingham, Peg Brown, Dave Lavallee, Kevin Logan, David Maslyn, Leo O'Donnell, Jan Sawyer, and Beverly Swan. Heartfelt appreciation is due departmental secretary Valerie Morgan-Addison. Too numerous to thank individually are the many undergraduate and graduate students who participated in the project over the years.

For assistance with research and editing, we thank Diane Fagan Affleck, Edna Anness, Martin Bide, Sharon Hussey, Gail Fowler Mohanty, Lisa Nolan, Steve Nowortorski, Ron Onorato, Alfred Ordoñez, Carol Smith, and staff at the Rhode Island Historical Society Library and at the Spaulding House Research Library in Pawtucket.

Rhode Island Quilt Documentation Project Personnel
Linda Welters, Project Director
Margaret T. Ordoñez, Quilt Examination
Catherine A. Cerny, Quilt and Quiltmaker History
Alda Louise Ganze Kaye, Volunteers and Documentation Sites

*Notes*

1. Shelly Zegert, "The Quilt Projects: 15 Years Later," *Folk Art* (Spring 1996): 28–37.

2. Richard L. Cleveland and Donna Bister, *Plain and Fancy: Vermont's People and Their Quilts as a Reflection of America* (Gualala, Calif.: Quilt Digest Press, 1991).

3. One quilt from RIQDP was included in Kathryn F. Sullivan, *Gatherings: America's Quilt Heritage* (Paducah, Ky.: American Quilter's Society, 1995): 136–37. RIQDP participated in the symposium "What's American about American Quilts? A Research Forum on Regional Characteristics" at the Smithsonian Institute on March 18–19, 1995 (Margaret T. Ordoñez, "Nineteenth-Century Album Quilts in Rhode Island," *What's American about American Quilts—A Research Forum on Regional Characteristics*, [Washington, D.C.: Smithsonian Institution National Museum of American History, 1997] 2:10–17). Likewise, Rhode Island quilts shared the limelight at the regional symposium "What's New England about New England Quilts?" at Old Sturbridge Village on June 13, 1998 (Margaret T. Ordoñez and Linda Welters, "New England Calico Printing Reflected in Rhode Island Quilts: 1820–1860," *What's New England about New England Quilts?* [Sturbridge, Mass.: Old Sturbridge Village, in press]).

FIG. 5. The "Rhode Island Block," official logo of the RIQDP.

4. Eight graduate students curated this exhibition as part of a class on curatorial and conservation issues of quilts, Spring 1994, University of Rhode Island. Their research appears as short essays in this book.

5. A publication resulted: Linda Welters, *Home from the Mill: French-Canadian Quilt-makers in Rhode Island* (Saint-Lambert, Quebec: Musée Marsil, 1996).

# Introduction

LINDA WELTERS *&* MARGARET T. ORDOÑEZ

RHODE ISLAND HAS A UNIQUE PLACE IN AMERICAN QUILT HISTORY. THE water-powered revolution that began in the 1790s at Slater Mill on the Blackstone River in Pawtucket quickly spread throughout southern New England. Aspiring manufacturers erected mills on brooks, streams, and rivers all over Rhode Island, from Westerly to Woonsocket. The mills that dotted the landscape transformed Rhode Island's agricultural and maritime economy to a manufacturing one. The products of textile mills found their way across the United States. Quilts in other states sometimes contain fabrics with Rhode Island mill names stamped on them, thus providing evidence for the far-reaching distribution of Rhode Island–manufactured textiles.

Technological innovation in the textile industry continued in the Ocean State throughout the nineteenth century and into the twentieth. Although many companies had relocated to the southeastern states by the mid–twentieth century, Rhode Island still is home to over forty textile manufacturing firms. This past and present association with textile mills directed the focus of the Rhode Island Quilt Documentation Project to technology.

This book grew out of a larger effort across America to document the quilt history of each state and province. The scholarly study of quilts aligns with a material culture approach; through study of an object, the researcher analyzes and interprets the past. Objects are laden with meaning on multiple levels. Quilts are emblematic of a potpourri of current issues in American history, particularly women's social history. Tactile and visually appealing, quilts provide a foundation for discussing women's roles in American life. Women more often left records of themselves in products of the needle than of the pen. Quilts are sometimes the only tangible evidence a family has of an ancestor's accomplishments.

Multiculturalism is another issue that can be studied through quilts. Native Americans in some parts of the United States practiced patchwork (the Seminole in Florida) and quilting (the Sioux in the Dakotas). Of the many nationalities who came to America, only some made quilts. The aesthetic choices of the various cultural communities brought diversity to American quiltmaking that exemplifies the development of traditions in the manner of folkways.

Using quilts in the RIQDP database, contributors to *Down by the Old Mill Stream* explore the relationship between technological change in the production of textiles and the corresponding change in consumption patterns. The Industrial Revolution began with the application of water-powered machinery to the cotton-spinning process. Machine-spun cotton yarns became power-loomed fabric that could be dyed and printed inexpensively. Cotton yarns also served as a more economical thread for stitching and quilting than hand-spun linen thread. Advances in the dye and printing industries fueled the demand for calico prints.

Rhode Island's contribution to this transformation is significant. By the nineteenth century the growing number of mills in the state constantly sought better, more efficient methods to produce textiles for consumers. Fabrics in quilts made throughout the United States represent the textile industry's development in Rhode Island and New England.

The story of Rhode Island's quilts began early. The only quilted textile surviving from seventeenth-century New England is a fragment of a rosy-red silk petticoat belonging to Elizabeth Alden Pabodie (1622/23–1707) who is buried in the cemetery of the Congregational Church in Little Compton, Rhode Island. Backed in green fustian and quilted in a clamshell pattern, the fragment is now in the collections of The Pilgrim Society, Plymouth, Massachusetts. (Little Compton was formerly part of the Plymouth colony.) Elizabeth was the daughter of John and Priscilla Alden, who came to New England on the *Mayflower*. Elizabeth's direct descendants, like other Rhode Islanders, continued to make quilts in the succeeding centuries— Lydia Braman Peabody of Middletown (1808–1886) made quilts for each of her nine children.

Rhode Island's quilting traditions are tied to English settlement patterns in the region. Quilting, known in England and elsewhere in Europe since the Middle Ages, came to Rhode Island early. Quilts appear in seventeenth-century merchant records and probate inventories in New England, although no whole quilts survive to inform us of their physical characteristics. Toward the end of the eighteenth century, Rhode Islanders began to make quilts in earnest. With the entry of plentiful, inexpensive cotton textiles into the marketplace around 1825, a distinct regional style emerged. Patchwork strongly prevailed over appliqué and other fancywork until the crazy quilt era of the late nineteenth century. Quilters often set blocks on point with sashing but included no borders. They often used fabrics from sample runs in printworks.

The old adage "use it up, wear it out, make it do, or do without" was not lost on Rhode Island quiltmakers. A strong element of thriftiness is evident in Rhode Island quilts in the reuse of materials. For example, the earliest of the patchwork quilts incorporate toiles and furnishing cottons previously used as bed hangings.

A number of changes in the nineteenth century simultaneouly diminished regionalism in Rhode Island quiltmaking, starting with the arrival of immigrants of differing cultural heritages. Of the many who came to work in the textile mills, Irish and French Canadians created quilts. A distinct aesthetic is evident among light-colored, pieced, French-Canadian quilts.

Improved transportation and communication brought another change to Rhode Island quilts. National trends in quiltmaking began to influence Rhode Islanders as the century ended. The Log Cabins and crazy quilts popular in the rest of the nation also were favored by Rhode Islanders.

RIQDP documented numerous early quilts, some dating from the last half of the eighteenth century. Rhode Islanders own many quilts from the nineteenth century, still tucked away in the family chests. Because of the strength of these early quilts in the database and their ability to reveal the development of the textile industry, authors throughout the book have emphasized quilts made before 1900. Fabrics in these quilts are keys to identifying the technological developments in the dyeing and printing of textiles. These keys include the presence of new dyes (e.g., chrome yellow, Prussian blue, aniline black, azoic red) and the commercial use of new technologies (e.g., multicylinder printing, die-and-mill engravings, etching).

The book is organized in two parts. The first consists of five essays that focus on the cultural and social history of Rhode Island quilts as well as their significance as records of technological change in the textile industry.

In her essay on "Cultural Legacies," Linda Welters explores historical and cultural influences on the stylistic aspects of Rhode Island quilts as determined by the cultural groups that produced them. She discusses the development of early quilts beginning with whole-cloth and early patchwork types and continuing to the establishment of Rhode Island patchwork traditions. The essay addresses the growth of mills and changing demographics as they affected quiltmaking in Rhode Island.

In "Woven Documents" Gail Fowler Mohanty uses quilts to illustrate textiles produced in Rhode Island during three periods. The preindustrial period was characterized by both home production and the importation of fabrics from abroad. At the end of the eighteenth century, a transition occurred that added American factory-made textiles into the mix of products available to consumers. After 1815 and the introduction of the power loom, cotton fabrics such as plaids, stripes, and checks grew to dominate Rhode Island production until printing technology developed.

Martin Bide, in "Secrets of the Printer's Palette," investigates the coloring materials and their associated chemistry that created the cloth in Rhode Island quilts. Indigo, madder, quercitron, woods, and mineral colors are discussed as well as the new synthetic dyestuffs that appeared during the last half of the nineteenth century. He also explains the chemistry behind the printing techniques employed to achieve color on cloth, including resist and discharge methods, raised style, madder style, steam style, direct printing, pigment style, and the process to achieve Turkey red.

The technology of printing cloth and the development of that technology in Rhode Island are addressed by Margaret T. Ordoñez in "Technology Reflected." Beginning in the eighteenth century printers in the state stamped color onto linen and cotton fabrics. In the nineteenth century expanded printing operations provided new life to an oversupplied market for plain woven cotton fabrics. Advances in technology helped establish a well-grounded printing industry by midcentury, resulting in a greatly expanded choice of cotton fabrics for consumers. Quilts from the state reflect all these changes.

Finally, Catherine A. Cerny uncovers the meaning quilts hold for those who made them and who now own them, in "Social Connectedness." She establishes that a quilt reinforces ties among the maker and family, community, and nation. Her essay relates many stories of the value Rhode Island quilts hold for the descendants of the makers.

The second part of the book, "Stitches through Time: A Selection of Rhode Island Quilts," presents short essays about specific quilts that reflect the history of Rhode Island, tell a unique story, or exhibit outstanding aesthetic qualities. The stories related to Rhode Island quilts draw on superstitions that persisted in rural areas, pride in ancestry, frugality, small-town life, love, marriage, friendships, and family life. Many quilts are directly connected to the textile industry; quiltmakers and their families often owned or worked at mills.

This is not a book about beautiful quilts. While many of the quilts qualify as works of art, some are purely utilitarian. This does not lessen their usefulness as documents in relating the history of the production and consumption of textiles in Rhode Island. Utility quilts show the transition from hand- to machine-spun yarns, hand- to water-power loomed cloth, block- to cylinder-printed cottons, and naturally to synthetically dyed goods. Likewise, the heavy wear patterns typical of utility quilts speak to the needs of Rhode Island families for warm bed coverings rather than fancy "show" quilts.

To speak of quilts made within the borders of Rhode Island is somewhat limiting; these changed during its history. Before 1812, parts of southern Massachusetts belonged to Rhode Island; for example, Seekonk was part of Providence until 1862. In Rhode Island, the smallest state in the union, borders seem arbitrary. Many quiltmakers moved across state lines during their lifetimes, taking their quilts and quilting frames with them. This is particularly true for families that sought work in the regional textile industry. Some quiltmakers crossed state lines just for a day to join their friends over the quilting frame. Many communities are close together in southern New England. Quiltmakers in the areas of Connecticut and Massachusetts that border Rhode Island probably produced quilts that are quite similar to those found through RIQDP.

In many ways this book is not just a regional study; it contributes to the scholarship of both quilting and textile history. A distinct regional style in quilt patterns and fabrics, on the order of a folkway, is identifiable. As other New England state quilt documentation projects end, data about regional characteristics can be compared and conclusions drawn about regional folkways in quilting and the factors that influenced their development.

# Part One

*Essays on Culture,*

*Technology, and*

*Quilts in Rhode Island*

FIG. 6. Quilted petticoat, signed "AW" and dated "1770." Wool calimanco, striped wool lining, wool batting. Hand-quilted, 8–11 stitches per inch. Made by Anne Waterman Clapp (1746–1844). Rhode Island Historical Society (1982.76.3). RIQDP #506. (The short gown is a reproduction.)

Quilted petticoats preceded quilted bed covers in popularity. Worn with open-fronted gowns, such layered wool garments provided warmth in drafty houses. The motifs in the border—deer, birds, and flowers—are in the English tradition. Ann Waterman was a descendant of Samuel Gorton, the founder of Warwick, Rhode Island.

# Cultural Legacies

LINDA WELTERS

IN THE EARLY 1770S ANNE WATERMAN (1746–1844) OF WARWICK, Rhode Island, made a quilted wool petticoat with flowers, birds, deer, pineapples, and a feather scroll stitched into the border (Fig. 6). Perhaps she wore the petticoat with a long, open-fronted gown when she married John Clapp in 1775. Anne learned her needlework skills from her grandmother, Susannah Gorton, who had made a similar quilted petticoat some years before.[1] These two women, grandmother and granddaughter, exemplify the English heritage of many Rhode Island quilters. Their ancestors came to southern New England in search of religious freedom, bringing English ways with them. Englishwomen were renowned for their needlework skills, which they applied to both clothing and furnishings. These needlework skills included quilting, the act of stitching together two layers of fabric with batting in between, which had been practiced in England as early as the Middle Ages.[2]

This essay explores the stylistic aspects of Rhode Island quilts as determined by the cultural groups that produced them. At the close of the colonial period, most of Rhode Island's inhabitants were of English descent. The once-robust Native American population had been reduced severely by disease and warfare. Slaves obtained from Africa's western coast constituted another minority. In the nineteenth century, demographic changes altered the Anglo-American dominance of Rhode Island. After the 1820s the burgeoning textile industry attracted new immigrants from countries other than England. By 1900 Rhode Island's strong English heritage was moderated by Irish, French Canadian, Italian, Polish, and Portuguese influences.

Who among these many different cultural groups made quilts, and what were the characteristics of those quilts? Not surprisingly, Rhode Island's earliest quilts had strong ties to England in both style and fabrication. By the second quarter of the nineteenth century, Rhode Islanders had developed their own distinctive quiltmaking practices, at least partially in response to the growing local availability of printed cottons. Although the successive waves of immigrants who arrived to work in the state's textile mills came in contact with Yankee pieced quilts, not all of these new arrivals adopted the practice of quiltmaking. Toward the end of the nineteenth century, Rhode Islanders, like their quilting counterparts in other states, participated in national quilting trends.

*Rhode Island's Colonial Period*

Rhode Island originally was inhabited by two Algonquian-speaking Indian tribes, the Narragansetts and the Wampanoags. English occupation began in 1636 when dissident clergyman Roger Williams and his small band of followers left Massachusetts and founded the city of Providence at the head of Narragansett Bay. Other political and religious nonconformists followed, establishing their own towns at natural harbors along the coastline. The colony of Rhode Island developed a reputation for religious tolerance; soon Antinomians, Baptists, Quakers, Sephardic Jews, and Calvinist French Huguenots arrived in search of religious freedom.

Deteriorating relations between New England colonists and Native Americans erupted in conflict in 1675–76. A Wampanoag chief known as King Philip led an ill-fated attempt to force the colonists from Rhode Island and southeastern Massachusetts. The Narragansetts joined the cause, which culminated in the massacre of hundreds of Indians in the Great Swamp Fight of 1675. Those Indians who survived sought refuge with the Niantic Indians in the southern part of the state. With the death of King Philip in 1676 and the virtual extinction of the Wampanoags, English dominance over Rhode Island was assured.[3]

Early English settlement was confined to coastal lowlands extending along the shores of Block Island Sound and Narragansett Bay, including the islands in the Bay. As the years went by, the scarcity of coastal land forced expansion into the interior uplands, where settlers struggled to farm the stony, less fertile soil. In the eighteenth century, the colony of Rhode Island grew and prospered. Its extended coastline and relative scarcity of natural resources encouraged the development of a maritime economy. Providence and Bristol were active ports, but the city of Newport emerged as the major commercial and cultural center. It rivaled Boston, New York, and Philadelphia in importance. Across the Bay the rich farmlands of South County (North and South Kingstown) fostered the development of a plantation system similar to that of the southern colonies. African and Indian slaves, as well as indentured servants, provided the labor. These large coastal farms produced meat, cheese, butter, flax, wool, and a famous breed of horses known as the Narragansett Pacer.[4]

Rhode Island's successful maritime and agricultural economies fueled the profitable, but nefarious, triangle trade, for which the colony was famous. Newport, Providence, and Bristol sea captains transported molasses and sugar from the West Indies to Rhode Island to be processed into rum which was then traded along the African coast for slaves. The ships then sailed for the West Indies where their human cargo was exchanged for money and the ingredients to make more rum. Although the West Indies' plantation economy absorbed most of the slaves, some slaves came to Rhode Island with the captains.[5]

Slaves in Rhode Island predominantly resided in Newport and South County. At the height of the Narragansett planters' prosperity in 1755, African slaves were 11 percent of Rhode Island's population.[6] The slave trade finally was outlawed in Rhode Island in 1787.[7] In that same year, John Brown of Providence widened maritime horizons by sailing for the Orient, thus leading Rhode Island ship captains into the lucrative China and East India trade.

Success at agriculture and maritime pursuits created a gentry class that enjoyed material comforts. Beginning in the 1690s a gradual rise in the standard of living brought an increase in demand for consumer goods. The houses of the wealthy merchant-shipping families and plantation owners grew larger, and rooms were furnished in the English style. Newport, as well as other thriving colonial towns, supported a number of tailors, cabinetmakers, silversmiths, and other artisans. Most of the colony's textiles, a significant portion of household wealth, were imported from factors in England who shipped cloth of English manufacture as well as specialty fabrics from other textile-producing countries like Ireland, France, and India (Fig. 7).

By the end of the colonial period, Rhode Island was an outpost of English culture. The descendants of the few Native Americans who had survived the seventeenth century without being sold into slavery lived a marginal existence on their tribal lands in Charlestown.[8] African Americans fared no better. Even if they had been granted freedom by Quaker abolitionists or purchased their own freedom, they still found themselves living on the social margins.[9]

Few Rhode Island quilts from the colonial period survive. Fewer still have firm dates and provenance. To determine when quilts, quiltmaking, and patchwork first came to the area we must turn to documentary sources. These

*Documentary Evidence for Quilting*

Juſt Imported from London, Mancheſter and Liverpool, by

# STEWART and TAYLOR,

And to be Sold at their Store, the Weſt End of the Great Bridge, in Providence, Wholeſale and Retail,

A Variety of ENGLISH and INDIA GOODS,

ſuitable for the Seaſon, among which are the following Articles, viz. broadcloths of various colours, ratteens and bearſkins, duffils and baiſes, Mancheſter velvets and checks, a good aſſortment of Iriſh linens, dowlas, lawns and cambricks, figured and ſprigged lawn aprons and handkerchiefs, a good aſſortment of calicoes and chintz, ſhaloons, durants and tammies of various colours, calimancoes, taffeties, perſians, ozenbrigs, wool and cotton cards, beſt German and Engliſh ſteel, gunpowder, ſhot, lead, an aſſortment of hard ware and nails, a few crates of ſtone, glaſs and delph ware, looking glaſſes, and a variety of other articles, too tedious to enumerate.

N. B. Said Stewart and Taylor expeſt (as one of them has been at the above Places, and purchaſed their Goods from the Manufaſturers) they will be able to ſell as cheap as any on the Continent.

sources include wills and estate inventories, diaries, and other written records. Wills generally are not so explicit as inventories for which every possession was recorded and assessed, room by room, after a person of property had died.

Colonial inventories often list "bedsteads," "beds," "bedding," and/or "furniture." The word "bedstead" indicated a wooden frame to support the "bed" and "furniture" and could be either a low bed or a high bed with posts. "Beds" were mattresses of ticking or tow-cloth filled with, in order of desirability, feathers, flocks of sheeps' wool, or straw. William Weeden, in his social history of Rhode Island, observed that until 1750 the feather bed was "the most constant unit of domestic comfort."[10] "Furniture" consisted of textiles used as bedding: sheets, blankets, bedspreads, coverlets, rugs, quilts, pillow biers (cases), bolsters, and hangings.

Evidence for quilts in Rhode Island first appears in early eighteenth-century inventories. A study of Providence probate records from 1670 to 1726 uncovered five quilt references ranging in date from 1712 to 1721.[11] The probate records of the town of South Kingstown, incorporated in 1723, reveal that in 1726 a quilting frame worth six shillings was stored in Thomas Mumford's garret.[12] Another South Kingstown "Quilting Frame & Barrs" in the chamber of English immigrant Jonathon Oatly's house was valued at £4 in 1756.[13] These early mentions of quilting frames suggest that the families of South Kingstown in the heart of plantation country were quilting as early as 1726. Such frames could have been used to quilt either bed covers or petticoats.

Other South Kingstown probate records listed mostly beds, bedsteads, and furniture until Capt. John Peck Rathbun's 1782 inventory which included two calico bed quilts, one with a colored ground and one with purple and white stripes.[14] Toward the end of the century, inventories listed quilts more frequently. Perhaps the appraisers' descriptions became more thorough, but another explanation is that the rise in popularity of quilts correlates with the growing availability and affordability of the fabrics, batting, and thread necessary for making quilts. The 1799 inventory of Ruhamah Champlin listed three bed quilts; her will, made one month prior to her death, bequeathed "one bed quilt of a litish colour" to her son.[15] Also in 1799 Mary Babcock bequeathed to her beloved daughter Polly Babcock "one blue bed quilt."[16] John Robinson's 1801 inventory contained a "moss coloured bed quilt" and a calico coverlet "of Patch Work" valued at $2.50.[17] The 1806 inventory of widow Elizabeth Potter listed two bed quilts and a quilted petticoat.[18]

The number of quilts in South Kingstown inventories grew in comparison to other bed coverings by the mid-1820s. William Browning's 1825 inventory listed four quilts and a copperplate spread.[19] The 1826 inventory of Taber Tucker listed six quilts and ten coverlets.[20] The 1825 inventory of Joseph Babcock valued what must have been a spectacular bed quilt at $15 and quilting frames at 33¢.[21] One can only wonder why the appraiser found the quilt three to six times more valuable than quilts in other inventories. Possible explanations include precious fabrics, detailed piecing, and fine stitching.

The names in these inventories—Champlin, Potter, Babcock, Robinson, Browning—are those of South County's prominent Narragansett planter families. Quilts appeared mainly in the inventories of these prosperous individuals. The probate records do not indicate under what types of bed covers South County's minority populations slept. Occasionally a decedent willed a bed and bedding to a "Negro" or an Indian in the household;

bedding might have included a quilt or coverlet. Both African Americans and Native Americans might have helped stitch quilts in the households in which they worked as servants.

Diaries are another source of information about quilting. Few eighteenth-century Rhode Island women's diaries exist.[22] One is the diary of Susannah Martin, a young woman coming of age in Providence in 1799 who mentions quilting often.[23] In one nine-day period, a succession of three quilts were put in the frame at her house, quilted by Susannah and a number of others. One of the quilts belonged to her grandmother. On April 10, the third day of quilting, Susannah and her sister arose before 8:00 A.M. and again "went to quilting" after which she complained, "Quilting I find is mighty lazy work & I shall be thankful when it is done to feel more active." Susannah enjoyed a lively social life that sometimes included assisting others with quilting when visiting. Interspersed among her entries are references to other types of needlework: "finished my bonnet," "start to work on my gown," and "tufted till past 8." She makes no reference to patchwork or piecing, implying that the quilts made in her mother's household were whole-cloth quilts. The speed with which they were quilted excludes elaborate quilting patterns.

These limited documentary sources, then, indicate that although quilts existed in Rhode Island households in the eighteenth century, they were not common. The infrequent mention of patchwork argues that early Rhode Island quilts were mostly whole-cloth quilts. These conclusions are supported by documentary research in other areas along the Atlantic seaboard settled by the English.[24]

*Early Whole-Cloth Quilts*

Rhode Island's earliest extant quilts reflect the descriptions in the written records. They also testify to colonial New England's emulation of European taste. Colonial gentry looked to London for the latest styles in both apparel and home furnishings. London, in turn, absorbed new fashions emanating from France, especially the court at Versailles. This fascination with European sources is especially evident in the fabrics from which Rhode Island's earliest quilts are made.

Fabrics in Rhode Island's earliest quilts came from England, France, and India. England was well known throughout the world for quality wools as early as the Middle Ages. By 1700 wool growers, manufacturers, and merchants had developed and marketed successfully a wide variety of woolen and worsted cloths for many end uses. In the eighteenth century fine silks from the looms of Spitalfields and printed cottons were added to the list of textiles manufactured in Britain. France was home to the world-famous silk weaving of Lyon, print works including the famous toiles de Jouy, and the stuffed white work known as Marseilles quilting. Indian cottons brought home on East India companies' ships had been received enthusiastically throughout Europe and America.

Wool fabrics were common in early quilted petticoats. An elaborately quilted wool petticoat is the earliest dated example of Rhode Island quilting.[25] It was quilted by three professional seamstresses from the village of Kingston and worn by Alice Tripp of Kingston at her marriage to Thomas Casey of Newport in 1745.[26] Quilted petticoats were at the height of their popularity in England in the mid–eighteenth century, and colonial belles like Alice copied this fashion. The petticoat's outer fabric is English calimanco, a glazed wool fabric in a twill weave. The manufacture of calimanco and other worsted cloths was the specialty of Norwich, England. Calimanco was popular in the colonies for men's banions (dressing gowns) and women's winter dresses as well as for home furnishings. Calimanco also was woven in Rhode Island by professional weavers such as Martin Read of Narragansett.[27]

Five other eighteenth-century quilted petticoats with a Rhode Island provenance survive in Rhode Island collections.[28] All but one were made of calimanco. These petticoats, as far as we know, belonged to women of the gentry class. However, indentured servants wore them also; an ad in *The Newport Mercury* described a twenty-five-year-old runaway Indian woman as dressed in a "light striped short gown and a black quilted petticoat."[29] Elaborate petticoats sometimes were recycled into the centers of bed quilts after they went out of fashion in the 1790s. The RIQDP database includes three such petticoat quilts, including one of pink calimanco that belonged to the John Browns, Providence's leading family.

New England historian Jane Nylander surmises that quilting was transferred from petticoat to bed around the middle of the eighteenth century.[30] Numerous quilted calimanco bed covers in solid colors of dark blue, light blue, green, red, and pink survive in American collections, attesting to the widespread use of this fabric for bed covers. Dark blue was the color of six of the nine wool whole-cloth quilts in Rhode Island, the finest of which is illustrated in Figure 8. This quilt could have been made in Rhode Island from imported calimanco or purchased ready-made. Quilted petticoats in silk and wool were made in English factories, then stored in petticoat warehouses for sale or distribution domestically and abroad.[31] Newspapers on both sides of the Atlantic advertised bed quilts and quilted petticoats.[32]

The calimanco quilt in Figure 8 is stitched in bold curvilinear motifs in an all-over pattern incorporating an urn of flowers, foliage, and scrolling borders. Its neoclassical elements help to date it circa 1800. The other eight Rhode Island wool whole-cloth quilts are not so elaborately quilted nor are the fabrics so highly glazed. These features suggest that perhaps they were

FIG. 8. Whole-cloth quilt, ca. 1800. Wool calimanco top, wool back, wool batting, 97 x 90 in. Hand-quilted, 9 stitches per inch. Maker unknown. Collection of Little Compton Historical Society. RIQDP #637.

English merchants exported both fabrics and ready-made goods to America in the eighteenth century, including a glazed wool called calimanco. John Banister of Newport placed an order for scarlet, brown, and "Blew emboss'd" calimanco in 1744. Boston merchants advertised "Callimancoe" quilts from London and Bristol in 1760. This quilt could have been purchased ready-made or stitched in Rhode Island from imported calimanco.

the products of domestic manufacture in imitation of imported calimanco quilts. They are quilted in simple diamond patterns or in repeated blocks (of radiating flower petals) arranged on point. The backs of these quilts are often pale yellow or undyed woolen cloth.

In the early years, Rhode Islanders made whole-cloth quilts from a wide variety of fabrics in addition to wool (see Table 1). Printed cottons represent the largest category. Typical printed fabrics found in whole-cloth tops are chintzes, calicoes, copperplate toiles in monochromatic color schemes (red, brown, blue), and blue resist prints. Such fabrics almost always were imported from England, France, or India.

The printed fabrics in the whole-cloth quilts display all of the major printing techniques: block, resist, copperplate, and cylinder. They range in date from 1760 to 1840 and correspond to the golden age of printed textile design. The earliest RIQDP-dated whole-cloth quilt belongs to a set of copperplate hangings made for a four-poster Chippendale bed.[33] Designs of printed fabrics in whole-cloth quilts include birds with arborescent motifs

TABLE I

*Whole-Cloth Quilts by Fabric Type*

|  | 1750–1839 | 1840–1899 | 1900–1949 | TOTAL |
|---|---|---|---|---|
| Wool Solids | 9 | – | – | 9 |
| Silk Solids | – | 1 | – | 1 |
| Cotton Prints |  |  |  |  |
|    copperplate toile | 4 | – | – | 4 |
|    chintz/calico | 10 | 5 | 5 | 20 |
|    blue resist/china blue | 1 | – | – | 1 |
| White work |  |  |  |  |
|    corded/stuffed | 5 | – | – | 5 |
|    candlewick | 1 | – | – | 1 |
|    embroidered | – | 1 | – | 1 |
|    loom–woven covers | 1 | 1 | – | 2 |
| Petticoat Quilts |  |  |  |  |
|    wool | 2 | – | – | 2 |
|    silk | 1 | – | – | 1 |
| TOTAL | 34 | 8 | 5 | 47 |

or urns, florals, stripes, and pillar prints. Many of the quilts made from glazed cotton prints were never washed, so their tops remain shiny and crisp. Quilting stitches range from four to eight stitches per inch and were executed in diamond, chevron, floral, and circular patterns. Some early quilts in the RIQDP database had complex quilting patterns, informing us that not all early quilts had plain quilting. The quilting on the earlier examples employed linen thread. Four examples of printed whole-cloth quilts can be seen elsewhere in this book.

Rhode Islanders continued to make whole-cloth quilts and comforters from printed textiles throughout the nineteenth and into the early twentieth century. The printed cottons in the post-1840 quilts lack distinction, placing them in the utility category. Often these bedcovers are tied rather than quilted. Two exceptions are a quilt belonging to a set of cylinder-printed bed hangings, circa 1840, that was handed down in the family of Governor Theodore F. Green; and a brown silk quilt, circa 1875, made from the 1734 wedding dress of Content Norton Thatcher of Martha's Vineyard, Massachusetts.[34]

Other whole-cloth quilts were made of plain white cotton. When English and Dutch merchants opened the East India trade in the early seventeenth century, the exporting of fine white Indian cottons began. The heyday of New England's China and East India trade, the 1780s through the 1820s, coincided with the neoclassical style in the decorative arts. This style popularized a number of techniques for making white-work bed covers—stuffed and corded work known as Marseilles quilting, candlewicking, and embroidery.

The Marseilles quilt originated in the seventeenth century in Provence, France, and was advertised in the colonies as early as 1749.[35] The British soon achieved a machine-made version, "quilted in the loom," which also was called a Marseilles quilt. The handmade, stuffed and corded Marseilles covers had all-over designs incorporating vases or baskets of flowers in the center surrounded by wreaths, grapes, and vines, or feather scrolls.

White-work bed covers in Rhode Island date from 1790 to 1856. Included in this group are five handmade Marseilles quilts, one candlewick spread (1827), one embroidered spread (1856), and two loom-woven Marseilles covers. A Marseilles quilt dated 1815 made by Mary Remington of East Greenwich is illustrated in Susan Swan's *Plain and Fancy*.[36] The tan-colored Marseilles quilt seen in Figure 9 was made by Mary Talbot Pitman in Providence or Wickford in 1807–8. The cotton lining of this quilt reportedly was brought from India. It is a tour-de-force of stitchery with sixteen stitches

FIG. 9. Whole-cloth quilt, 1807–8. Cotton top and back, handmade fringe, 102 x 95 in. Hand-quilted, 16 stitches per inch. Made by Mary Talbot Pitman. Collection of the Cocumscussoc Association. RIQDP #681

Mary Talbot of Providence made this exquisitely worked Marseilles-style quilt to commemorate her marriage to John Pitman. The marriage took place when Rhode Island was active in the China and East India trade. The plain white backing of this quilt reputedly came from India, where fine cotton fabrics were made long before the Industrial Revolution.

per inch and handmade netted fringes on three sides. Unlike the other white-work bed covers in our database, it has a radiating flower at the center instead of a basket. Interestingly, Rhode Island's Marseilles quilts with a known provenance come from some of the state's oldest towns established by English settlers along the upper part of Narragansett Bay—Wickford, East Greenwich, Warwick, and Providence. Only one of the white-work bed coverings belonged to a family not of English extraction. This woven Marseilles cover, circa 1870, was originally owned by Josephine LaFleche Ferron of France, who gave it to her daughter Josephine when she married in Providence, Rhode Island, in 1920.

The English had a long tradition of both pieced and appliquéd textiles, which they incorporated into quiltmaking as early as 1700. England's oldest extant patchwork quilt, the so-called Levens Hall quilt, circa 1708, is pieced and appliquéd from seventeenth-century Indian chintzes.[37] This quilt exemplifies the two methods for making quilt tops that would later develop in the United States—patchwork and appliqué.

*Early Patchwork Quilts*

Patchwork was the method used to make America's oldest quilt, dated 1726, in Montreal's McCord Museum.[38] It is made of silk triangles arranged around a central element; such an arrangement is known as a medallion quilt. Paper templates were used to piece the top with exactness. Examples of later eighteenth-century patchwork similar to the McCord quilt are found in British, Dutch, and American museums, indicating that the style was fairly widespread by 1800.[39] A medallion quilt made by the mother of Anna Tuels for her wedding in 1785 is New England's earliest extant example. Alice Morse Earle, the antiquarian, wrote of an elaborate quilt completed in the 1790s that she had seen in Narragansett. It contained pieces of a 1738 wedding dress. The quilt was sent to Newport when George Washington visited "to grace the bed upon which the hero slept."[40]

Another type of early quilt, the appliquéd chintz style, is known today as *broderie perse*. This type of quilt is absent from the RIQDP database. In other areas of the country, old Indian palampores (printed cotton bedspreads) or European calicoes were cut apart and stitched to new white grounds to create quilts and spreads in all-over patterns. Examples are illustrated in numerous quilt and folk art books.[41] Appliquéd chintz quilts are said to be the forerunners of the appliqué block quilts that appeared in the 1840s in the mid-Atlantic states and rapidly spread west and south. Rhode Island quiltmakers in our database produced only six nineteenth-century cotton appliqué quilts. The lack of eighteenth-century appliquéd chintz quilts implies that appliqué was not the technique of choice among early Rhode Island quiltmakers.

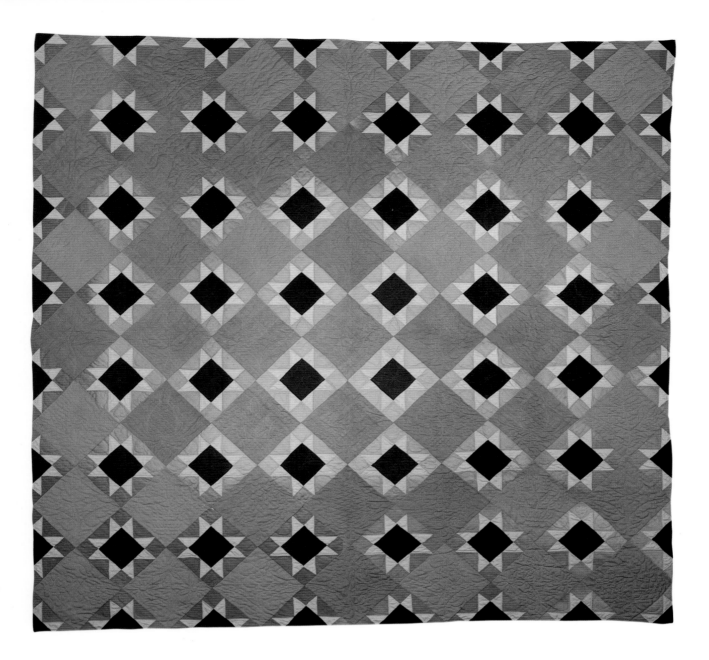

Rhode Islanders preferred piecing to appliqué when forming whole tops from two or more fabrics. The transition from whole-cloth quilts to patchwork quilts in Rhode Island began late in the eighteenth century when women began assembling strips, squares, and triangles of fabrics into tops for quilts. A few of the oldest quilts were pieced from wool fabrics, such as the one illustrated in Figure 10, but the majority were made from printed cottons. Strip, medallion, and block styles resulted.

Strip quilts capitalized on the vertical patterns of printed cottons, particularly those with pillars, floral stripes, and rainbows. The oldest strip quilt incorporates a pillar print and dates from the 1790s.[42] One from a century later utilizes a striped fabric recycled from a full skirt of the hoopskirt era (1855–69); the fold marks of cartridge pleats where the skirt joined the bodice are still visible.[43] The other early patchwork quilts were pieced from rectangles of fabrics that had either irregularly shaped patches arranged around a center block (medallion style) or repeating blocks of simple patchwork (block style). A number of these quilts were made for four-poster beds as evidenced by their cut-out corners. Strip quilts and simple patchwork patterns continued to be made throughout the nineteenth century and were among the first styles to be picked up by immigrant families.

The RIQDP uncovered only a few medallion-style quilts from the early decades of the nineteenth century. The quilt illustrated in Figure 11 has a newer patchwork section, whose fabrics date from about 1840, applied to the center of a much older quilt. It was passed down through a family with many old Rhode Island names, all descended from English settlers. Its fabrics suggest that it was renovated around 1838 when the owner's great-great grandmother, Elizabeth Bailey (1800–1888), married George Stanhope (1799–1862) in Newport. A similar quilt dated 1790–1825 is illustrated in *Clues in the Calico*.[44]

FIG. 10. (*Opposite*) Star quilt, ca. 1800. Wool top, wool and linen back, 107 x 98 in. Hand-quilted in decorative designs, 10–12 stitches per inch. Maker unknown. Varnum House, East Greenwich, Rhode Island. RIQDP #769.

This quilt exemplifies early patchwork in Rhode Island. Simple patchwork blocks are arranged on point without a border. The quiltmaker's sewing skills show in the details—the plain blue blocks are quilted in basket, wreath, pineapple, and flower motifs. The top is a professionally made wool fabric while the back appears to be a homespun, home-woven linsey-woolsey.

FIG. 11. Medallion quilt, ca. 1840. Cotton top, back, and batting, 97 x 95¾ in. Hand-pieced and hand-quilted, 10 stitches per inch in border, 4 stitches per inch in pieced section. Possibly made by Elizabeth Bailey Stanhope (1800–1888). Private collection. RIQDP #1.

This quilt for a four-poster bed descended through a family with many old Rhode Island names such as Almy, Babcock, Potter, Watson, Weeden, Bailey, and Stanhope. The quilter used the medallion format, an early form of patchwork with blocks of varying sizes and patterns. An Eight-Pointed Star is visible as well as small blocks of triangles known as Yankee Puzzle or Broken Dishes. The fabrics in the medallion section date to the 1830s whereas the cylinder-printed toile in the border is much older. The original quilt was possibly renovated around the time of Elizabeth Bailey's marriage to George Stanhope in Newport in 1838.

FIG. 12. (*Opposite*) Honeycomb or Hexagon quilt, inscribed "Abigail Hunt, 1807." Cotton top and back, 104½ x 98½ in. Hand-pieced and hand-quilted in clamshell pattern (border) and outline pattern (hexagon section), 9–11 stitches per inch. Made by Abigail Hunt. Collection of Alice C. Baxter. RIQDP #346.

This quilt is an early example of English piecing, a method of making patchwork that employs paper templates to achieve precise edges. Fabric patches are folded around templates, then stitched to other patches, and so on until the desired size is reached. The templates could be any geometric shape although hexagons are among the most popular template style in the history of quiltmaking. *Godey's Lady's Book* published directions for hexagon work in 1835, setting off a national fashion for this style. The hexagon or honeycomb pattern also was called mosaic work and was revived in the twentieth century as Grandmother's Flower Garden.

The quilt in Figure 11 was the first quilt documented by the project. It displays the pattern blocks common to the beginnings of patchwork, when women began experimenting with the simple patterns formed by placing triangles and squares of dark colors against lighter ones. It has a large central block with an Eight-Pointed Star surrounded by smaller blocks of varying patterns. These patchwork blocks are the prototypes for the patterns that later became mainstays in the repertory of Rhode Island quiltmakers. Few quilts had standard pattern names until the authors of quilt books began to attach names to the most popular patterns in the early twentieth century. In this quilt the pattern known as Star of LeMoyne is visible as well as the four-patch block known as Broken Dishes and the simple Diamond in a Square block.

Another type of early patchwork quilt inherited from England is the Honeycomb quilt, also called hexagon or mosaic work. Honeycomb quilts employed the English piecing method in which each patch was folded around a hexagonal template, usually stiff paper, then stitched to another patch along one side, continuing until larger units were built up.[45] The pieced units were then sewn together to form the quilt top. Sometimes the papers remained, which aids researchers in determining provenance. Honeycomb quilts provided an ideal format to use up small amounts of printed fabrics as each ring consisted of a different print. They were time-consuming to make, and their carefully sewn pieces showed off the maker's needlework skills. Eliza Coffin must have occupied herself for months when, at seventy-four years of age, she pieced together 4,295 hexagons each measuring just one-and-a-half inches across.[46]

The oldest English Honeycomb coverlet, in London's Victoria and Albert Museum, is assigned a late eighteenth-century date.[47] The Honeycomb quilt illustrated in Figure 12, signed "Abigail Hunt 1807," is the earliest dated American example.[48] Abigail used copperplate-, block-, and cylinder-printed cottons to make her quilt. Some of the white fabrics separating the hexagon units are striped cotton dimity, a popular apparel fabric around 1800. For the wide border Abigail used a glazed arborescent bird print of the type common to Rhode Island's printed whole-cloth quilts. The back is a brown, block-printed cotton calico; the printer's mark, "T. P. D. Belle-couche," is barely visible above the binding.

After *Godey's Lady's Book*, the popular Victorian woman's magazine, published directions for making hexagon work in January 1835, these quilts became enormously popular in Rhode Island as elsewhere in the United States. One Honeycomb quilt, dated 1830–40, had a handwritten note attached that said, "Godey's Lady's Book came out with this pattern. Fabrics are probably English, dress scraps."[49] Ten other Honeycomb quilts in the

FIG. 13. (*Opposite*) Nine-Patch quilt, inscribed "Ann Thankfull Mathewson, 1815." Cotton top and back, 105 x 101¼ in. Hand-pieced and hand-quilted, 7 stitches per inch. Made by Ann Thankfull Mathewson. Museum of Art, Rhode Island School of Design (39.005). Walter J. Kimball Fund. RIQDP #701.

This quilt contains calicoes in the patchwork blocks, furnishing prints in the plain blocks, and an appliquéd butterfly (possibly cut from an Indian chintz) in the center block. These fabrics were surely imported since the American calico-printing industry was in its infancy in 1815. The quiltmaker lived in the growing port city of Providence, whose shops sold all kinds of textiles to those who could afford them.

RIQDP database date before 1850; another three were begun in Charleston, South Carolina, in the 1830s and were finished a century later in Rhode Island.

Honeycomb quilts were made mostly by quiltmakers of English heritage living in Rhode Island's oldest towns. Ten quilts of this type came from the Newport-Portsmouth-Tiverton area of Aquidneck Island. Two of these were made in the 1840s by Lydia Braman Peabody (1808–1886), a direct descendant of John and Priscilla Alden's daughter Elizabeth. She reportedly made a quilt for each of her nine children.[50]

Rhode Island quiltmakers continued to make Honeycomb quilts throughout the nineteenth century, altering the fabrics and their arrangement to suit current taste. Sometimes the hexagons were large. Crisp silks or deep-hued wools sometimes substituted for calicoes. If the quiltmaker had many printed cottons on hand, as was possible in the latter nineteenth century, she could attempt to make a quilt where every patch was made from a different print, thus creating a "charm" quilt. The Honeycomb style was revived in the twentieth century under the rubric Grandmother's Flower Garden.

The appearance of numerous patchwork quilts in the first quarter of the nineteenth century coincided with the growing availability of printed cottons in small, colorful patterns. According to Barbara Brackman, most quiltmakers preferred the medallion format for pieced quilts until the block style became popular around 1840.[51] The quilts in the Rhode Island project indicate that although the medallion style was made in the state, strip quilts, single-pattern block quilts, and hexagon styles were more popular (see Table 2).

TABLE 2
*Quilt Styles to 1850*

| Whole-Cloth | Medallion | Strip | Hexagon | Pieced Block | Appliqué |
|---|---|---|---|---|---|
| 35 | 4 | 7 | 11 | 47 | 1 (wool) |

The earliest dated block-style quilt is a magnificent Nine-Patch made and signed by Ann Thankfull Mathewson in 1815 (Fig. 13). Nine-Patch blocks of small-scale calico prints alternate with single blocks of large-scale furnishing chintzes. All four sides are bordered with a large-scale floral and bird design. A small butterfly, perhaps cut from an old Indian palampore, is appliqued to the center block on which Ann cross-stitched her name and the year. The printed fabrics are not of American manufacture as the quilt

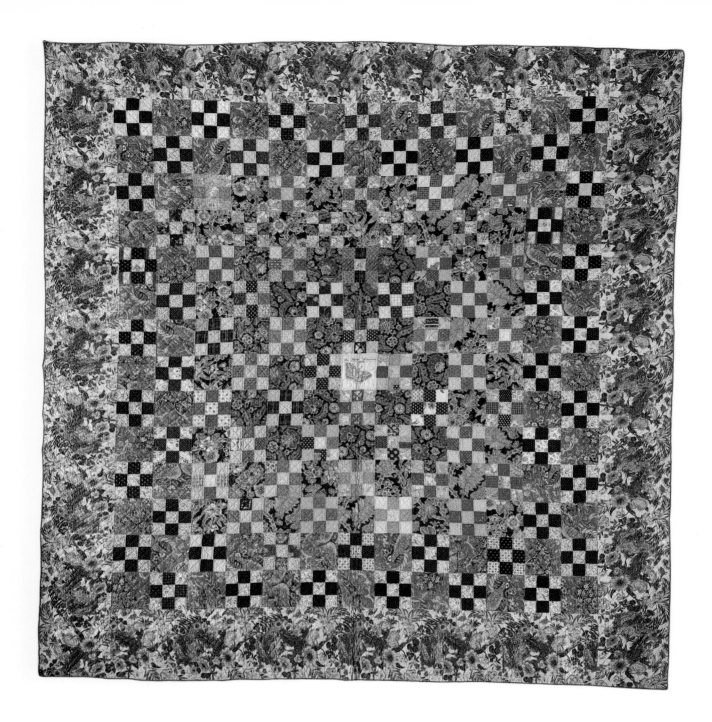

predates the development of New England's print works. This is a high-style quilt, for the Mathewsons were a prominent Providence family. Not every Rhode Island family had the resources to purchase the many printed cottons necessary to produce a quilt such as this. Although English and French prints were readily available for use in patchwork quilts, they were still costly in 1815.

Patchwork quilting was adopted at all economic levels as inexpensive printed fabrics became available from Rhode Island's new mills. Rhode Island had entered the business of manufacturing cotton textiles by water power in 1790 on the Blackstone River in Pawtucket. The numerous rivers and streams on the west side of Narragansett Bay were ideal for the development of cotton spinning, weaving, and then printing. The first mills spun yarn only; the power loom was incorporated successfully into the manufacturing process around 1815. Rhode Island's first print works, A & W Sprague (now Cranston Print Works), opened in 1824 and ushered in the era of abundant, inexpensive, domestically printed cottons.

An 1826 article from the *Pawtucket Chronicle* describes the effect of the entry of southern New England's calico printers into the textile marketplace on prices of foreign and domestic goods:

### MANUFACTURING OF CALICO

Till within a very short time it is well known that this article has demanded a high price among retailers who have kept none but such as was imported from Europe. Manufacturers have at length introduced the business of making Calicoes of their own, and there are now many valuable establishments in the country which produce this kind of cloth of the first quality. Within two years the article has been reduced in price 30 per cent, which is doubtless to be attributed to the success of our manufacturers. In our immediate vicinity, one manufactory has been in operation about a year and a half, another is now nearly finished of no inconsiderable dimensions. This is situated in Seekonk, on Bucklin's Brook, and we understand that preparations are making to manufacture Calico of the first rate in this mill. It has to be worked by machinery altogether new, and which never before has been introduced in this country. Mr. Wilkinson and others are the proprietors of the works, and a small village already appears rising around them in the middle of a forest.

We trust that we shall have occasion little longer to apply to foreign markets for this species of manufacture since our own have already surpassed the use of those imported from France and Great Britain. The domestic Calicoes we are happy to say, meet the approbation of the ladies in preference; owing to the superior strength of their texture, and the permanency of their colors.[52]

The characteristic Rhode Island quilt of the mid–nineteenth century— pieced blocks of simple construction—often contained fabrics typical of those manufactured in area mills. Block-style quilts used the calicoes well, as clever juxtapositioning of opposing hues and contrasting values showed the new textiles to advantage. The single-pattern block style soon dominated Rhode Island quilts, taking over from the whole-cloth, medallion, and Honeycomb styles. Even the wide chintz borders disappeared.

The quilts made during this critical period—the 1830s and 1840s—established Rhode Island's quilt traditions. The quilts shared these characteristics: pieced, single-pattern, block style positioned on point, borderless, with quilting pattern related to piecing. Common patterns for the block quilts were One-Patch, Four-Patch, Nine-Patch, Sixteen-Patch, stars (LeMoyne, Variable, Rising), Irish Chain, Broken Dishes, and Yankee Puzzle. The Flying Geese pattern, where strips of pieced triangles alternated with uncut strips of printed fabrics, also appeared. Quilts illustrated throughout this book show these common pieced patterns and the more complex offshoots that developed later in the nineteenth century (e.g., Ocean Waves). Many quilts of simple patchwork blocks, especially Four-Patch and Nine-Patch, were made in Rhode Island through to the end of the 1940s (see Table 3).

TABLE 3

*Frequencies of Patchwork Block Patterns in Rhode Island Quilts*

| Pattern | 1800–1849 | 1850–1899 | 1900–1949 | TOTAL |
|---|---|---|---|---|
| Crazy | 0 | 55 | 13 | 68 |
| Log Cabin | 0 | 47 | 9 | 56 |
| Star | 8 | 19 | 20 | 47 |
| Four-Patch | 6 | 15 | 5 | 26 |
| Nine-Patch | 7 | 13 | 4 | 24 |
| One-Patch | 4 | 9 | 7 | 20 |
| Chr. Cross | 3 | 8 | 0 | 11 |
| Irish Chain | 0 | 7 | 3 | 10 |
| Album Patch | 2 | 6 | 0 | 8 |
| Basket | 0 | 5 | 3 | 8 |
| Diamond in Sq. | 2 | 3 | 3 | 8 |
| Broken Dishes | 2 | 3 | 2 | 7 |
| Sixteen-Patch | 1 | 2 | 3 | 6 |
| Baby Blocks | 0 | 5 | 0 | 5 |
| Sunburst | 1 | 3 | 1 | 5 |
| Kaleidoscope | 0 | 2 | 2 | 4 |
| Pinwheel | 1 | 2 | 1 | 4 |

*Note:* These patterns occurred four or more times in the RIQDP Database.

Rhode Island quilts reveal Yankee thriftiness in that older materials frequently were used for backs, interlinings, and tops. The quilts on the whole showed a mentality of "use it up, wear it out, make it do, or do without." Recycled fabrics included scraps from dresses, flour sacks, old blankets, and sometimes even other quilts. We found several examples of a quilt that had an older quilt inside, or had been inside another quilt. Rhode Islanders with connections to textile mills incorporated into their quilts discarded fabric "seconds" that had dyeing or printing mistakes. Utility quilts outnumbered show quilts in the RIQDP database, often telling of many years' use on beds and later of such lowly roles as painters' drop cloths or dogs' beds.

How did Rhode Island's young women learn how to quilt and where did they obtain their patterns? At first quiltmaking skills were transferred through an informal network of female relatives and friends. Quilting parties had been held in the state since the eighteenth century.[53] In rural communities through the mid–nineteenth century, women met at quilting parties "to sew together little bits of calico, and at the same time take the characters of their neighbors to pieces."[54] Friendships made through church affiliation might have been another source of information about quilting patterns. Women might have shared patterns through sewing societies, a phenomenon of the Victorian era. In East Greenwich, sewing societies existed from at least the 1850s through the 1870s.[55] Perhaps young women who worked in textile mills shared ideas about how to piece together mill seconds for bed covers.

Quilts exhibited at fairs offered another place for obtaining pattern ideas. New England's first agricultural fair was held in Massachusetts in 1808.[56] In 1821 the Rhode Island Society for the Encouragement of Domestic Industry began the Rhode Island Cattle Show and Exhibition of Manufactures, held annually in Pawtuxet, now part of Cranston. "Household manufactures" was a category at the Rhode Island Exhibition, to encourage "female labour, so as to render that labour in some degree as productive as the like skill and application in man; at the same time preserving the moral and even elevated standing of the female in society."[57] The items awarded premiums in 1826 were lace, straw bonnets, baskets, blankets, stockings, hearth rugs, shawls, carpets, linen cloth, linen diaper, blanketing, and counterpanes (an early term for quilts and coverlets).

As we have seen, publication of the directions for hexagon work in *Godey's Lady's Book* had an effect on the production of these quilts in Rhode Island in the late 1830s and 1840s. *Godey's* and other women's magazines published more patchwork patterns in the 1850s and 1860s, thereby fostering the popularity of certain patterns on a national level.[58] A direct link between *Godey's* and a Rhode Island quiltmaker occurred in 1864, when the magazine published a novel design for an autograph quilt submitted by a young Providence woman.[59] She first conceived of the idea for her quilt, a tumbling blocks design, in 1857. This pattern had been published in *Godey's* April 1850 issue in a group of template styles. The woman, now identified as Adeline Harris Sears, had collected autographs on silk patches from famous persons including Abraham Lincoln, Charles Dickens, and Ralph Waldo Emerson. The quilt, now in the Metropolitan Museum of Art, appears as Figure 1 in this book.[60]

The widespread popularity of crazy quilts in the 1880s and 1890s attests to the influence magazines had on women's needlework. More than 10 percent of the Rhode Island quilts in our database were crazy quilts. By the early twentieth century, daily newspapers and other printed sources published quilt patterns such as Dresden Plate, Double Wedding Ring, and Butterfly, further extending the range of quilt patterns stitched by Rhode Island women. Conversely, widely distributed publications virtually eliminated regional distinctions in piecing.

The textile industry expanded rapidly in the years after the factories successfully incorporated the cotton gin, the power loom, and the cylinder printing machine. The biggest growth in Rhode Island was along the Blackstone and Pawtuxet Rivers. By 1830 manufacturing was an important component of the economy. Rhode Island's textile companies, mostly limited partnerships, continued developing during the next thirty years. Although some of the companies failed or were bought out, many responded to the challenges of the larger, corporate-owned mills in Massachusetts and New Hampshire as well as to foreign competition. Rhode Island mill owners found their niche in the marketplace, primarily in the manufacture of cotton (see Table 4). By 1860 Rhode Island produced 29 percent of all the printed cotton manufactured in the United States, more than any other state including Massachusetts.[61]

*Growth of Mills and Changing Demographics*

TABLE 4
*Rhode Island Cotton and Woolen Mills*

|        | 1809–10 | 1812 | 1815 | 1819 | 1832 | 1840 | 1850 | 1860 |
|--------|---------|------|------|------|------|------|------|------|
| Cotton | 25      | 38   | 100  | –    | 126  | 226  | 174  | 176  |
| Wool   | 3       | –    | –    | 24   | 22   | 41   | 57   | 57   |

*Source:* Data developed from Peter J. Coleman, *The Transformation of Rhode Island 1790–1860* (Providence: Brown University Press, 1963), 86, 87, 93, 96, 98, 124, 127, 135, 137, 140.

This rapid industrial growth required unskilled labor. The earliest factory hands were Yankees, a fact of which the mill owners were proud. As the industry grew, labor shortages forced acceptance of foreign-born workers. From 1830 to 1860 the state's population increased by 77,000; of this number, 32,500 were factory workers.[62] Rhode Island mills were known to employ whole families, including women and children, who lived in company-owned housing. A swelling tide of immigrant families moved to the state to fill this need. When the first state census to record the nativity of the population was taken in 1865, one-fifth of Rhode Island's population was foreign born.[63]

This first wave of immigrants was Irish tenant farmers. They began arriving in small numbers in the 1820s, but the exodus increased as potato crops failed almost every year in the 1830s and 1840s. The Irish, who had dug the canals at Lowell in the 1820s, began working inside textile mills when worsening labor conditions caused the industry to open its doors to foreign workers in the late 1840s. Irish immigration continued so that by 1865 the Irish comprised 68 percent of the foreign-born residents of Rhode Island.[64]

Irish newcomers settled in communities throughout the state. Roman Catholic, impoverished, and often illiterate, they faced discrimination from Protestant Yankees and from other immigrant groups. The men worked as unskilled laborers and the women as factory workers, seamstresses, and domestics. Mass was held in taverns and town halls until they could build their own churches. Eventually, acculturation and assimilation were achieved when their children grew up, sometimes intermarrying with other ethnic groups.[65]

The next wave of immigration began in the 1860s. Labor shortages in the mills during and after the Civil War sent recruiters to rural Quebec in search of workers. Many impoverished French Canadians, living on farms subdivided too many times, moved south for economic gain. From 1860 to 1910, 35,000 French Canadians entered Rhode Island.[66] They preferred to settle in small mill villages or sections of cities where other French Canadians lived (Fig. 14). In this way they could retain their French language and customs. They built Gothic-style Roman Catholic churches and established church-affiliated schools.

Mill owners found French Canadians ideal workers. They adapted to mill-village life easily, settling into mill-owned housing and sending their large families to work in the mills for lower wages than others would accept for unskilled jobs.[67] They resisted organized labor and refused to strike. The state's largest concentrations of French Canadians were in the West Warwick village of Arctic and the city of Woonsocket, where linguistic and cultural individuality was preserved well into the twentieth century.[68]

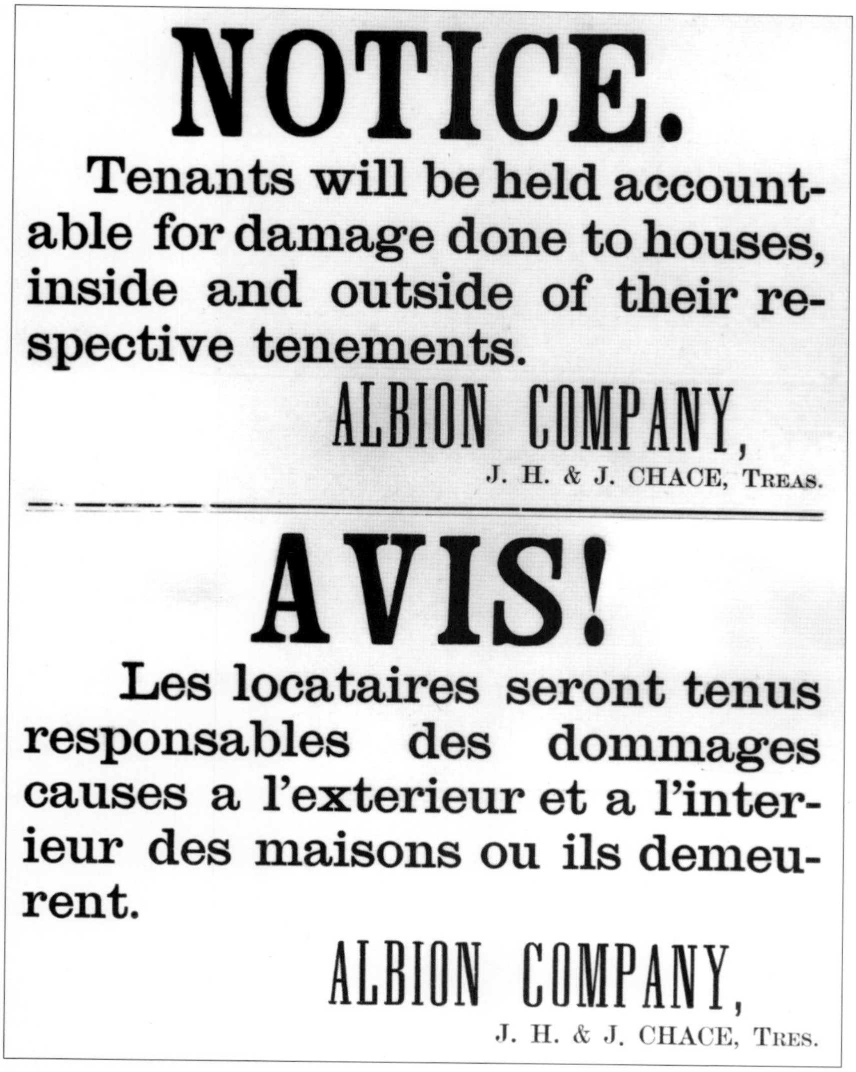

**NOTICE.**

Tenants will be held account-able for damage done to houses, inside and outside of their respective tenements.

ALBION COMPANY,

J. H. & J. CHACE, TREAS.

**AVIS!**

Les locataires seront tenus responsables des dommages causes a l'exterieur et a l'interieur des maisons ou ils demeurent.

ALBION COMPANY,

J. H. & J. CHACE, TRES.

FIG. 14. Notice to tenants of mill housing in English and French, Albion Company, Lincoln, Rhode Island. Courtesy of Slater Mill Historic Site, Pawtucket Rhode Island.

Immigration during the post–Civil War period included British, Swedish, and German settlers as well. Skilled mechanics from England and Scotland were attracted to Rhode Island through advertisements in British newspapers. Settling mostly in Pawtucket, North Providence, and Providence, they assimilated easily with the native Yankees because of language and their Protestant religions. A small number of Swedish immigrants came to Rhode Island in the wake of famine and a decline in the agricultural sector of the Swedish economy. They settled on the South Side of Providence and in Cranston. Mostly Lutheran, they built their own churches as well. A few thousand Germans settled mainly in Pawtucket and Providence in the second half of the nineteenth century, finding employment in the skilled trades.[69]

Another group joined the northern Europeans at the time of the second wave of immigration into Rhode Island—freed slaves who came north after the Civil War. These newcomers settled mostly in Providence and Newport, where they boarded with family or friends until they found work. Rhode Island's mill owners, who had profited from the manufacture of Negro Cloth for southern plantations prior to the Civil War, did not welcome African Americans as employees. Instead, African Americans found work in service industries. Some rose to positions of wealth and influence, like George Downing of Providence who built a profitable restaurant, hotel, and catering business. Most survived through a community network that included extended families, churches, and fraternal organizations.[70]

The third great wave of immigration began in 1880 and ceased in 1924 when the U.S. Congress passed the National Origins Quota Act. During this forty-four-year period America opened its doors to a tidal wave of immigrants. Italians, Portuguese, Greeks, Arabs, and Armenians came from the Mediterranean countries, while Russian Jews, Polish Catholics, Lithuanians, and Ukrainians came from eastern Europe. Rhode Island's bigger textile mills along the Blackstone served as a magnet for these newcomers. The two largest ethnic groups to arrive at this time were the Italians and the Portuguese. From 1911 to 1934, the Fabre Line operated passenger ships that sailed to Providence from Marseilles, stopping in Italy and Portugal along the way to pick up passengers. The Portuguese settled in certain neighborhoods of Providence and throughout the entire East Bay region. Italians settled in Providence, Johnston, Cranston, and Westerly. Predominantly Catholic, both the Portuguese and the Italians built churches around which self-contained communities developed.[71]

How did these new arrivals integrate into long-established Yankee communities? Language, religion, and race were keys to the degree of assimilation. Immigrants whose native tongue was English integrated more easily, as did those of the Protestant denominations. Those who clung to their native language, practiced a non-Protestant religion, or were not Caucasian experienced more difficulties with assimilation. The French Canadians became the most insular of all the nineteenth-century immigrants by recreating provincial Quebec culture in rural mill towns.[72]

*Quilts and Cultural Heritage*

Which of the many immigrant groups made quilts? What did these quilts look like? Rhode Island quiltmakers were overwhelmingly Yankee, that is Protestant of English heritage, but the French Canadians and the Irish also made quilts according to our data (see Table 5).

Only four quilts made by quiltmakers with Scottish ancestry have been documented. Few Scots settled in Rhode Island compared to the Carolinas and West Virginia.

TABLE 5

*Ethnicity of Rhode Island Quiltmakers (when reported)*

| | Number of Quiltmakers $n = 276$ | Percentage of Total Quiltmakers | Number of Quilts $n = 394$ |
|---|---|---|---|
| English | 222 | 80 | 308 |
| French Canadian | 28 | 10 | 55 |
| Irish | 16 | 5.7 | 23 |
| Scottish | 5 | 1.8 | 7 |
| German | 4 | 1.4 | 4 |
| African American | 2 | 0.7 | 2 |
| Welsh | 2 | 0.7 | 2 |
| Swedish | 1 | 0.3 | 1 |
| Italian | 1 | 0.3 | 5 |
| Dutch | 1 | 0.3 | 1 |
| French | 1 | 0.3 | 1 |
| TOTAL | 280 | 100 | 408 |

*Note:* Total may be higher than *n* because of mixed ethnic background.

Few quilts belonging to families from other northern European countries were documented; they reveal little to distinguish them from other quilts made in Rhode Island during the same time period. Women who lived in culturally integrated communities apparently made quilts like those of the Yankees around them, particularly if they came to the United States before the end of the nineteenth century. The Magnusson family is a case in point (Fig. 15). Anders Peter Magnusson and his wife Britta emigrated from Sweden to New England in 1852, eventually settling onto a farm in the Pontiac section of Warwick. They were the first Swedes to settle in this region, and Anders Magnusson fought in the Civil War. The Magnussons helped found the Swedish Lutheran Church in Pontiac in 1874. Either Britta or her daughter Jennie Hallene made the Honeycomb quilt in Figure 16, using so many different calico fabrics, including Centennial prints, that it qualifies as a charm quilt. Although quilts are not unknown in Sweden, the Swedish traditionally used woven covers for their beds. This quilt is decidedly an adoption of the Yankee quiltmaking tradition.

Quiltmakers with Irish heritage adapted readily to the quiltmaking traditions around them, perhaps aided by a long tradition of quiltmaking in Ireland.[73] Connections to the old country are apparent in several quilts: one quiltmaker's mother, back in Ireland, quilted also; another used the Irish

FIG. 15. Three generations of the Magnusson family, ca. 1890. Anders and Britta Magnusson came to New England from Sweden in 1852. After settling on a farm in Warwick, they helped found the Swedish Lutheran church in Pontiac. Their daughters married two brothers. In the photograph, the couple is seated in the center surrounded by the two daughters and their husbands and the grandchildren. Both Britta and daughter Jennie Hallene are remembered as having made quilts. In the photograph, Jennie is seated on the right with her children. She died in 1895 after giving birth to her third set of twins. RIQDP Archives.

Chain pattern to commemorate her Irish roots; a third quiltmaker made a Turkey red and white appliqué in the Heart and Spade pattern popular with quiltmakers in Ulster, Ireland.[74] The sixteen Irish quiltmakers documented in this study had varying backgrounds ranging from one whose ancestors arrived in the early eighteenth century to four quiltmakers who were born in Ireland. Some of the quiltmakers came from families who suffered economic hardships as evidenced by stories of the potato famine, going to Ohio to work on the railroad, and moving from town to town in southern New England in search of mill work (Fig. 17).

Six of the Irish quiltmakers had connections to the textile industry; two worked at Cranston Print Works where mill seconds were the source of fabrics for the family quilts. The Irish quiltmakers lived predominantly in the state's industrial towns and cities such as West Warwick, Providence, North Providence, and Pawtucket. One quiltmaker's son, John Quinn, was the mayor of Pawtucket from 1932 to 1936. Despite stories of prejudice against Irish Catholic immigrants, the ancestors of four of our quilt owners married English or French Canadian immigrants.

Fig. 16. (*Previous page*) Hexagon quilt, ca. 1890. Cotton top, new cotton back and batting, 88 x 68 in. Hand-pieced, tied. Made by Britta Magnusson (1822–1894) or Jennie Magnusson Hallene (d. 1895). Rhode Island Historical Society (1994.16.1). RIQDP #120.

This quilt exemplifies the cross-cultural aspects of quiltmaking in Rhode Island. Hexagon work originated in England in the late eighteenth century and arrived shortly thereafter in New England, where quiltmakers of English heritage adopted the technique. Nineteenth-century immigrants to Rhode Island, in this case from Sweden, utilized English piecing to make quilts in the style of their adopted locale.

Fig. 17. (*Right*) Mary Jane Ward Broderick and her daughter-in-law, Florence Murphy Broderick and grandson Bill Broderick. Mary Jane Ward was born in Wilton, New Hampshire, to parents who had emigrated from Ireland. The family moved numerous times to find factory work, including in Woonsocket textile mills. RIQDP Archives.

Fig. 18. (*Opposite*) Double Wedding Ring quilt, 1930s. Cotton top and back, 90 x 75 in. Hand- and machine-pieced, tied. Made by Mary Jane Ward Broderick (1873–1964). Collection of Mary L. Averill. RIQDP #200.

Rhode Islanders of Irish heritage made quilts in patterns popular with quiltmakers of other cultural backgrounds. Pattern companies began publishing patterns for Double Wedding Ring quilts in the late 1920s. Mary Jane Broderick reportedly made this quilt for her great-granddaughter, the present owner, upon the occasion of her birth.

Irish quiltmakers made a variety of quilts ranging in date from the 1870s to the 1930s. The patterns they chose were popular with other Rhode Island quiltmakers as well, such as Variable Star, Star of LeMoyne, Irish Chain, Log Cabin, Album Patch, Churn Dash, Yo-Yo, Dresden Plate, and Double Wedding Ring (Fig. 18). No color preferences are apparent; the quiltmakers seem to have used whatever cotton fabrics were available. However, the quilts as a group show an emphasis on function and thrift not unlike the dominant Yankee quiltmakers. No crazy quilts or silk template quilts

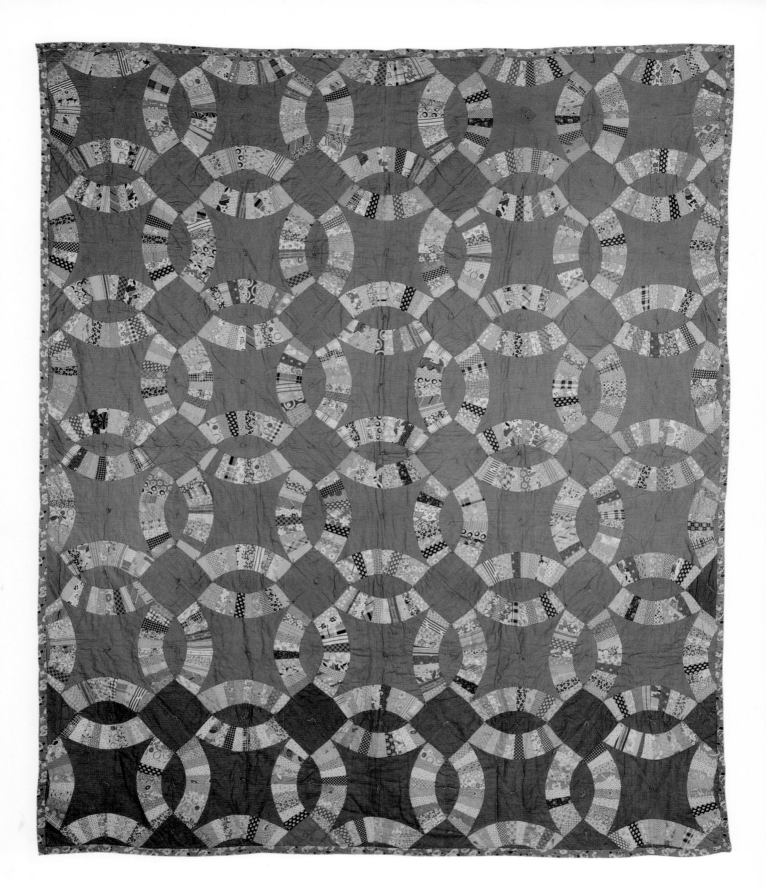

FIG. 19. (*Below*) Louise Cloutier *(left)* and Virginie Gurtin, 1920s. Born in Quebec, these two sisters emigrated to Marlboro, Massachusettes, in the latter part of the nineteenth century. Louise married Charles Cloutier, and Virginie worked in textile mills until her marriage in 1899. The sisters made many quilts together. Descendants who live in Rhode Island remember them cutting out quilt patches on the floor of their home. RIQDP Archives.

FIG. 20. (*Opposite*) Crazy quilt, dated "Fevrier 15, 1899." Wool, silk satin, silk velvet, 73½ x 79 in. Hand-pieced, embroidered, tied. Made by Catherine Plante Ethier. Collection of Anne Seitsinger. RIQDP #62.

Catherine Plante Ethier of Maskinongé, Quebec, made this crazy quilt as a gift to her daughter Virginie on her wedding day, February 15, 1899. Catherine, reputed to have been a Native American, married Moîse Ethier, a miner, probably in the 1840s. The quilt has been handed down through five generations; the present owner brought it to Rhode Island. Recently three generations of women in this French Canadian family got together to reminisce over this quilt.

emerged from Irish American trunks. Instead, quilts made from cotton flour sacks, feed sacks, and mill seconds were brought for documentation. One worn-out quilt even had another, older quilt inside. For the most part the quilts made by quiltmakers with Irish ancestry reflect the degree to which their makers had adapted to American culture.

French Canadians were the largest group of quiltmakers in Rhode Island after those with English heritage. Quiltmaking was practiced throughout eastern Canada, and the Quebec natives brought their quiltmaking skills with them. Quiltmakers settled in mill towns like Arctic, Providence, North Providence, Central Falls, Warren, and Woonsocket. They attended French-Canadian churches like St. Joseph's in West Warwick, Notre Dame in Central Falls, and L'Eglise des Canadiens in Bristol. Canadian relatives came to visit them, sometimes making quilts to pass the time. Many of the French Canadian immigrants, like Virginie Gurtin and Louise Cloutier, continued speaking French all their lives (Fig. 19). When Virginie married, her mother made a crazy quilt for her dated "Fevrier 15, 1899" (Fig. 20).

Upon arrival in Rhode Island, French-Canadian women appear to have taken to quilting with a passion, perhaps because of the availability of free or low-cost remnants from the mills. Eleven of the quiltmakers made more than one quilt. At least fourteen of the quiltmakers had someone in their families working in the mills as a machinist, weaver, printer, or quality con-

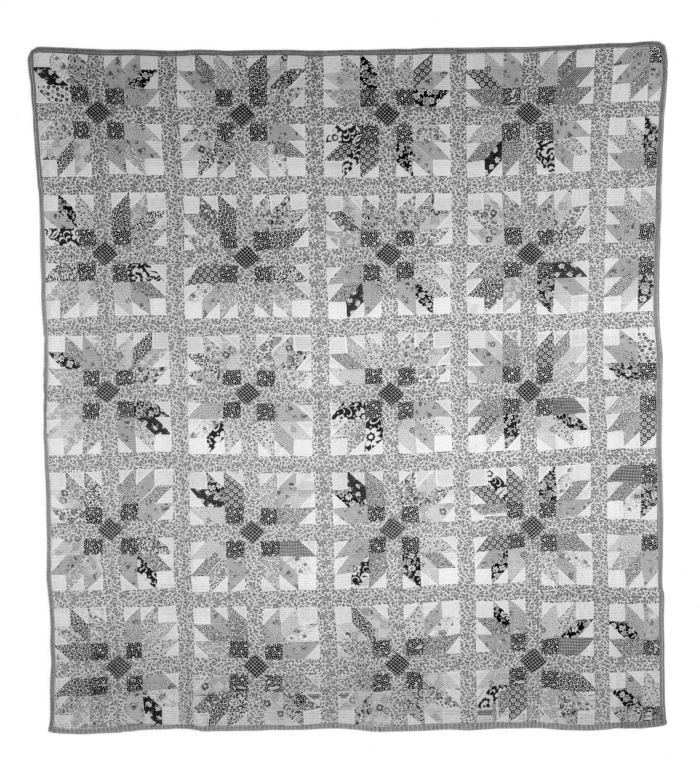

trol supervisor. Sometimes the women worked in the mills themselves; one started at age eleven when her mother died. These quiltmakers had large families—twelve, fourteen, eighteen children—yet found time to make quilts to brighten beds or to commemorate a birth or wedding. Perhaps

40    *Down by the Old Mill Stream*

quiltmaking offered a creative release while living in mill housing where overcrowding, poor ventilation, and contaminated water bred tuberculosis, cholera, and other diseases. Only three of the fourteen children born to Delima Mercier Mailhot, maker of numerous extant quilts, lived to adulthood.[75]

In several instances quilt owners commented that their French Canadian great-grandmother or great-aunt had made many quilts; one had stitched thirty or forty quilts. Lucie Belleau Duchesneau quilted day and night during the Depression (Fig. 22). Her daughter-in-law, with whom she lived as a widow, wished she would slow down so they would not have to buy so many quilting supplies. Lucie probably used published patterns for her quilts, for two of them are identical to those shown in rural or farm magazines (Fig. 21).

The fifty-five quilts made by French Canadians date from the 1890s through the mid–twentieth century. Many, constructed during the 1930s and 1940s, display the popular patterns of the day including Grandmother's Flower Garden, Wedding Ring, Fan, Dresden Plate, and Butterfly. The earlier quilts are in well-known patterns such as Log Cabin, Pineapple, Nine-Patch, and Bear's Paw. What sets these quilts apart from the quilts made by other ethnic groups is a preference for light colors. Only five of the French Canadian quilts were in medium to dark tones; four of these were crazy

FIG. 21. (*Opposite*) "Old Fashion Quilt," 1930s. Cotton top and back, blanket filler, 82 x 72 in. Hand- and machine-pieced, hand-quilted, 2 stitches per inch. Made by Lucie Belleau Duchesneau (1858–1942). Collection of Helen Pajak. RIQDP #66.

Judging from Lucie's other surviving quilts, she preferred Star and Fan patterns in pastel colors. Money was scarce so she used old clothes for the pieces. This well-worn quilt was used by Lucie's granddaughter, the present owner, when she attended boarding school. The pattern for this quilt is similar to one that was published as "Old Fashion Quilt" in the *Oklahoma Farmer Stockman*.

FIG. 22. Lucie Belleau Duchesneau at the quilting frame in her West Warwick home. The French Canadians who came to work in Rhode Island's textile mills quilted with enthusiasm. Lucie Belleau, born in Canada, married Zephir Duchesneau and moved to Arctic, a mill village in the West Warwick section of Rhode Island, where he worked as a millwright. They had six children. Lucie loved to quilt. After she was widowed during the Great Depression, she quilted day and night, producing quilts so fast that her daughter-in-law wished she would slow down so she would use less fabric. RIQDP Archives.

FIG. 23. (*Opposite*) Dresden Plate top, 1930s. Cotton top (unfinished), 75 x 92½ in. Machine-pieced. Made by Marie Louise "Babe" Brown McCastor (1896–1983). Collection of Arline Allston Seaforth. RIQDP #694.

Babe McCastor liked sewing, crochet, trapunto, and other handicrafts. She did not make many quilts and left this Dresden Plate unfinished.

quilts. The remaining fifty quilts had large amounts of white, usually combined with pastel colors like pink, yellow, blue, or blue-green. The liberal use of white is also a characteristic of quilts made by Francophones in Quebec.[76]

Few of the later immigrants from southern and eastern Europe took up quiltmaking. The project documented no quilts by quiltmakers with Greek, Armenian, Jewish, Lithuanian, or Polish heritage. And despite the large number of Italians in the state, only one Italian quiltmaker appeared in the database; she had lived in France before emigrating to the United States.

Is the lack of Italian American quilts because Italians did not come forward on quilt documentation days or because they did not make quilts? Between 1898 and 1932, the Fabre Line brought 54,973 Italians to Providence.[77] Many of these immigrants came from economically disadvantaged southern Italy. Although southern Italy has a strong needlework tradition, the inhabitants did not make quilts. According to one study, girls and women in Sicily expended much time and energy on white-work bedding, embroidered and trimmed in handmade lace for display as part of their trousseaux.[78] Trousseaux were carefully enumerated in wedding contracts. Despite the labor and cost associated with this deeply embedded cultural practice, it continued in a time of great poverty. Trousseaux symbolized sexual purity in a society imbued with the Mediterranean concepts of honor and shame. Italian colonies in Providence, Cranston, and Westerly were self-contained communities that continued to practice traditions from the old country. Members of Italian families in Rhode Island recall their grandmothers making doilies and lace pillow edgings, but not quilts. Additionally, by the time the Italians arrived in Rhode Island, Yankee quiltmakers already were being influenced by colonial revival styles.

Rhode Island's African American population is small compared to that of other states, and so is the number of African American quilts documented by the project. Although long-time African American residents remember having quilts on their beds when growing up, no quilts appeared on documentation days. Instead, we searched out African American quilts in the Ocean State. One of the two quilts we found was a fashionable silk quilt in the Pineapple pattern made by a descendant of Providence's prominent George Downing family. The other was an unfinished Dresden Plate top (Fig. 23) stitched by Babe McCastor (Fig. 24), who enjoyed numerous textile crafts as hobbies. Both the Downing quilt and the McCastor quilt reflect styles popular throughout the United States during the periods in which they were made. Unfortunately, not many Rhode Island quilts made by African Americans survived the passage of time. One woman told me that she remembered having many quilts while growing up in Newport, but

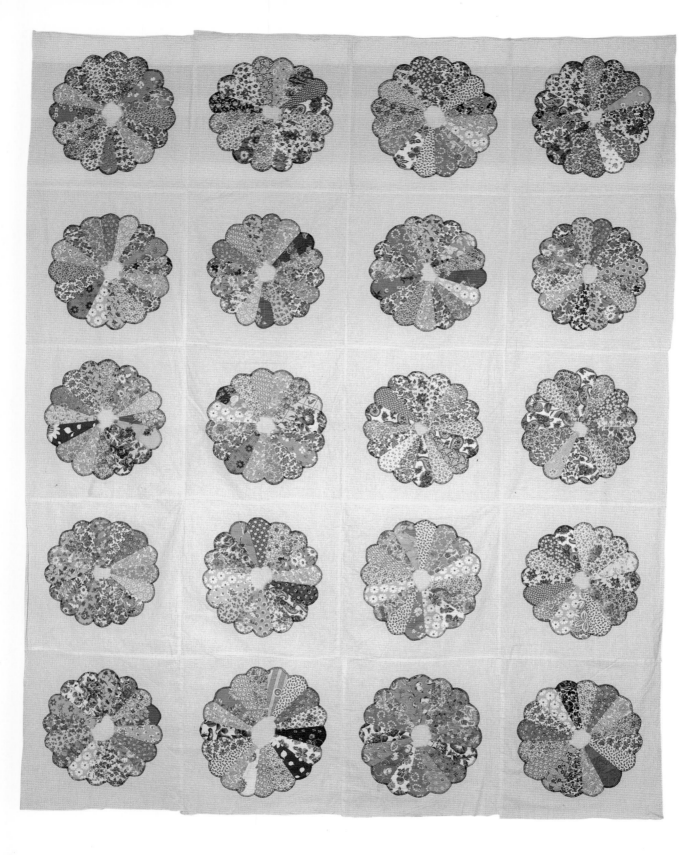

FIG. 24. Babe McCastor and her husband, Paul. Babe, an African American who lived in Newport, was adopted by her great-aunt and great-uncle Mary and Samuel Brown after her mother died. In 1918 she married Paul McCastor (1890–1976), who was listed as "white" on their marriage license. He was actually part Native American, and in 1933 he became a certified member of the National Algonquian Indian Council. When Paul, a WWI veteran, became disabled in the 1940s, she assumed his duties as a janitor at Rogers High School. She was a frequent and outspoken visitor at city council meetings. RIQDP Archives.

that they were sent out to the "wet wash," where they were too vigorously laundered and eventually were destroyed.

In the twentieth century, African Americans from the southern states came to the industrial north bringing their southern quilts and quilting traditions with them. The seven women who made up the St. Martin dePorres Center Quilting Club in Providence in the early 1980s came from varied geographical backgrounds—Virginia, South Carolina, North Carolina—where they learned quiltmaking at a young age.[79] Several related stories of growing up in the South in conditions of extreme poverty. The quilts they made were patched together out of feed sacks and flour bags and were stuffed with straw. Quilts were the only way to keep warm in unheated, uninsulated houses where wind whistled through the cracks. One of the quiltmakers had never seen a factory-made blanket until she went away to college. The quiltmakers reminisced fondly about quilting as an activity that provided

*Down by the Old Mill Stream*

socialization and recreation for African American women living in the rural South in the days before television.[80]

What of Rhode Island's Native Americans? Did they make quilts? Quilts are not part of Narragansett or Wampanoag culture. Textile crafts of southern New England Indians are based on the off-loom techniques of twining and plaiting rather than manipulation of woven cloth through needlework skills. In the nineteenth century native crafts included manufacture of baskets, brooms, and mats to sell to Anglo-American farm families. The chances of a Narragansett-made quilt's surviving from the 1800s are further limited by the fact that the population living on Narragansett tribal lands in Charlestown never totaled more than a few hundred people. By the first quarter of the twentieth century, a cultural revival was under way among New England's Indians in which quiltmaking had no place. Consequently, it is not surprising that no quilts appeared during our documentation days. Even recently made quilts were not forthcoming.

*Conclusion*

Rhode Island's quilt heritage reflects the English ancestry of its early settlers. The oldest quilted textiles in Rhode Island's family and public collections—wool and silk petticoats, whole-cloth quilts, medallion quilts, and hexagon work—represent the influence of Old England on New England in style, pattern, and fabrication. Only after Rhode Island's textile industry began printing cotton calico in the 1820s did an independent style emerge. By 1840 the typical Rhode Island quilt was pieced in the block style, sewn without a border, and arranged on point.

These quilts leave a legacy of Rhode Island's textile history in their creases and folds. Quilts in the database reveal an early dependence on imported European cloth for quilt tops. The changes wrought by the Industrial Revolution that began in Rhode Island are evident in the materials and processes found in these quilts. The mills located on Rhode Island's many streams and rivers produced cotton thread for quilting and many yards of sheeting, muslin, and calico used by quiltmakers both in the state and beyond.

In addition to increasing the availability of inexpensive cottons, the area's mills attracted many new residents to the state, some of whom made quilts. Families from northern Europe or Canada who immigrated in the early to middle nineteenth century were more likely to make quilts after they came to Rhode Island than the southern Europeans who arrived during the "Great Migration" from the 1880s to the 1920s.

Regardless of a quilt's age or beauty or the quiltmaker's ethnic origin, each Rhode Island quilt leaves a legacy of the past. From the earliest whole-cloth quilts belonging to Rhode Island's leading Anglo-American families to the Depression-era Fan quilts stitched by French Canadian women, the history of the state's cultural landscape unfolds. Even the absence of a strong quiltmaking tradition in the Native American, African American, and Italian American communities contributes to our understanding of culture.

*Notes*

1. Susannah was the granddaughter of Samuel Gorton, an Englishman who founded Warwick in 1642. Her petticoat is owned by the Rhode Island Historical Society (acc. no. 1982.76.2).

2. The *Oxford English Dictionary*'s earliest reference to "quilt" is 1290.

3. William S. Simmons, "Narragansett," in *Handbook of North American Indians*, vol. 15, *Northeast*, Bruce C. Trigger, ed. (Washington, D.C.: Smithsonian Institution, 1978), 194–95.

4. Peter J. Coleman, *The Transformation of Rhode Island* 1790–1860 (Providence: Brown University Press, 1963), 5–14.

5. Patrick T. Conley, *An Album of Rhode Island History, 1636–1986* (Norfolk, Va.: Donning Co., 1986), 42.

6. Irving H. Bartlett, *From Slave to Citizen: The Story of the Negro in Rhode Island* (Providence: Urban League of Greater Providence, 1954), 9.

7. Although trading in slaves was outlawed in the state, Rhode Island slave traders continued to operate by delivering slaves to Charleston, N.C. Conley, *Album*, 9.

8. Simmons, "Narragansett," 195–96.

9. *Creative Survival: The Providence Black Community in the 19th Century* (Providence: R.I. Black Heritage Society, n.d.), 40.

10. William B. Weeden, *Early Rhode Island* (New York: Grafton Press, 1910), 235. Weeden remarks that "In the seventeenth century, feather beds were of the very most important personal effects. After a roof for shelter and a fire in the chimney, the best comfort was to be found in a good nest of feathers" (125–26).

11. Sally Garoutte, "Early Colonial Quilts in a Bedding Context," in *Uncoverings 1980*, Sally Garoutte, ed. (San Francisco: American Quilt Study Group, 1981), 23, 26.

12. April 8, 1726, Probate and Council Records, 1723–35, Town of South Kingstown, King's County, Colony of Rhode Island, 22. The total estate was valued at £154.18.4.

13. January 12, 1756, Probate Records, 1754–72, Town of South Kingstown, Wakefield, R.I., 356. Jonathon Oatly was born in London in 1689, came to America in the early 1700s, and bought land in South Kingstown in 1728. The will specified his wife, Mary Oatly, as the executor. Perhaps she was the quilter.

14. October 12, 1782, Probate Records, 1772–1800, Town of South Kingstown, Wakefield, R.I., 135.

15. July 10, 1799 and June 2, 1799, Probate Records, 1799–1807, Town of South Kingstown, Wakefield, R.I., 19, 16.

16. September 2, 1799, Probate Records, 1799–1807, Town of South Kingstown, Wakefield, R.I., 50–52. The range of bedding textiles in her home included coverlets, bedspreads of calico and check fabrics, and sets of bed curtains in calico, diaper, and copperplate. In her will, she ordered her daughter Polly to weave one piece of "blue and white chex" and one piece of tow-cloth, keeping half for herself and giving the other half to a sibling.

17. July 13, 1801, Probate Records, 1799-1807, Town of South Kingstown, Wakefield, R.I., 111.

18. March 10, 1806, Probate Records, 1799–1807, Town of South Kingstown , Wakefield, R.I., 304–5.

19. 1 bedspread quilted @ $2.50, 1 bed quilt $2.50, 1 woolen bed quilt @ $2, 1 red copperplate spread and suit curtains, 1 old bed quilt (May 9, 1825, Probate Records, 1823–28, Town of South Kingstown, Wakefield, R.I., 96–98).

20. August 7, 1826, Probate Records, 1823-28, Town of South Kingstown, Wakefield, R.I., 179.

21. November 16, 1825, Probate Records, 1823-28, Town of South Kingstown, Wakefield, R.I., 130.

22. Lynn Bonfield studied 118 diaries of New England quilters, but none from Rhode Island. The earliest reference to quilting in New England was dated 1766, in the diary of Elizabeth Porter Phelps of Hadley, Mass. Phelps quilted both petticoats and bed quilts. Other women from Massachusetts, Connecticut, and Maine recorded quilting in their diaries starting in the 1770s. Lynne Bonfield, "Diaries of New England Quilters Before 1860," in *Uncoverings 1988,* Laurel Horton, ed.(San Francisco: American Quilt Study Group, 1989), 175–76, 189–92.

23. Diary of Susannah Martin, 1799, Manuscript Collection, R.I. Historical Society, Providence.

24. Although quilts were mentioned in the early inventories of Kent County, Md., the 1800–1820 period experienced a dramatic increase. Two-thirds of the total 311 quilts were in inventories dated 1800 or later. Gloria Seaman Allen, "Bed Coverings, Kent County, Maryland, 1710–1820," in *Uncoverings 1985,* Sally Garoutte, ed. (San Francisco: American Quilt Study Group, 1986), 19. See also Lynne Z. Bassett and Jack Larkin, *Northern Comfort: New England's Earliest Quilts, 1780–1850.* (Nashville: Rutledge Hill Press, 1998), 11.

25. RIQDP #507 (R I. Historical Society acc. no. 1985.7.1).

26. The assertion that this petticoat was quilted in Rhode Island is supported by the use of homespun for the waistband and blue-and-white striped homespun for the lining. The motifs in the border resemble those found in other petticoats made in Rhode Island and Connecticut.

27. Alice Morse Earle, *In Old Narragansett* (New York, Charles Scribner's Sons, 1898), 29. Earle mentions that Read wove coverlets, blankets, broadcloth, flannel, worsted, linen, tow-cloth, and calimanco.

28. Three are at the Rhode Island Historical Society (RIQDP #498, #506, #508). Two are at the Rhode Island School of Design Museum of Art. Susan Anderson Hay, *A World of Costume and Textiles: A Handbook of the Collection* (Providence: Museum of Art, Rhode Island School of Design, 1988), 142.

29. The Indian woman's name was Vice Hill and she ran away from James Hardy, Innholder. *The Newport Mercury,* September 23, 1760.

30. Jane Nylander, catalog entry, "Quilt," *The Great River: Art & Society of the Connecticut Valley, 1635–1820* (Hartford, Conn.: Wadsworth Atheneum, 1985), 378.

31. Beverly Lemire, "Redressing the History of the Clothing Trade in England: Readymade Clothing, Guilds, and Women Workers, 1650–1800," *Dress* 21 (1994): 67–69. According to Lemire, women workers in and around London quilted petticoats on frames for the domestic and overseas ready-to-wear trade. Prices ranged from six shillings for the least expensive to sixty shillings for the fanciest ones.

32. Nylander, *The Great River*, 378; Tandy Hersh, "18th Century Quilted Silk Petticoats Worn in America," in *Uncoverings 1984*, Sally Garoutte, ed. (San Francisco: American Quilt Study Group, 1985), 87; Bassett and Larkin, *Northern Comfort*, 13.

33. RIQDP #499 quilt, #500 valence, #501 headcloth, and #503 pillow shams. The quilt is backed with linen. The toile is a historical scene in brown.

34. RIQDP #705 and #618, respectively. T. F. Green was Governor of Rhode Island from 1933 to 1937.

35. Sally Garoutte, "Marseilles Quilts and Their Woven Offspring," in *Uncoverings 1982*, Sally Garoutte, ed. (San Francisco: American Quilt Study Group, 1983), 117; Susan Burrows Swan, *Plain and Fancy* (New York: Rutledge Books, 1977), 154; Kathryn Berenson, *Quilts of Provence* (New York: Henry Holt and Co., 1996), 19.

36. Swan, *Plain and Fancy*, 158.

37. Jacqueline Beaudoin-Ross, "An Early-Eighteenth-Century Pieced Quilt in Montreal," *Canadian Art Review* 6, no.2 (1979–80). This quilt is also discussed in Jonathon Holstein, "The American Block Quilt," in *In the Heart of Pennsylvania*, Jeannette Lasansky, ed. (Lewisburg, Pa.: Oral Traditions, 1986), 21. A second pieced quilt, dated 1704 through circumstantial evidence and family history, is located at the Essex Institute in Salem, Mass. Known as the Saltonstall quilt, its early date has been questioned by textile specialists. The quilt is illustrated in Patsy and Myron Orlofsky, *Quilts in America* (1974; reprint, New York: Abbeville Publishers, 1992), 33.

38. Beaudoin-Ross, "Pieced Quilt in Montreal." Although it is not known where the quilt was made, ownership suggests an English origin.

39. Deborah Kraak, "American Pieced Silk Quilts," paper presented at the Dublin Seminar for New England Folklife, Deerfield, Mass., June 28, 1997.

40. Alice Morse Earle, *Home Life in Colonial Days* (New York: Macmillan, 1898), 276. The Narragansett attribution comes from the index, which lists "old quilt in" under the heading "Narragansett" (462). Earle states that the marriage of Esther Powell to James Helme took place in 1738. However, the marriage of Esther Powell to Capt. James Helme is recorded as taking place in South Kingstown in 1746, not 1738. *Rhode Island Vital Records, New Series*, vol. 5, *Washington County, Rhode Island, Marriages from Probate Records 1685–1860*, 175.

41. The Heritage Quilt Project of New Jersey, *New Jersey Quilts 1777 to 1950* (Paducah, Ky.: American Quilter's Society, 1992), Plate 23; Roderick Kiracofe, *The American Quilt: A History of Cloth and Comfort, 1750–1950* (New York: Clarkson N. Potter, 1993), figs. 48–50, 50–53, 61, 63; *An American Sampler: Folk Art from the Shelburne Museum* (Washington, D.C.: National Gallery of Art, 1987), Plates 78, 81, 83, 85, 88.

42. RIQDP #771, Varnum House, East Greenwich, R.I.

43. RIQDP #808, Paine House, Coventry, R.I.

44. Barbara Brackman, *Clues in the Calico* (McClean, Va.: EMS Publications, 1989), 125. A quilt with a fabric similar to the boder in Figure 11 was displayed at the Vermont Quilt Festival in 1994; it was dated 1808–9 and probably was made in Gloucester or Marblehead, Mass.

45. The pattern for the templates was made of tin or firm cardboard, and the individual templates were brown paper or letter paper according to Earle, *Home Life in Colonial Days*, 272.

46. RIQDP #88; made just before her death in 1888.

47. Department of Textiles, *Notes on Applied Work and Patchwork* (London: Victoria and Albert Museum, 1938), 12.

48. Barbara Brackman's earliest Hexagon quilt is dated 1813. *Encyclopedia of Pieced Quilt Patterns* (Paducah, Ky.: American Quilter's Society, 1993), 30; Amelia Peck states that Elizabeth Clarkson's Honeycomb quilt, made circa 1830, "is a very early example of this type of template quilt in America," *American Quilts & Coverlets in the Metropolitan Museum of Art* (New York: Metropolitan Museum of Art and Dutton Studio Books, 1990), 24.

49. RIQDP #776; Varnum House, East Greenwich, R.I.

50. RIQDP #457 and #458; the current owner is the great-granddaughter of the maker.

51. Brackman, *Clues*, 123–25.

52. *New England Farmer,* December 8, 1826, 156–57.

53. Weeden mentions that a Rhode Island seamstress named Joanna Dugglass was paid for overseeing quilting in South Kingstown in 1765. *Early Rhode Island,* 287. Antiquarian Alice Morse Earle wrote that she knew of a 1752 quilting bee of ten days' duration in Narragansett. *Home Life in Colonial Days,* 274.

54. Howard A. Keach, *Burrillville; As it was, and as it is,* (Providence: Knowles, Anthony & Co., Printers, 1856), 143. The author referred to both quilting parties and quilting bees.

55. November 24, 1856, September 3,1856, Mary M. Dawley, *Diary,* 1856–1864, Manuscripts Collection, R.I. Historical Society, Providence. The East Greenwich Soldier's Aid Society reorganized as the Ladies' Freedmen's Aid Society in 1865 and began making quilts to be distributed to freed slaves through the National Freedmen's Relief Association in Washington, D.C. D. H. Greene, *History of the Town of East Greenwich and Adjacent Territory from 1677 to 1877* (Providence: J.A. & R.A. Reid, 1877), 237–45. Fig. 93 was made by members of the Frenchtown Sewing Society in 1874.

56. Jane C. Nylander, "Flowers from the Needle," in *An American Sampler: Folk Art from the Shelburne Museum* (Washington, D.C.: National Gallery of Art, 1987), 42.

57. *New England Farmer*, October 27, 1826, 108–9.

58. Virginia Gunn, "Victorian Silk Template Patchwork in American Periodicals 1850–1875," in *Uncoverings 1983,* Sally Garoutte, ed. (San Francisco: American Quilt Study Group, 1984), 9–25.

59. Ibid., 20–21

60. "Recent Acquisitions, A Selection: 1995–1996," *The Metropolitan Museum of Art Bulletin* (New York: Metropolitan Museum of Art, 1996), 50. The quilt was first illustrated in Orlofsky, *Quilts in America* (1992 reprint), Plate 142.

61. J. Leander Bishop, *A History of American Manufactures from 1608 to 1860* (1866; reprint, New York: Augustus M. Kelley, 1966), 457.

62. Coleman, *Transformation,* 108

63. Ibid., 299.

64. Patrick T Conley, *The Irish in Rhode Island* (Providence: Rhode Island Heritage Commission, 1986), 9.

65. Ibid., 10–15, 25.

66. Albert K. Aubin, *The French in Rhode Island* (Providence: R.I. Heritage Commission, 1988), 14.

67. Steve Dunwell, *The Run of the Mill* (Boston: David R. Godine, 1978), 113.

68. Aubin, *The French in Rhode Island,* 14-15.

69. Conley, *Album,* 118.

70. Conley, *Album,* 113; Bartlett, *From Slave to Citizen,* 60–61; *Creative Survival,* 28–51.

71. Conley, *Album,* 162.

72. Dunwell, *Mill,* 116.

73. Valerie Wilson, "Quiltmaking in Counties Antrim and Down: Some Preliminary Findings from the Ulster Quilt Survey," in *Uncoverings 1991*, Laurel Horton, ed. (San Francisco: American Quilt Study Group, 1982), 142–75.

74. RIQDP #399,#4 and #423, RIQDP #847. Wilson states that among 130 Ulster quilts made between 1860 and the 1890s, the Irish Chain was one of the most popular pieced patterns, and that Turkey red and white Heart and Spade or Heart and Dove patterns stood out among the appliqué quilts. Wilson, "Ulster Quilt Survey," 154.

75. RIQDP #174, #176, #242. Delima's sewing basket still exists. It contains wooden templates for patchwork and appliqué quilts, commercial quilt patterns, unfinished blocks, and hexagons intended for a Grandmother's Flower Garden.

76. Marie Durand, "La Courtepointe Québécoise: Création ou emprunt?" *Material History Review* 34 (Fall 1991): 30.

77. Carmela E. Santoro, *The Italians in Rhode Island: The Age of Exploration to the Present 1524–1989* (Providence: R.I. Heritage Commission, 1990), 4.

78. Jane Schneider, "Trousseau as Treasure: Some Contradictions of Late Nineteenth-Century Change in Sicily," in *Beyond the Myths of Culture: Essays in Cultural Materialism*, ed. Eric B. Ross (San Francisco: Academic Press, 1980), 323–56.

79. Michael Edward Bell and Carol Bell, *Quilting: Folk Tradition of the Rhode Island Afro American Community* (Providence: R.I. Black Heritage Society and the St. Martin de-Porres Senior Citizens Center, n.d.); study of tape recordings, slides, and newspaper clippings at the R.I. Preservation Commission revealed that the quilts were not made in Rhode Island before 1950.

80. Tape-recorded interviews (tapes RI81-MB-R22, RI81-MB-R24, RI84-MLH-CI), Rhode Island Preservation Commission, Providence, R.I.

# Woven Documents

GAIL FOWLER MOHANTY

*Technological &*

*Economic Factors*

*Influencing Rhode*

*Island Textile*

*Production to 1840*

THE FABRICS IN A QUILT, WHETHER NEW OR RECYCLED, OFFER CLUES for tracing consumption patterns, technological developments, and economic cycles over time. On the basis of the quilt alone, the sources and manufacture of the fabrics are difficult to discern. With additional documentation such as factory swatch books, business records, or accurate provenance, researchers may estimate when the maker created the quilt, where the textiles came from, and how they were manufactured.[1] To determine whether fabrics are of domestic or foreign manufacture and of home or industrial production remains problematic, but clues inherent in the material become evident when paired with documentary evidence and historical interpretation.[2]

The study of a quilt begins with an examination of the material evidence and then moves to other sources such as comparable dated fabrics and maker's genealogy. If researchers make interpretations based largely on visual identification, some clues remain hidden. Few authors place quilting or quilts in the larger contexts of domestic livelihood, commercial manufacture, and household economy. Often quilts are viewed as significant in and of themselves.[3] Knowledge of technological capability and product availability offers useful temporal evidence. In this essay, the history of domestic and industrial textile manufacture provides a lens that brings quilt fabrics into focus. Centering on hand- and power-processing of woven fabrics with an eye to demand and availability, this essay links the major technological and economic developments to quilts through their fibers, yarns, and fabrics.

The three time frames discussed are colonial preindustrial textile production from 1636 through 1789, early textile industrialization prior to power loom mechanization from 1790 through 1814, and the period from 1815 to

1840 when Rhode Island textile manufacturers gradually implemented power-loom mechanization. These time frames relate to technological and economic issues as well as to the material selected for study. The first period is characterized by both home production and the importation of all varieties of fabrics from abroad. During the middle period, a transition occurred that added American factory-made textiles into the mix of products available to Rhode Island consumers. After the 1815 introduction of the power loom into New England factories, cotton fabrics grew to dominate the market. The early plaids, stripes, and tickings continued in importance until printing technology enabled firms to duplicate these woven designs and textures.

*Preindustrial Textile Manufacture in Rhode Island: 1636–1789*

Myths obscure preindustrial textile manufacture in the American colonies with the same force as those shrouding quiltmaking. Historians struggle to dispel mistaken assumptions concerning the growth and exportation of raw materials, self-sufficiency, textile importation, and domestic cloth production.[4] Importation loomed large as the provider of the most necessary fabrics to homes, both urban and rural. However, a review of documentary material pertaining to preindustrial textile production in Rhode Island and the rest of New England suggests that a large percentage of the population either produced or processed textile fibers. Plentiful wool and flax fibers resulted from the raising of sheep for meat and growing of flax for flaxseed exportation or linseed oil production. Probate inventories and account books verify the relationship between agriculture, fibers, and domestic textiles. Documentary information regarding textile manufacture offers clear evidence of the kinds of domestic materials available to Rhode Islanders.[5]

WOOL

The production of both wool and flax began in New England almost immediately after the establishment of the colonies. William Coddington of Newport sent sheep to John Winthrop of Boston in 1648 and provided Winthrop with the following instructions to aid in sheep breeding: "I could have sent yow longe leged and biger sheepe but these are better breed. I have sent yow five blacke and five whit. I judged it best so to doe, yow not expressinge your desire to me. . . . If you desire to have more whit sheepe than black, then rambe your ewes with whit rambs; if more blacke then yow may save a blacke rambe out of your breed of blacke ewes but by all means put not to your rambes till the latter end of next month, November."[6] The emphasis in this correspondence on the color of the wool indicates that the fiber as well as the meat was of importance to Winthrop. Rhode Island was known for its flocks of sheep even during the seventeenth century.[7]

Rhode Islanders began fabricating their own textiles during the mid–seventeenth century out of necessity because British domestic problems inhibited the exportation of fabrics to the colonies. Sheep, raised initially to support the European provisions trade, now provided Rhode Islanders with a source of woolen fibers for domestic production. These animals grew thick coats of fairly long-staple wool. The wool gathered from these sheep supplied Rhode Islanders with enough material for flock beds,[8] felt hats, stockings and fabric, with ample wool left for domestic and foreign coastal trade.

The presence of fulling mills also indicates domestic textile production in the colony. Woolen fabrics often were fulled to increase the density of the weave. Fulling involves soaking, shrinking, and beating woolens with water-powered hammers, which felt and soften the fabric. Fullers also might finish the cloth by napping, shearing, or glazing it to modify the cloth's surface texture. The medallion quilt illustrated in Figure 25 is typical of the preindustrial period because of its woolen face, batting, and back. The existence of numerous fulling mills throughout Rhode Island verify that Rhode

FIG. 25. Medallion quilt, late eighteenth or early nineteenth century. Wool top, back, and batting, 93 x 86½ in. Hand-pieced and hand-quilted in crosshatch and squares, 6 stitches per inch. Maker unknown. Slater Mill Historical Site, Pawtucket, Rhode Island (72.050.76). RIQDP #674.

Woolen fabrics frequently appear in Rhode Island's preindustrial quilts. Nearly every town had a fulling mill where local weavers could have their woolen fabrics fulled. The fulling operation cleaned, shrank, and felted the fabrics. The beige wool is printed with a small pin-dot pattern, implying that it was not homemade. This quilt, with its large block in the center surrounded by simple square blocks, was made to fit a four-poster bed.

Islanders produced woolen fabrics at a level that made fulling a commercially viable occupation.[9] In 1719 Thomas Hazard's father gave Thomas Culverwell land for a fulling mill implying that Kingston farmers produced enough wool to support a mill.[10]

FLAX  Seventeenth-century Rhode Islanders raised flax and made fabric from the fibers. The author of *New England's First Fruits* described the promotion of flax and hemp along with sheep raising around 1642: "In prospering hempe and flaxe so well that it is frequently sown, spun and woven into linnen cloath; and so with cotton wool (which we have at very reasonable rates from the Islands) and our linen yarne we can make dimitees and fustians for our summer cloathing; and having a matter of 1,000 sheepe which prosper well to begin withall, in a competent time we hope to have woolen cloath there made."[11]

By the mid–eighteenth century Rhode Island exported flaxseed grown in East Greenwich and other towns to Ireland to support the Irish linen trade. Seed exportation and oil processing left flax stalks that farmers and the community processed for a variety of purposes. Upholsterers used flax waste to stuff furniture. Farmers stuffed ticks with dried vegetable waste including corn shucks and flax dross. In addition, individuals processed the flax stalks to produce both line (long fibers) and tow (short fibers).

Rhode Island's eighteenth-century linseed oil mills indicate a flax culture centered on processing seeds into oil for making paint for houses and sailing vessels. Apparently South Kingstown and Hopkinton had the earliest Rhode Island linseed oil mills. These two communities differed in population and economy. South Kingstown's economy centered on raising sheep, flax, and horses. As did other Rhode Island farmers, South Kingstown's planters produced crops of flaxseed for exportation to Ireland. This trade fostered the erection of linseed oil mills to process surplus seed. Hopkinton, populated by some 200 people at the end of the seventeenth century, had fulling, carding, and oil mills, suggesting that manufacturing focused on products secondary to the predominantly subsistence farming characteristic of the region.[12]

COTTON  A third fiber available to Rhode Islanders during the seventeenth century was cotton. The colony received long-staple cotton from Barbados. Weavers mixed cotton with other fibers to extend its usage because of the fiber's relative scarcity and expense. In 1674 William Harris pointed out, "As to cloth there are made there linsey woollseys, and others of cotton and wool, and some all sheeps-wool, but the better sort of linnen is brought from England. They have many wool combers, spin their wool very fine of which make some Tammyes but for their own private use."[13] By 1674 cotton appears in probate inventories in Providence and Newport. The quantities ranged from three to fifteen pounds. Probate records commonly list cotton along with fiber-processing tools after 1710.[14]

Like cotton, raw silk was not a readily available fiber in Rhode Island during the colonial period and the years of the early republic. Britain encouraged the establishment of sericulture in the colonies, expecting to develop a product for export. Silkworms were raised in the colonies by 1762, yet Britain passed its last bounty to support colonial sericulture in 1769. Britain's failure to renew this incentive was a response to inadequate production and the changing political climate with its colonies.

SILK

Colonial governments also used bounties to encourage textile production including flax, hemp, wool, and silk. In 1734, Connecticut offered bounties on sewing silk, silk stockings, and silk stuffs. For a time, Moses Brown grew mulberry bushes in anticipation of raising silkworms in Providence. Pennsylvania silk growers succeeded in producing yarns and fabrics from their own worms. Yet P. Brocket's 1769 report of domestically produced silk fabric was less than complimentary: "Those home made silks were fuzzy as well as stiff. The colors did not stand well. They were defective in luster." News reports of individuals wearing mantuas and gowns of domestic silk, however, praised the spinners and weavers for their industry and skill in producing a material ordinarily imported. Despite efforts to raise silkworms and to manufacture silk domestically in Rhode Island and elsewhere during the preindustrial era, silk growers never produced a marketable quantity of fiber.[15]

The colonial government of Rhode Island sought to encourage weavers to fabricate cloth from the fibers produced. During the seventeenth century, communities provided male artisans with the land and resources to build shops and establish trade along traditional lines. Between 1675 and 1700, Providence had six weavers and at least two fulling mills finishing woolen fabrics for the weavers and the community of 1,179.[16]

DOMESTIC FABRIC PRODUCTION

On the basis of Providence probate inventories from 1675 to 1720, families performed some portion of textile manufacturing in their homes including carding, flax processing, spinning, knitting, and weaving. In Rhode Island's more agricultural communities such as Portsmouth and East Greenwich, civil records and family business accounts describe extensive domestic textile processing and fabrication within the home for family use and to assist neighbors. For over three generations the Carder family of Warwick, Rhode Island, exchanged agricultural labor, weaving, knitting, and fulling with their neighbors for goods they could not produce themselves. Their accounts document a complex series of exchanges with their neighbors.[17]

FIG. 26. (*Opposite*) Whole-cloth quilt, late eighteenth century. Wool top, back, and batting, 94 x 88 in. Hand-stitched and hand-quilted in diamond pattern, 8 stitches per inch. Descended in the Howland family, Hope, Rhode Island. URI Historic Textile and Costume Collection (1958.02.03). RIQDP #886.

Whole-cloth quilts like this one are often made from fine wool fabrics. This quilt's glazed surface is said to have been achieved with an egg wash. The quilting thread is wool, and the thread used to piece the top is linen, which is characteristic of preindustrial quilts in Rhode Island.

In urban areas, weavers subsisted primarily on their weaving, while those operating in less densely populated areas combined weaving with farm-related activities.

Throughout the seventeenth and eighteenth centuries, Rhode Islanders produced a variety of utilitarian fabrics to use within their homes and to trade. Household accounts and store records detail Rhode Island's preindustrial textile manufacture. A minimum of fifty individuals titled "weaver" pursued the trade in nine Rhode Island towns between 1680 and 1780. This does not account for the individuals who wove fabric and were not identified as weavers in civil records. Catherine Greene, wife of Governor William Greene, recorded the kinds and quantity of fabric produced at her family home in Potawomut during the Revolutionary War period. Mrs. Greene hired a series of artisans to weave her cloth including several African Americans. From 1776 through 1780, the fabric produced in the Greene household included worsted, flannel, kersey, checks, plain linen, handkerchiefs, coverlets, blankets, bedtick, diaper, and tow. No cotton was woven into any of the fabrics; her coverlets were made of linen and wool.[18] The home-produced fabrics consisted entirely of simply constructed utilitarian goods with the exception of diaper cloth and coverlets.

Thomas B. Hazard of South Kingstown, known as Nailer Tom, maintained a diary from the mid–eighteenth century through the mid–nineteenth century that documented both social and economic interchanges. Hazard's diary details fiber production, weaving, fulling, and tailoring. The account clearly shows how work was organized and links the work directly to specific exchanges. Weavers and spinners who exchanged their skills for Nailer Tom's goods are identified.[19] Nailer Tom's list of fabrics includes curtain material, coating, and cloth for children's clothes.

Probate, legislation, and personal accounts show an increasingly active level of textile production. This increase corresponded to the level of the fiber production resulting from both the raising of sheep for the provisions' trade and the growing of flax for either oil making or flax seed exportation. Textile manufacture grew continuously from the 1640s onward. The consistent increase in the number of sheep, weavers, and fulling mills demonstrated the rate and extent of that growth.

Whole-cloth quilts with wool fronts, backs, and battings formed common preindustrial quilts. The quilt shown in Figure 26 is made of a plain, possibly homespun and home-woven, fabric made from unusually fine wool. It has a glazed surface said to have been achieved with egg wash. The use of linen sewing thread for piecing indicates that this is a preindustrial quilt. The wool waste interlining evidences the common availability of the animal fiber in Rhode Island.

Although Rhode Islanders manufactured goods from domestically produced fibers, they could not produce enough for their household and apparel needs. Fashion played a role in determining the uses of domestic and imported goods. While domestic goods proved suitable for everyday toweling and handkerchiefs, imported goods provided homes with bed hangings, fine linens, and fancy fabrics unavailable in quantity through domestic channels. In 1729, Englishman Joshua Gee described the efforts of New England traders to provide sufficient goods to exchange for foreign cloth and clothing:

> New England takes from us all sorts of woolen manufacture, linen, sail cloth cordage for rigging their vessels, haberdashery, etc. To raise money to pay for what they take of us, they are forced to visit the Spanish coast where they pick up any commodity they can trade for. They carry lumber and provisions to Sugar Plantations, exchange provision for Logwood with Logwood cutters in Campeachey. They send pipe and barrel staves and fish to Spain, Portugal and the Streights. They send Pitch tar and turpentine to England with some skins. But all those commodities fall very short of purchasing their clothing in England.[20]

Assessing the percentage of domestic or imported fabrics used by colonists presents problems. Probate inventories of household goods and the terminology used to describe them varies based on the knowledge of the surveyor. Occasionally inventories use the terms "home cloth" or "homespun cloth." While these terms imply local production, they do not indicate whether the cloth was made in a shop or home. The quality of the cloth also is not described. Inventories sometimes identify a "piece at weaver's" or "piece of cloth at fulling mill." These citations place the fabric firmly in the realm of domestic manufactures. Typically fabric is identified by its type, for example sheeting or woolen cloth. The ticking that covered flock beds or feather beds is not described, nor are toweling and handkerchiefs because they may not be listed individually in inventories. In addition lists specify flock or feather beds and as a consequence do not identify the fabric used for the cover.[21]

Fabrics cited in Providence civil records between 1680 and 1726 include blanketing, kersey, homespun cloth, bagging, checks, handkerchiefs, linen and woolen cloth, coverlet, serge, flannel, and tow. These fabrics differed greatly in quality as compared to imported silks, mohair, satins, and baronette. Domestic manufactures supplied families with blankets, coverlets, workshirts, toweling, baby diapers, coarse sheets, and other everyday household fabrics. Later these materials were used as rags or sold to the local paper manufacturer. These domestic cloths filled a distinct need but were not as dear as the imports. People bartered to obtain imported goods not available through the local network or produced in the home.[22]

During the eighteenth century, merchants encountered resistance to imported fabrics of sleazy quality, inappropriate color, or out-of-date style. The responses of buyers suggest that style and contemporary taste were significant factors in imported cloth consumption. Merchants, unable to sell out-of-fashion fabrics or unpopular colors, constantly requested the precise goods that would be salable.[23] Taste influenced colonial choice of imported fabric rather than the meeting of basic needs. Domestically manufactured utilitarian goods reduced demand for imported materials of the same quality and enabled colonists to look toward fashion when purchasing imported fabrics.

Remnants of well-documented seventeenth- and eighteenth-century fabrics of American domestic manufacture are few. Textiles required intensive labor from seed or lamb to finished cloth and were used until they no longer existed. Some everyday fabrics were saved and reused to patch garments, piece into bed coverings, or provide stuffing. Imported fabrics were treasured, saved, and made into pieced bed coverings or quilts. The use of fabric remnants as part of a quilt indicates that some fabrics were prized beyond their ability to cover nakedness or shelter a body from the elements. Quilts extended the usefulness of old bed hangings. Recycling provided a new life for an imported fabric no longer strong enough on its own but still considered beautiful.

The whole-cloth quilt illustrated in Figure 27 is made of an imported pillar print. It is backed with a pair of old hand-spun, hand-woven linen sheets with cross-stitched initials, evidence of reuse (Fig. 28). In this case quilting the fabrics extended the life of valued goods and created a decorative bed covering cherished by its owners for generations.[24]

Eighteenth-century American quilts document textile importation from European nations. Their value as evidence of British textile manufacture has generated study and comment.[25] Historians of American textile manufactures might find domestic textiles surviving in museum collections, but not always in the expected places. These textiles, overlooked by their use and placement in quilts, offer valuable evidence of domestic production and the transformation of life and livelihood with the coming of industrialization.[26] A coat, dress, or petticoat might be disassembled and incorporated into a quilt. A bed cover might include both imported textiles dating to the pre- and early industrial period on the backside, while the quilt top might include newer imported and domestic manufactures. A case in point is the One-Patch quilt in Figure 29, whose front is pieced from ginghams,

stripes, and printed cottons dating to the mid-nineteenth century, while its back (Fig. 30) incorporates textiles dating to the late eighteenth and early nineteenth centuries.

As a result, examples of colonial American manufactures in quilts are rarely displayed because they compose the underside and sometimes the inside. Quilt batting is sometimes an old blanket, woolen fibers, or cotton material. New tops and backs rejuvenated older quilts, hiding early fabrics from view. Sometimes the backs are made of various pieces of ordinary utilitarian fabrics such as sheeting, plaid, check, or gingham or even inex-

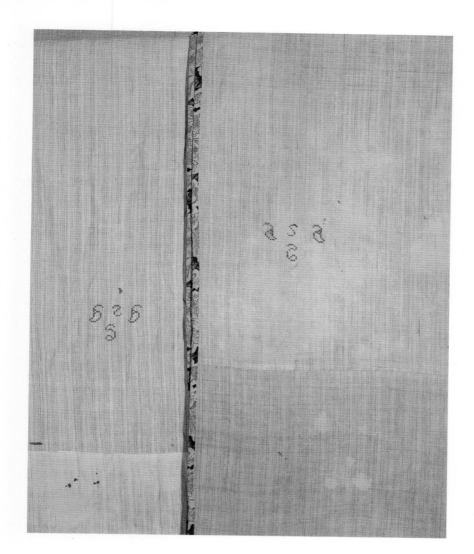

FIG. 27. (*Opposite*) Whole-cloth quilt, ca. 1800. Cotton top, linen back, 104 x 106 in. Hand-sewn and hand-quilted in interlocking circle pattern, 7 stitches per inch. Descended in the Bailey family, Little Compton, Rhode Island. Collection of the Little Compton Historical Society. RIQDP #619.

This whole-cloth quilt is made of an imported pillar print. Pillar prints first appeared in the late eighteenth century when neoclassical taste influenced the design of printed textiles. Fabrics with such large-scale designs were used as furnishing fabrics, particularly for bed hangings. Often old furnishing fabrics found a second life as parts of quilts.

FIG. 28. Detail. The back of the whole-cloth quilt illustrated in Figure 27 is seamed from a pair of old linen sheets and embroidered with two sets of cross-stitched initials "A.S.A." and the number "6." Such markings enabled the housewife to rotate the sheets, allowing for even wear. The linen yarns display uneven coloration, a clue that the sheets might have been made from locally grown flax.

pensive yardage bought new.[27] That the textiles span both pre- and early industrialization is indicated in the style of the prints, the kinds of fabric, and the less visible characteristics such as fiber content of quilting thread and batting. In Rhode Island the use of cotton is suggestive of postindustrial periods because of its relative scarcity during preindustrial times. The use of domestically produced fiber stuffing such as wool flock or flax waste indicates the greater availability of these fibers; the presence of such materials is not helpful in dating quilts because they continued to be used for long periods before and after industrialization.

The thread used to stitch a quilt and the method of quilting also provides us with some indicators of date. For instance, cotton thread was not used or perhaps rarely used in Rhode Island until after 1794, when Samuel Slater's first wife Hannah developed machine-spun sewing thread with her

husband.[28] A hand-stitched quilt could represent any time period, but a machine-stitched quilt must have been made after the invention of the sewing machine. A thread containing synthetic fibers indicates a post-1960 date for piecing, quilting, and / or finishing.[29] These factors all focus on the functional and not the aesthetic features of quilts, and these clues are pertinent to determining the age and the context of quilt production.

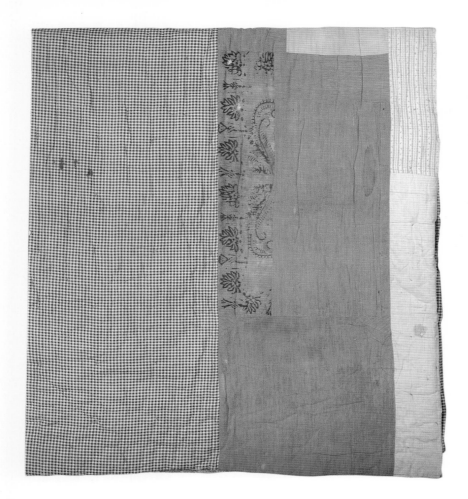

*Early Industrialization: 1790–1814*

By the late eighteenth century, merchants and traders sought land-based investments to counteract risky maritime trade. These investers looked toward the developing textile industry as a source of potential growth income. In Rhode Island, merchants including Daniel Anthony, Andrew Dexter, Moses Brown, and Lewis Peck initiated mechanized fiber-preparing processes in Providence. Moses Brown and William Almy, Brown's son-in-law, formed a partnership that led to the establishment of the first successful water-powered, cotton spinning mill in the United States. Initially their enterprise mirrored the innovations used by other such establishments in Worcester, Beverly, Hartford, Norwich, New York City, Baltimore, and Philadelphia.[30]

Brown encouraged Almy to acquire the most advanced machinery locally available. By 1789, the partners had acquired spinning, carding, and roving machines from Rhode Island businessmen and a Hanover, Massachusetts, clockmaker. Brown also hired artisans to make a few machines based on the "state models" that Massachusetts state senator Hugh Orr displayed at his house in Bridgewater. The spinning mill in Providence included hand-driven spinning frames, carding machines, and roving equipment. Unfortunately, because the frames were hand-driven rather than water-powered, the yarns produced were too weak to be used as warp. Brown and Almy used the yarn for filling in their own cloth, which mixed cotton and linen. They also sold the product to local weavers to be used as weft. Brown and Almy and other textile firms relied on locally hand-spun woolen or linen for warp yarns.[31] Commercial cotton cloth production was limited to just a few kinds of linen-cotton or woolen-cotton mixtures such as double jean back corduroy and materials that incorporated flax warp with cotton weft such as fustian, velvet, and velveteen.

Independent professional weavers purchased machine-spun yarns in Rhode Island during this era (Fig. 31). David and George Buffum operated a workshop in Newport's courthouse where they produced velvet and flannel. Buffum fashioned the flannel from woolen weft spun by Thomas Bush of Newport. Buffum's weavers also wove nankeen and weaverette. John Reynolds opened a shop in East Greenwich producing woolen-cotton fabric mixtures. William Potter operated a textile business in 1789 in Providence where he produced goods of mixed wool and cotton. Peck and Dexter's workshop manufactured 2,164 yards of cloth, and Lewis Peck's weavers fabricated 2,500 yards of material in a shed he operated independently of his former partners during 1790.[32]

By 1790 Samuel Slater replaced hand-cranked mechanisms with water-powered spinning throstles in Ezekiel Carpenter's clothier's shop at the falls in Pawtucket. Moses Brown, and William Almy financially supported and eagerly encouraged Slater's efforts. With the successful completion and operation of the machinery, Slater formed a partnership with William Almy and Smith Brown called Almy, Brown, and Slater. In so doing, Slater not only introduced water-powered spinning but produced yarns by machine that were of a strength and hardness to be used as both warp and weft. Almy and Brown produced fabrics made from Almy, Brown, and Slater yarns in Providence and later Pawtucket weave-sheds and sold the product to weavers throughout the United States. Figure 32 illustrates a sample of checked cotton made from Slater-spun yarns around 1792. The variety of domestic fabrics increased after 1790 because the firm could produce both mixtures and all-cotton fabrics for customers who guided and shaped the product line.[33]

In 1793, Rogerson Dabney of Alexandria, Virginia, replied unfavorably to Almy and Brown about the goods they had sent him for sale. "Your favor of the 17th instant was duly received accompanied with a box of cotton goods. We are sorry to say we have as yet met with no sale for thee and

Fig. 31. "Weaver," *Panorama of Professions and Trades*, 1837. Courtesy of Slater Mill Historic Site, Pawtucket, Rhode Island.

indeed there is little prospect of selling them to advantage here as Nankeens are unusually worn by all ranks of people of consequence. The jeans and jeanettes are quite out of fashion. The season is also too far advanced to make sale of such goods to advantage, however you may rely on our utmost exersions to sell them to advantage."[34]

In 1794 Jackson and Nightengale of Savannah, Georgia, wrote to Almy and Brown regarding fabric samples sent in exchange for unprocessed

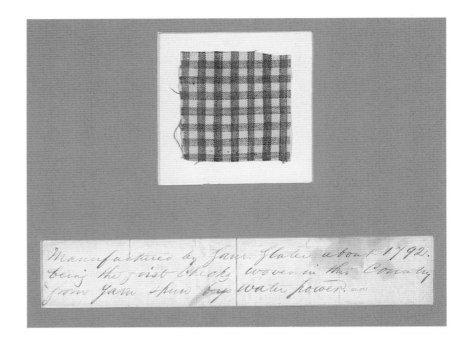

FIG. 32. Swatch of checked cotton made from yarns spun at Slater Mill, ca. 1792. Slater Mill Historic Site, Pawtucket, Rhode Island (52.077).

domestic cotton. At Almy and Brown's request, Jackson and Nightengale provided the firm with an estimate of the demand for certain textile commodities: "Should it prove so the consumption of this country would favor any considerably quant. of light cotton goods of every description particularly jeanettes and fustians. . . . The dark olive is the best color for the jeanettes and fustians and other fashionable colors for which the striped nankeen and white for Dimities, muslinettes etc. The prices of the articles will be regulated by the price at which the foreign articles of equal quality can be imported."[35] Jackson and Nightengale recognized that they were on the leading edge of domestic manufacture. They indicated that theirs was probably the first such source of domestic manufactures in quantity, and as such, they sought to assist Almy and Brown in making their establishment a success. Hence, they noted which colors and fabrics sold with speed and regularity. Neither weaverette nor velvet is mentioned among the fabrics of highest demand. Durable everyday fabrics such as dimity, jean, nankeen, and muslin competed with traditional nonindustrial manufactures but not necessarily with imports.

In 1797 Catharine Haines of New York contacted Almy and Brown with her reaction to the goods they had sent to her shop. She states:

The coarsest whitened cotton was very sailable and perhaps when our citizens return the fine may prove so too, but the unwhitened remains unsold neither do I think it will sell at all. . . . if it is not too much trouble

MS mentioned your having good homespun linen. I have had very good from New England. I mean tow cloth, if you have any I shall be obliged by puting in same box with cotton from 30–40 yards of good whitened tow linen sheeting width. I don't know the price but I have had the brown for 16 to 18p per yd tho I expect the withened will come higher if you have none bleached send 20 to 30 yds of brown.[36]

Clearly Haines desired standard utilitarian goods for household rather than fashionable use. Initially, Brown and Almy endeavored to compete with textiles imported from abroad by manufacturing velvets, baronettes, caronettes, and other pile fabrics, but this proved uncompetitive because domestic prices were higher.

The manufacture and use of hand-woven, hand-processed fabrics persisted after the introduction of water-powered cotton spinning and the rise in cotton cultivation in the southern parts of the United States. Quilts of this period were fabricated in simple pieced fashion. The hexagon quilt shown in Figure 33, made by Abigail Reynolds Greene, consists of a top pieced from solid-colored wool with a wool backing and batting. The wool probably came from sheep raised on Greene's farm in East Greenwich; surviving family account books reveal that wool was exchanged for cloth at local mills.[37] In this case the wool backing fabric includes the initials "A. R. 5," indicating that the backing fabric predates the quilter's marriage in 1811. Because of the relative scarcity of imported textiles during the early nineteenth century due to the Napoleonic Wars and the Embargo Act, indi-

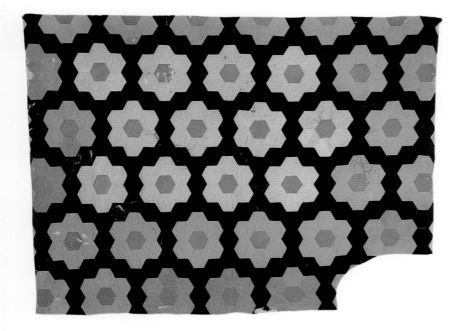

FIG. 33. Hexagon or Honeycomb quilt, early nineteenth century. Wool top, back, and batting, 93 x 70½ in. Hand-pieced and hand-quilted in outline pattern, 5 stitches per inch. Made by Abigail Reynolds Greene (1794–1889). Private collection. RIQDP #567.

The wool blankets that Abigail Reynolds Greene used to back this quilt are marked "A.R.5," her maiden initials, which tells us that the blankets predate her 1811 marriage. The wool for the front of the quilt and the batting could have been products of the Greene family farm in East Greenwich, since sheep were raised there. The quilt has been cut down from its original size.

FIG. 34. (*Opposite*) Nine-Patch quilt, ca.
1820. Wool top and back, cotton batting,
82 x 54 in. Hand-pieced and hand-quilted
in echo and fan pattern, 5 stitches per
inch. Maker unknown. Slater Mill
Historical Site, Pawtucket, Rhode Island
(72.050.74). RIQDP #675.

This much-used quilt is composed of
the types of fabrics manufactured by
Rhode Island's many small woolen mills
in the early nineteenth century. Checks,
stripes, and a variety of solid-colored
fabrics make up its patches.

viduals might have tended to recycle domestic textiles and to utilize older
blankets by quilting them to sturdy domestic textiles.

Another example of early nineteenth-century woven fabrics is shown in
Figure 34. The fabric could have been woven at home or at any of Rhode
Island's many small woolen mills.[38] This quilt is made of checked red and
black wool, striped red and green fabric, and plain fabric including a few
squares of jean. Some of the pieces are seamed. Either the maker prized the
fabrics used in the quilt and only had limited pieces available, or the quilter
recycled previously seamed fragments. The woolen back is composed of
two pieces of similar fabric seamed to span the quilt's full width. The material is a stripe pattern of green and red. The filler is a thin cotton batting.
Cotton was not commonly available until the fiber was brought to Rhode
Island in great quantity at the turn of the century. Expanded southern cotton production greatly increased the availability of cotton to the industrial-
izing centers of the north; the batting suggests a post-1790 date for assembling and completing the quilt. The pieces of the fabric were hand-stitched
with brown thread. The cotton thread is indicative of a post-1794 date. Although we do not have the provenance of this quilt, it probably was made
during the first quarter of the nineteenth century.

With the transatlantic transfer of British textile technology, the industrialization of textile manufacture burst forth onto the landscape of southern New England with tremendous speed and force after 1790. These early
businesses did not entirely eliminate the involvement of skilled craftsmen
in textile manufacture but changed the ways the involvement took place.
Independent and domestic textile manufacture continued alongside industrialization especially in woolen and flax production. Cotton availability
increased, and the fiber was introduced into commonly used fabrics such as
jean, diaper, and toweling. Additional quantities of machine-spun cotton
yarn and thread, and fabric woven from industrially produced yarns altered the fabrics available to consumers. In 1799 Daniel Waldo described
the response of the local population in Worcester, Massachusetts, to the
machine-spun yarns then available from Providence: "As people in this part
of the country are getting into the way of purchasing your yarns instead of
spinning for themselves, to keep them in these habits, it will be necessary
that I should always be supplied with a large quantity of assorted yarns
with every number and kind and in the proportion which your exporters
show to be propre."[39] By 1820 twenty-one out of eighty-two Rhode Island
mills produced thread or yarn alone, and thirty-one sold textiles as thread,
yarn or fabric.[40]

The whole-cloth quilt illustrated in Figure 35 suggests that domestic
weavers purchased warps to weave at home for their own use just as Waldo
indicated. The back of the quilt is a hand-woven cotton check of indigo and

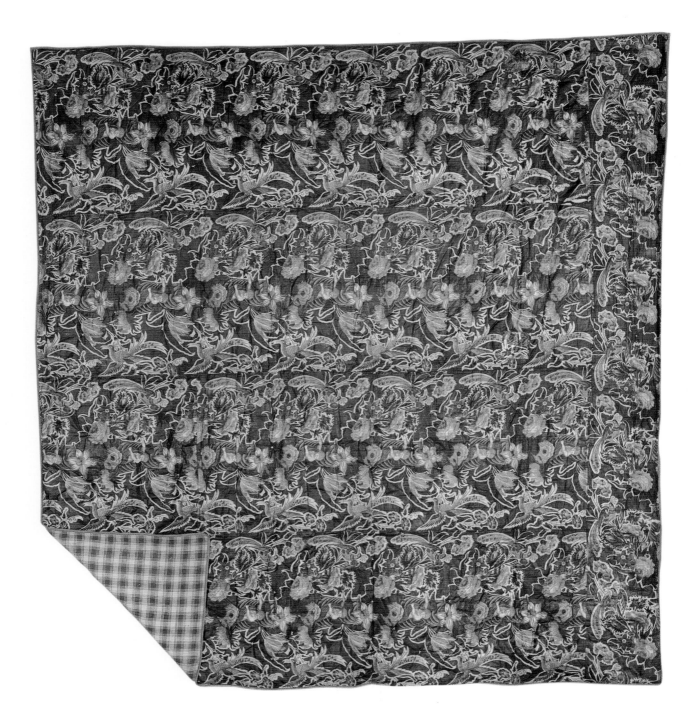

white machine-spun yarns. The top is a block print that probably was imported. Machine-spun warps and wefts saved families time and effort in producing textiles for their own use.

As more spinning mills competed with one another for the sale of their products, their survival necessitated bringing other commodities to market, namely woven fabrics. The manufacture and sale of simple utilitarian fabrics proved profitable, particularly prior to 1816, when foreign trade was disrupted by the Napoleonic War and the War of 1812. Mill owners took advantage of this situation and instituted various forms of fabric manufacture: they contracted with weavers to produce fabric in independent weave sheds, issued warps to individual part-time weavers, and commissioned cloth agents to issue warps to weavers.[41]

From 1794 to 1806, Almy and Brown engaged Benjamin Shepard's small jenny-spinning and weaving business in Taunton, Massachusetts, to produce bed ticking from machine-spun yarns. Silas and Benjamin Shepard, the older of Benjamin's sons, contracted with Almy and Brown to fabricate bed ticking from their machine-spun warps by dyeing or bleaching the yarns and weaving the fabric. The Shepard brothers' weave shed employed sufficient weavers to produce almost 1900 yards of fabric for Almy and Brown. Satisfied with the resulting materials, Almy and Brown continued to employ the Shepards exclusively to weave their warps until 1806. In the end the brothers had overseen the weaving of over 14,000 yards of ticking for Almy and Brown alone. The shed probably produced more materials for other manufacturers as well.[42]

Both the market for domestic fabrics and the skills of the available outworkers determined a manufacturer's choice of product line. Most textile manufacturers put out warps to hand-loom weavers to produce two- and four-harness plain-weave or twill fabrics. These simply constructed fabrics had a wide appeal and required little knowledge beyond basic weaving skills and limited weaving experience. The availability of a workforce with limited skill and experience, the need for simple and inexpensive domestic fabrics, the absence of foreign competition during the period of the War of 1812, and the complementary demands of the rural population and textile mill owners influenced fabric choices.[43]

Almy, Brown, and Slater's spinning mill was such a success that in three years, the firm outgrew its building and erected a new one at Pawtucket Falls at a man-made dam. The building became the prototype for subsequent mill buildings, but the original structure looked more like a barn than the larger mills that sprouted up along the banks of almost every river in the state. The Old Slater Mill, as it came to be called, was enlarged in 1801 and again in 1810. Like the industry itself, Slater Mill grew rapidly to keep pace with the ever-increasing demand for its goods.

By 1809 seventeen mills operated within a thirty-mile radius of Providence.[44] Thirty-six mills had been established by 1811 within the state of Rhode Island alone. The textile industry grew, sheltered from European competition because of the 1807 Embargo Act and deteriorating relations with Britain. In 1815, Samuel Ogden wrote a treatise entitled *Thoughts on What Probable Effect the Peace with Great-Britain Will Have on the Cotton*

FIG. 35. (*Opposite*) Whole-cloth quilt, 1800–25. Cotton top and back, 2-ply linen tie, 92 x 88 in. Hand-pieced, tied. Maker unknown. Collection of the Little Compton Historical Society. RIQDP #620.

Quilts from the first quarter of the nineteenth century exhibit characteristics of technological transition. The front of this quilt is an imported furnishing fabric with a hand-blocked bird motif. The back is a checked fabric woven by hand from machine-spun cotton yarns. The quilt is tied with hand-spun linen thread.

*Manufactures of This Country: Interspersed with Remarks on Our Bad Management in the Business and the Way to Improvement so as to Meet Imported Goods in Cheapness at Our Home Market, Pointed Out,* foretelling the devastating effect foreign goods would have on the market following the end of the War of 1812.[45]

## The Maturing of Rhode Island's Textile Industry: 1815–1840

The War of 1812 boosted Rhode Island's textile manufacturing, but after the war low-priced British goods flooded the market, driving many mills out of business. Depressed economic conditions, which initially impeded textile manufacture between 1814 and 1820 in all of the textile producing regions of the United States, also prevailed in Rhode Island resulting in a high level of bankruptcy. This depression caused numerous New England textile mills to cease operation and others to curtail production severely. Protective tariffs introduced from 1816 onward failed to help Rhode Island mills overcome the prevailing economic environment. The state's textile factories had an average of one-third less capital available to them than larger, better capitalized Waltham- or Lowell-style textile firms. As detailed below, these factors inhibited Rhode Island textile entrepreneurs from investing in technological developments until about 1826.[46]

The 1820 Census of Manufactures records the complaints of many Rhode Island textile factory agents. The mill agents charged that low-priced foreign goods, the lack of federal aid, poorly repaired or maintained equipment, and low or no profit margins contributed to their inability to overcome indebtedness. When McLane issued his 1833 Report on Manufactures, fewer than half the textile mills founded during the predepression era had survived the poor economic conditions. Eighty-four textile companies reported to McLane. Thirteen of the 84 mills reported periods of bankruptcy and shutdowns. Few of the reporting firms had dates of establishment prior to 1815. In 1816, Nathan Appleton visited Pawtucket in preparation for writing his work on power-loom development. He reported that most of the mills were not operating. The dramatic failure of the industry was striking after its strong start. In particular Rhode Island's industry had grown very rapidly during the golden years of 1790 to 1815; however, Massachusetts firms soon handily overtook Rhode Island's growth. Between 1820 and 1830 Rhode Island's textile industry had an annual growth of 12.4 percent, while in Massachusetts textile manufacturing grew 21.2 percent annually.[47]

The tariff of 1816 protected the cotton textile industry from foreign importation after the War of 1812, and the U.S. normalized trade with both England and France. In addition to the tariff, a minimum-valuation proviso levied greater duties on fabrics of cheap, simple construction such as sheeting and shirting than on those of more complex manufacture. The heavier

FIG. 36. (*Opposite*) Medallion quilt, after 1828. Cotton top and back, 76 x 64 in. Hand-pieced, tied, decorated with pom-poms. Maker unknown. Varnum House, East Greenwich, Rhode Island. RIQDP #766.

A testimonial to both British printed cottons exported to the United States and to the frugality of a Rhode Island quilt-maker, this top is pieced from selvages and ends of fabrics from England's leading print works. Visible in the patches are style numbers, dates, British manufacture stamps, and names of print works, including Hargreaves Brothers, William Allen of Manchester, and William Grant & Brother. Numerous scraps are printed with the dates 1827 and 1828. Manchester was the center of the cotton industry in England, and many English immigrants to Rhode Island trained in that city's textile mills.

duty on less expensive, coarse imported fabrics protected the kinds of fabrics that could be produced on early power looms.[48]

Rhode Island textile entrepreneurs avoided direct competition with inexpensive and doubly protected machine-made fabrics from Massachusetts and other states by producing multiharness and multishuttle weaves such as bed ticking, check, or plaid. Such fabrics were still woven by hand. Manufacturers temporarily accepted lower percentage profits until they invested in the new power-loom innovations between 1826 and 1828.

These technological limitations provided mill entrepreneurs with a market unaffected by power-loom technology but vulnerable to imported printed cottons. The medallion quilt pictured in Figure 36 is composed of British bolt ends with the names of many major British printing mills of the late 1820s. This quilt is a testimonial to the value of British printed cottons

An unknown quilter made this utility quilt and four other ones with similar fabrics and patterns. She (or he) must have had access to fabrics from local mills. Each quilt is pieced from industrially made fabrics including plaids, checks, stripes, and glazed cambric. These were typical products of Rhode Island mills during the 1830s. This quilt shows a range of patchwork blocks of the period including Pinwheel, Nine-Patch, Broken Dishes, Flying Geese, Four-Patch, and Two-Patch. In the other strip quilts, the most common blocks are Diamond in a Square, Album Patch, and Broken Dishes. Perhaps the quiltmaker was British; quiltmakers in rural England at this time favored strip quilts known as "strippies."

during this period. Printed cottons may have been relatively scarce due to the expense of paying the extra cost of tariff on imports and the rarity of competitive domestic products.[49]

Skillfully orchestrated capital management between 1816 and 1826 enabled Rhode Island firms to invest in technological innovations. Rhode Island's relatively limited cash resources shaped the mechanical textile innovations that developed and the ability of the firms to acquire them. Rhode Island manufacturers invested a larger percentage of their capital into fixed assets than the better-capitalized Massachusetts firm owners. The limited liquid assets available to buy new equipment prevented the immediate modernization of the factories. The financial structure of the businesses forced entrepreneurs to restrict investments on improvements to profits earned. When Rhode Island mill owners acquired power looms, they changed their production to fabrics that were protected by the minimum valuation proviso. Manufacturers could not power weave the same fabrics that they had made by hand but rather competed with their domestic producers to benefit more greatly from the tariff. They produced inexpensive single-shuttle, two-harness weaves such as plain-weave printing cloth, sheeting or shirting. Those Rhode Island businessmen continued to produce more expensive hand-woven fabrics until they acquired sufficient numbers of power looms to weave fabric from all the yarns they spun in their factories.[50]

Because contemporary power looms were somewhat deficient and limited investment capital prevented firms from purchasing a large number of power looms at one time, businesses continued to hire hand-loom artisans to produce ticking, plaid, gingham, and chambray. Such fabrics were the primary textiles hand-woven in Rhode Island. Power looms wove almost all the simple two-harness, plain-weave fabrics manufactured in the state by the early 1820s. Manufacturers sought to change entirely from hand to power manufacture thus simplifying their record keeping, reducing their risk, and facilitating the production process. To get the most from the tariffs, mill owners changed their product lines.[51] Figure 37 illustrates a quilt composed of mill remnants from this period: poorly dyed plain-weave sheeting, glazed cambric, checks, plaids, stripes, and a single-printed cotton.

Rhode Island firms had shifted entirely from hand to power production of cotton goods by 1830. Of the thirty-eight Rhode Island firms responding to McLane's 1830 questionnaire, all but four mills manufactured only power-loom fabrics. Few mills produced the variety of fabrics that characterized manufacture between 1816 and 1826. Five textile mills responded to both the 1820 and 1830 Census of Manufactures. Their answers documented a shift from hand-woven four-harness twill weave fabrics to plain weave goods after investing in power loom technology. Denton Thurber, agent for the United Manufacturing Company of Providence, provided McLane with this

general observation concerning this across-the-board change in product line: "It would require much time and labor to go into particulars, and I will only observe that prior to 1817, we made various kinds of goods but since the introduction of the powerloom, we have manufactured principally powerloom stripes."[52]

In terms of economic and technological change, much happened during the last two decades of the eighteenth century and the first three of the nineteenth. Both economy and technology shaped product lines by establishing limits for profitablility. Technological development was not the sole factor that enabled American manufacturers to compete with European production. Periods of trade disruption vitally contributed to the growth and development of both preindustrial and industrial manufacturing by limiting competition. Duties on imports served to create markets for certain types of American products.

By 1830, the basic developments for producing fabrics by power-loom weaving had been integrated into Rhode Island manufacturing. Mills with power looms specialized in either wool manufacture or cotton manufacture (Fig. 38). For producers of cotton goods, attention had turned to printing

cotton cloth to produce a marketable product. Cranston Print Works and other printing firms had begun using blocks and cylinders to add decorative designs to cotton print cloths. Calico printing in Rhode Island expanded rapidly in the 1830s, producing a myriad of fabrics put to use by quilters across the United States. This subject is addressed in the essay by Margaret Ordoñez.

Advances in textile production significantly changed the availability and the price of fabrics and thread. This ultimately affected the choices open to quiltmakers in Rhode Island and elsewhere. With the numerous textile mills within the state and the percentage of the population involved in textile manufacture, the effect of machine-spun threads and cloth may have been greater on local quilters than on quilters in nonindustrial states. Quilts document the transition from hand-spun to power-spun yarns and threads. Linen thread used for piecing or quilting exemplifies the preindustrial technology of hand spinning. The advent of power spinning and the consequent increase of domestically grown cotton introduced a new thread fiber to the market. The availability of the machine-spun cotton thread, commercially carded cotton batting, and power-loom-woven calico made pieced and quilted bedcovers an economical and convenient choice for warm bedding. Quilts could be stitched by anyone with needle skills, whereas not everyone had been skilled enough to weave the coverlets and blankets that had predominated as bed coverings previously.

As manufacturing developed and a wider variety of materials became available, the variety of quilting designs and the incorporation of new types of fabrics indicates that cloth became less expensive and more accessible. A transition from whole cloth to pieced tops suggests that the makers did not hesitate to cut pieces into specific shapes and risk wasting fabric to create the desired effect.

Well after industrialization made textiles available in urban areas, rural and frontier areas persisted in producing textiles by hand, particularly with wool, because of the availability of that raw material and the slower development of the woolen industry. People who continued to produce textiles at home by hand did so because of the production of fibers as a by-product of agricultural pursuits and the desire to continue hand weaving. Since the supply of raw material and the availability of unprocessed fibers continued to support domestic production, some quilts include both domestic and industrial textiles. The transition occurred first with machine-spun yarns, then proceeded to simple fabrics woven on power looms. The basic power-loom fabrics were then enhanced and made more fashionable or marketable by dyeing and printing. With the advent of machine printing, a wide variety of patterned fabrics became available at inexpensive prices. The choices offered quilters and other consumers had greatly increased.

*Notes*

Material in this chapter was previously published by the author in an article entitled "Rhode Island Mills," that appeared in the *Journal of the Early Republic* 9 (Summer 1989): 191–216.

1. Roderick Kirocofe, *The American Quilt: A History of Cloth and Comfort, 1750–1950* (New York: Clarkson Potter, 1993); Gail Van der Hoof, "Various Aspects of Dating Quilts," in *In the Heart of Pennsylvania Symposium Papers*, Jeanette Lasansky, et al., eds., (Lewiston, Penn.: Oral Traditions Project, 1986), 77–82; Rachel Maines, "Paradigms of Scarcity and Abundance: The Quilt as an Artifact of the Industrial Revolution," in *Heart of Pennsylvania*, 84–88.

2. Katharine R. Koob, "Documenting Quilts by Their Fabrics," in *Uncoverings 1981*, Sally Garoutte, ed. (San Francisco: American Quilt Study Group, 1982), 3–9; Diane Fagan Affleck, "Identification of Professionally and Home Woven Textiles," *Ars Textrina* 11 (1989): 153–70; Patricia L. Fiske, ed., *Imported and Domestic Textiles in Eighteenth Century America: Proceedings of 1975 Irene Emery Round Table on Museum Textiles* (Washington, D.C.: Textile Museum, 1975); Barbara Brackman, *Clues in the Calico: A Guide to Identifying and Dating Antique Quilts*, (McLean, Va.: EPM Publications,1989).

3. *The Knopf Collector's Guides to American Antique Quilts with Coverlets, Rugs and Samplers* (New York: Alfred A. Knopf, 1982); Sally Garoutte, "Early Colonial Quilts in a Bedding Context," in *Uncoverings 1980*, Sally Garoutte, ed. (San Francisco: American Quilt Study Group, 1981), 18–25. For a discussion of using material culture to learn about history and culture see Jules David Prown, "The Truth of Material Culture: History or Fiction," in *History from Things: Essays on Material Culture*, Steven Luber and W. David Kingery, eds. (Washington, D.C.: Smithsonian Institution, 1993), 1–19.

4. Inaccurate images of colonial and frontier home life are included in Alice Morse Earle, *Homelife in Colonial Days* (1898; reprint, New York: Macmillan, 1964) and Carl Bridenbaugh, *The Colonial Craftsman* (Chicago: University of Chicago, 1961). For more information about the myth of the Golden Age of Women or the age during which women are credited with being able to perform a wide variety of household tasks see Mary Beth Norton, "The Myth of the Golden Age," in *Women of America*, Mary Beth Norton and Carol Ruth Berkin, eds. (Boston: Houghton Mifflin, 1979), 37–47, and Claudia Goldin, "The Economic Status of Women in the Early Republic: Quantitative Evidence," *Journal of Interdisciplinary History* 16 (1983): 379–80. Winifred Rosenberg, "The Market and Massachusetts Farmers, 1750–1855," *Journal of Economic History* 41 (1981): 283–314; Carole Shammas, "How Self-Sufficient Was Early America?" *Journal of Interdisciplinary History* 12 (1982): 247–72; Laurel Thatcher Ulrich, *Goodwives: Image and Reality in the Lives of Women in Northern New England, 1650–1750* (New York: Knopf, 1982), "Housewife and Gadder: Themes of Self-Sufficiency and Community in Eighteenth-Century New England," in *To Toil the Livelong Day: America's Women at Work, 1780–1980*, Carol Groneman and Mary Beth Norton, eds. (Ithaca, N.Y.: Cornell University Press, 1987), 21–34; James Henretta, "Families and Farms: *Mentalité* in Pre-Industrial America," *William and Mary Quarterly* 35 (1978): 12–14; Michael Merrill, "Cash Is Good to Eat: Self Sufficiency and Exchange in Rural Economies in the United States," *Radical History Review* 4 (1977): 52–57; Christopher Clark, "Household Economy, Market Exchange and the Rise of Capitalism in Con-

necticut Valley, 1800–1860," *Journal of Social History* 12 (1979–80): 169–89; Alan Kulikoff, "The Transition to Capitalism in Rural America," *William and Mary Quarterly* 46 (1989): 120–44. See also Adrienne Dora Hood, "Organization and Extent of Textile Manufacture in Eighteenth-Century Rural Pennsylvania: A Case Study of Chester County" (Ph.D. diss., University of California at San Diego, 1988).

5. Carl Bridenbaugh, *Fat Mutton and Liberty of Conscience: Society in Rhode Island, 1636–1690,* (Providence: Brown University, 1976); Robert Cooper Krapf, "History of the Growth of the Woolen Worsted Industry in R.I." (master's thesis, Brown University, 1938); George J. Lough, Jr., "The Champlins of Newport: A Commercial History," (Ph.D. diss., University of Connecticut, 1977); and Thomas M. Truzes, "Connecticut in the Irish-American Flaxseed Trade, 1750–1775," *Eire Ireland* 12 (1977): 34–63.

6. Clarence Saunders Brigham, *Early Records of the Town of Portsmouth* (Providence: E. L. Freeman and Sons, 1901), 217, 222.

7. In 1656, Dutch New Yorker Adriaen Van der Donck understood the value of sheep husbandry in New England, "where the weaving business is driven and much attention is paid to sheep." See Bridenbaugh, *Fat Mutton*, 56, for Van Der Donck's words. Thomas Budd, *Good Order Established in Pennsylvania and New Jersey* (reprint, Ann Arbor: University of Michigan Press, 1966), 11.

8. The stuffing in flock beds was the wool trimmed from the fleece from around the tail area and underbelly of the sheep. It was coarser and dirtier than the rest of the fleece and unusable for spinning and weaving and used for other purposes. The coarse, often dirt-stained fibers were scoured and used to stuff tickings.

9. As of 1700 at least five fulling mills operated in the towns of Warwick, Providence, South Kingston, and East Providence. By this date the colony consisted of nine cities and towns. Apparently Rhode Island colonists constructed and finished woolen fabrics by the end of the seventeenth century. By 1750 fifteen Rhode Island fulling mills were located in Warwick (one), Hopkinton (one), Pawtucket Village (two), S. Kingston (eight), Providence (one), Westerly (one), and East Providence (one). The state comprised twenty cities and towns by then. Thomas Cochran, *Frontiers of Change: Industrialization in America* (New York: Oxford University Press, 1981), 56; Oliver Payson Fuller, *The History of Warwick* (Providence: Angell, Burlingame, and Company Printers, 1875), 52, 95, 191, 247; S. S. Griswold, *Historical Sketch of the Town of Hopkinton* (Hope Valley, R.I.: L. W. A. Cole, 1877), 25, 58, 64; Brigham, *Town of Portsmouth*, 128, 157, 186–87, 217; Horatio Rogers, George Moulton Carpenter, and Edward Field, eds., *Early Records of the Town of Providence*, 21 vols. (Providence: Snow and Farnum, 1894), 2:14, 83; 4:153–54; Thomas Steere, *History of the Town of Smithfield* (Providence: E. L. Freeman, 1881), 101, 113–14; Massena Goodrich, *Historical Sketch of the Town of Pawtucket* (Pawtucket: Nickerson and Sibley, 1876), 34, 61; Franklin Stuart Coyle, "Welcome Arnold (1745–1798) Providence Merchant: The Founding of an Enterprise," (Ph.D. diss., Brown University, 1972), 56; William R. Bagnall, *The Textile Industries of the United States Including Sketches and Notices of Cotton, Woolen, Silk and Linen Manufactures in the Colonial Period* (Boston: W. B. Clarke, 1893; reprint, New York: Augustus Kelley Publishers, 1971), 280, 284, 213; Caroline Hazard, ed., *Thomas Hazard Son of Robert Called College Tom* (Boston: Houghton Mifflin, 1853), 101; Walter Nebiker, *Historic and Architectural Resources of South Kingston* (Providence: Rhode Island Historic Preservation Commission, 1984 ), 13, 17; Nebiker, *Historic and Architectural Resources of Westerly* (Providence: Rhode Island Historic Preservation Commission, 1978), 13, 3; John G. Erhardt, *A History of Rehoboth, Seekonk, Swansea, Attleboro, East Providence, Barrington and Pawtucket*, 2 vols. (Seekonk, Mass.: Erhardt, 1982), 1:43, 71.

10. Hazard, *Thomas Hazard*, 101–2.

11. *New England's First Fruits* quoted in Bagnall, *Textile Industries*, 6. Information about flaxseed trade in Rhode Island is in Lough, "The Champlins of Newport," 117, 172–81; Truzes, "Connecticut in the Irish-American Flaxseed Trade," 34–63; J. Leander Bishop, *A History of American Manufactures from 1608 to 1860*, 3 vols. (Philadelphia: Edward Young, 1868; reprint, New York: Augustus M. Kelley, 1966), 1:34, 335–37, 378; James Henretta, "The War for Independence and American Economic Development," in *The Economy of Early America: The Revolutionary Period 1763–1790*, Ronald Hoffman, et al., eds. (Charlottesville: University Press of Virginia, 1988), 65.

12. Bagnall, *Textile Industries*, 284; Nebiker, *Resources of South Kingston*, 13, 17; Griswold, *Historical Sketch of Hopkinton*, 25, 58, 64. Elizabeth Johnson and James L. Wheaton, IV, comps., *History of Pawtucket, Rhode Island: Reverend David Benedict's Reminiscences and New Series* (Pawtucket, Spaulding House, 1986), 7, 11, 12, 70; Erhardt, *A History*, 1:43, 71; Goodrich, *Town of Pawtucket*, 34, 56, 61; Christian McBurney, "The South Kingstown Planters: Country Gentry in Colonial Rhode Island," *Rhode Island History* 45 (1986): 81–94.

13. William B. Weeden, *Economic and Social History of New England, 1620–1785* (New York: Houghton Mifflin, 1890; reprint, New York: Hillary House, 1963), 305; also Weeden, *Early Rhode Island: A Social History* (New York: Grafton Press, 1910), 115; Howard Chapin, *Documentary History of Rhode Island* (Providence: Preston Rounds, 1919); Krapf, *Woolen Worsted Industry*, 3.

14. Gail Fowler Mohanty, "Unnoticed Craftsmen Noted," in revision.

15. Victor S. Clark, *History of Manufactures in the United States*, 3 vols. (New York: Peter Smith, 1949), 1:34, 36, 318; Bagnall, *Textile Industries*, 24, 60–62.

16. In 1704 the need for weaving services was great enough that Providence awarded William Smith a forty-square-foot piece of land on which to build and set up a weaver's shop. Smith was not the only weaver during this period. Thomas Olney, Joseph Smith, John Angell, John Warner, and Thomas Barnes also wove cloth. The maximum population in Providence during this period was about 175 families. Rogers, Carpenter, and Field, *Town of Providence*, 5:121, 239; 6:7; 13:164, 177; John Osborne Austin, *Genealogical Dictionary of Rhode Island* (Albany: Munsell, 1887), various pages; "Appendix of Weavers: Providence and Newport," in Bridenbaugh, *Fat Mutton*, records Thomas Applegate, Newport weaver (1641); Robert Bennett, Newport tailor (1646); John Swallow, Newport cloth worker (1649); Mathew West, Newport tailor (1666); Thomas Waterman, Aquidnessett weaver (1673); John Wood, Portsmouth weaver (1674); William Clarke, Newport weaver (1674); Richard Knight, Portsmouth weaver (1680); John Carder, Warwick weaver (1689); Joseph Barker, Newport tailor (1688); Richard Cadman, Portsmouth weaver (1688); Henry Hall, Westerly weaver (1693); William Smith, Providence weaver (1702); Jonathan Rue, Providence weaver (1680); William Austin, Providence weaver (1674); Moses Lippitt, Providence weaver's apprentice (1674–1689); and two unnamed artisans in Providence, a weaver (1674) and a dyer.

17. John Carder, Account Book, 1689–1759, Rhode Island Historical Society, Providence, R.I.

18. Catherine Greene, Account Book, ca. 1776, Rhode Island Historical Society, Providence, R.I.

19. Hazard, Caroline, ed., *Nailer Tom's Diary: Otherwise the Journal of Thomas B. Hazard of Kingstown, R I, 1778–1840* (Boston: Merrymount Press, 1930), 106–8. The account identifies several weavers and spinners who worked for Thomas Hazard including Affabe Exchange (1794–95), Pattee Brown (1795), John Holloway (1795), James Gardiner (1793), and Joseph Oately (1793–95). Spinning was also performed by neighbors including Selar

Rodman, Anna Champlin (1795), Molly Fowler (1795), Robe Congdon (1795), Jonathon Locke's wife (1794), and Hannah Jack (1790).

20. Linda R. Baumgarten, "The Textile Trade of Boston, 1650–1700," in *Arts of the Anglo American Community in the Seventeenth Century,* Ian M. Quimby, ed. (Charlottesville, Va.: University of Virginia Press, 1970), 222.

21. Mohanty, "Unnoticed Craftsmen Noted"; Mohanty, "Oil, Seed and Flock," in Mohanty, *Labor and Laborers of the Loom: the Impact of Mechanization on Handloom Weavers, 1780–1840,* unpublished manuscript.

22. Mohanty, "Unnoticed Craftsmen Noted." Fabrics listed in weavers' account books for Essex County, Massachusetts, prior to 1790 included tow, cradle coverlets, bagging, blanketing, diaper, cheesecloth, cotton blend, coverlets, kersey, stripe, check, fustian, lawn, serge, waled fabrics, chambray, and drugget.

23. Florence Montgomery, "Fortunes to Be Acquired: Textiles in Eighteenth Century Rhode Island," *Rhode Island History* 31 (1972): 52–63; Mohanty, *Labor and Laborers of the Loom,* 44.

24. Montgomery, "Fortunes to be Acquired," 54–55; Baumgarten, "Textile Trade in Boston," 223.

25. Hood, "Textile Manufacture"; Kirocofe, *American Quilt;* Garoutte, "Early Colonial Quilts"; Brackman, *Clues in the Calico.*

26. Montgomery, "Fortunes to Be Acquired," 52–63; Montgomery, *Printed Textiles: English and American Cottons and Linens 1700–1850* (New York: Viking Press, 1970); Baumgarten, "Textile Trade of Boston," 219–73.

27. During a 1990 conference honoring two hundred years of textile manufacturing in the United States, sponsored by the Museum of American Textile History, noted British historian, Joan Thirsk, indicated that British textile historians looked for suviving evidence of their seventeenth- and eighteenth-century textiles in museum collections across the United States. See the reuse of fabrics in RIQDP quilts #503, 765, 766, 805, and 808; and Brackman, *Clues in Calico,* 39.

28. Grace Rogers Cooper, *The Sewing Machine: Its Invention and Development* (Washington, D.C.: Smithsonian Institution, 1985), 216; Bagnall, *Textile Industries,* 164; and Brackman, *Clues in Calico,* 50.

29. Cooper, *The Sewing Machine,* 216; Brackman, *Clues in Calico* 50–51.

30. Mohanty, "Experimentation in Textile Technology, 1788–1790, and Its Impact on Handloom Weaving and Weavers in Rhode Island," *Technology and Culture* 29 (1988): 2–4.

31. Ibid., 4–10.

32. Mohanty, "Experimentation in Textile Technology," 11–14.

33. Almy and Brown Papers, Rhode Island Historical Society, Providence, R.I.

34. Rogerson Dabney, Alexandria, Va., to Almy and Brown, August 6, 1793, Almy and Brown Papers.

35. Jackson and Nightingale, Savannah, Ga., to Almy and Brown, February 20, 1794, Almy and Brown Papers.

36. Catharine Haines, New York, N.Y., to Almy and Brown, October 16, 1797, Almy and Brown Papers.

37. Thomas Fry, Account Book, 1815–22, Private Collection, East Greenwich, R.I.

38. Cynthia Dimock, "Rhode Island Military Uniforms: Conservation and Exhibition" (master's thesis, University of Rhode Island, 1997), 166–73.

39. Daniel Waldo, Worcester, Mass., to Almy and Brown, 1799, Almy and Brown Papers.

40. *U.S. Census of Manufactures,* 1820, Schedules for Rhode Island.

41. Mohanty, "Handloom Outwork and Outwork Weaving in Rural Rhode Island 1810–1821," *American Studies* 30 (1989): 41–50.

42. Ibid., 45–46.

43. Ibid., 49–50; Mohanty, "Putting Up with Putting Out: Power Loom Diffusion and Outwork for Rhode Island Mills, 1821–29," *Journal of the Early Republic* 9 (1989): 195.

44. "Cotton Manufacturing within a thirty mile radius of Providence, 14 Nov. 1809." Miscellaneous Manuscript, Rhode Island Historical Society, Providence, Rhode Island.

45. Samuel Ogden, *Thoughts on What Probable Effect the Peace with Great-Britain Will Have on the Cotton Manufactures of This Country: Interspersed with Remarks on Our Bad Management in the Business and the Way to Improvement so as to meet Imported Goods in Cheapness at Our Home Market, Pointed Out* (Providence: Goddard and Mann, 1815).

46. In Mohanty, "Putting Up with Putting Out," 201, see Slater swatch illustration; this simple two-shuttle plain-weave check was impossible to reproduce on early power looms, which would have required a drop-box mechanism not developed until later.

47. Ibid., 202, 204; *U.S. Census of Manufactures,* 1820, Schedules for Rhode Island; *Documents Relative to Manufactures in the United States* (known as the *McLane Report on Manufactures*), House Executive Document #308, 22nd Cong., 1st sess., 2 vols. (Washington, D.C., 1833) 1:970–76. Nathan Appleton, "Introduction of the Powerloom and the Origin of Lowell," in *The Early Development of the American Cotton Textile Industry* (1858; reprint, New York: J. and J. Harper Editions, 1969); David Jeremy, *Transatlantic Industrial Revolution: The Diffusion of Textile Technologies Between Britain and America 1790–1830s* (Cambridge, Mass.: MIT Press), 204.

48. Mohanty, "Putting Up with Putting Out," 202–3.

49. Ibid., 203.

50. Ibid., 204–5.

51. Blackstone Manufacturing Company, Rhode Island Historical Society, Providence, R.I.; *U.S. Census of Manufactures,* 1820, Schedules for Rhode Island; and *McLane Report on Manufactures,* 1:970–76.

52. Mohanty, "Putting Up with Putting Out," 215; *U.S. Census of Manufactures,* 1820, Schedules for Rhode Island; and *McLane Report on Manufactures,* 1:970–76.

# Secrets of the Printer's Palette

MARTIN BIDE

A QUILT IS A FABRIC COLLECTION OF THE PERIOD IN WHICH IT WAS made. Although some recycled fabrics in a quilt might be considerably older, many are current to the time the quilt was constructed. The range of colors in fabrics of the early nineteenth century can surprise those who imagine that fabrics colored in an age of natural dyes must be limited in range and dull in color, particularly when bright mineral colorants are included. The Star quilt (Fig. 39) of the 1830s has bright red, yellow, green, and blue, together with a range of more subtle shades. Nor were these colors loose: the fastness of the majority to washing would meet today's requirements, and the resistance to sunlight fading was often good.

To achieve this array of fast colors required considerable ingenuity on the part of printers and dyers. The balance between fastness, colorfulness, and economy was a delicate one. Cheap fabrics were produced with a minimum of processing. High quality and unique color effects required fabrics that could be produced only by using a long sequence of steps. Rapid advances in chemical knowledge and the large-scale availability of "new" chemicals meant that the technologists of the time were experimenting constantly. By producing a new color or color combination, or by achieving the same pattern in fewer steps, they hoped to outdo their rivals.

This essay deals with the colors that appear in printed fabrics commercially produced in western Europe and the United States and used in quilts, mainly of the nineteenth century. Drawing heavily on primary sources from Rhode Island's nineteenth-century textile printers, it covers the coloring materials applied to textiles, explains the background processes, and follows the major changes that came as the dyeing and printing industry progressed. In doing so, the review should provide to the aficionado clues to the origin of a quilt and deepen the understanding of its colors. A word of

caution, however: with such a range of methods in an era of relatively rapid change, it can be surprisingly difficult to look at a printed fabric, even one that is well dated, and know for certain what printing methods and what coloring materials were used unless sophisticated analytical methods are available.

The calico printing industry in Europe was established in the late seventeenth century. The suggested date for the founding of the industry in England is 1676.[1] It was inspired by the import of Indian cotton textiles with their array of fast and bright colors. Previously Europe had known only crude oil-painted textiles or fugitive designs. Indian printers used painstakingly long processes, and typically painted on mordants and resists by hand rather than printing them.[2] The methods were brought to Europe and modified to allow more rapid production by block printing. The use of thickeners to give a sharp mark and methods to remove the thickeners after printing were important European developments.[3] Most dyed and printed material in North America was imported until a domestic printing industry was established in the 1820s.

The period from 1750 to 1850 saw the birth of the inorganic chemical industry. Inorganic chemicals are, broadly speaking, those of mineral origin, as opposed to carbon-based "organic" chemicals of vegetable and animal origin. Inorganic chemicals such as chlorine, sulfuric and hydrochloric acids, soda ash, lead acetate, and ferrous sulfate became widely and cheaply available. They had a great effect on textile coloration. Such chemicals allowed for more, better, and quicker fabric preparation; expanded the range of mordants, essential to the production of fast colors on cotton; and provided newer discharging methods. Inorganic or "mineral" colorants (such as Prussian blue and chrome yellow) produced in situ on the fiber were also developed as products of this branch of chemical industry.

The mineral colors supplemented the natural dyes, chiefly madder and indigo. With international trade well established, dyers and printers were able to use the best technical colorants from around the world. The New World dye, cochineal, had long displaced kermes from European use; indigo from India had supplanted the European woad; and tropical dye-woods (such as brazilwood) were widely available.[4] At the end of the eighteenth century quercitron bark from the United States supplemented weld in Europe as a source of yellow. The story of quercitron's commercial development is a fascinating one and indicative of the importance of dyes and dyeing during this period.[5] Synthetic dyes became available from 1856, a date that has become a benchmark in any discussion of dyes and dyeing in the nineteenth century. Over the next half century they achieved the dominance that they enjoy today, and in the few cases where science could not immediately do better, it copied nature and produced indigo and alizarin synthetically.

Cotton was and continues to be the major substrate for printing. By the late eighteenth century in Europe, cotton imported from India replaced linen in major use, particularly for printed goods, and the Industrial Revolution introduced the methods for producing cotton fabrics in large volume.

*Background*

FIG. 39. (*Opposite*) Star quilt, 1830s. Cotton top and back, cotton batting, 87 x 81 in. Hand-pieced and hand-quilted in outline pattern, 4–6 stitches per inch. Descended in the Gardner family of Exeter, Rhode Island. URI Historic Textile and Costume Collection (1955.36.116). RIQDP #127.

This quilt incorporates the color palette available to textile printers using natural dyes and mineral colors. The fabrics are either block- or cylinder-printed, or a combination of the two methods. (See details in Figures 44 & 45.)

Printed fabrics were exported to North America, and when the U.S. printing industry was established, it printed chiefly on fabrics of domestic manufacture. Ultimately, of course, U.S. cotton became a major source of the fabrics produced in both the United States and Britain. The majority of printed fabrics in quilts are cotton. Quilters also used silks, wools, and some mixed wool-cotton fabrics such as delaines.

Most chemicals have no particular attraction for fibers: they can be applied by soaking, or by a dipping followed by a uniform squeezing between rollers. The dip-and-squeeze sequence is referred to as *padding*. In other cases a chemical, particularly a dye, does have an attraction for the fiber; this attraction between a dye and a fiber is referred to as *substantivity*. A dye with substantivity will be attracted from a bath to a fiber and penetrate it. Thus "dyeing" takes place. Direct printing with dyes can be considered as localized dyeing in which the "bath" is moist print paste. Substantivity derives from physical forces of attraction. Hydrogen bonds and other polar forces are easily formed with protein fibers such as wool, and many natural dyes have substantivity for protein fibers. To this day, home dyers of natural dyes overwhelmingly prefer to color wool for this reason. Substantivity for cotton relies more heavily on nonpolar dispersion forces, which in turn require dye molecules that match the shape of the cellulose molecules of cotton. Few natural dyes have substantivity for cotton. Dyers and printers using them had to exercise great ingenuity to achieve fast colors. In effect, this essay is a study of that ingenuity.

Dyers attempted to change the cotton fiber to make it more receptive to dyes. The use of animal products like dung, urine, and blood in old dyeing processes such as that for "Turkey red" suggested that these had some way of fixing dye. Linking this suggestion with the greater substantivity of dyes for protein fibers led to attempts to provide cotton with similar properties. The efforts were classified as "animalizing" cotton, and mostly consisted of depositing protein material on the fiber. Albumen from eggs or blood, and casein and lactarine from milk were used in these attempts.[6] As chemical knowledge has increased many other more sophisticated efforts have been made and continue to this day.[7] The early efforts were unsuccessful, and modern methods have yet to be widely adopted. Successful dyeing and printing of cotton came about through clever coloring techniques rather than through modification of the fiber.

Such successful printing requires more than just fast color with unstained white areas; it needs patterns with clearly defined edges, known in the trade as a "sharp mark." Colors mixed simply with water and then printed wick and bleed. To achieve the necessary sharpness some control of print paste flow properties, *rheology*, is required. *Thickeners* provide the rheology necessary to allow a color to flow onto the fabric during printing yet hold it firm until drying and fixation take place. For the most part, wheat flour or starch, with gum tragacanth or gum senegal, were used to thicken pastes. Overall success also includes contribution from the machinery used and is measured by good registration and avoidance of the variety of mistakes that machinery can cause, such as scrimps, snaps, streaks, scumming, and so on. Such faults are addressed in the following essay on the machinery of textile printing.

In the history of printed textiles, many subtly different styles of printing have been used. *Style* refers to the methods used to achieve coloration, rather than the pattern itself, although certain styles did lend themselves to particular pattern types. The choice of a particular style was based on the pattern being printed, the colors in the pattern, the fastness and sharpness required, and the cost. A brief description of the various styles is given in Table 6.

Numerous other styles of printing appear in the literature but were, for the most part, simply variations of the styles in Table 6. They generally referred to a particular colorant or printing method. For example, the *bronze style* involves the raised mineral color manganese bronze, and the *cover and pad style* refers to the application of a continuous background design in the madder style. The need for these fine distinctions came and went with the importance of each. The major styles are detailed in what fol-lows, although it is not practicable to deal strictly on a style-by-style basis.

Textile dyeing and printing are major industries worldwide, and the transfer of information has always been of interest. The depth and quality of understanding directly parallels that of the chemistry on which it is based. The importance of the industry and its relation to chemistry can be gauged by a comment on the title page of a 1790 chemistry text: "It is a pity so few chemists are dyers and so few dyers chemists."[8] Early technical dyeing manuals such as that by Bemis are little more than cookbooks, and they represent the state of chemical knowledge of the time.[9] Bancroft wrote a text that was criticized for its lack of practicality but which now is viewed in a better light. His concept of substantivity for dyes that color successfully without mordants remains valid and is widely used today.[10] Partridge is interesting for his experience on both sides of the Atlantic.[11] The need for the United States to adopt the latest methods and to build a first-rate industry was evident in 1833.[12] In 1846 an anonymous "experienced dyer" produced a lengthy tome that described in full detail most of the dyeing and printing processes of the day and demonstrated the greater understanding of chemistry that had developed by that time.[13] Unraveling the chemistry involved is not too challenging for the chemist of today. Other books of the same era seem to be very similar, and the summary represented by O'Neill's dictionary, printed in London in 1862, is quite thorough.[14] Once again the

TABLE 6
*Printing Styles*

| Style | Description | Notes |
|---|---|---|
| Madder or Dyed Style | Fabric is printed with a mordant that is fixed by ageing. In a madder dyebath, the dye binds with the mordant in the printed areas. Other dyes could be added or used instead. | The original Indian process. Replaced in the late nineteenth century when synthetic alizarine allowed for direct (steam style) printing of madder colors. |
| Steam Style | All ingredients to form fast color are mixed, printed, and fixed by steaming. | Introduced after 1830 following development of "rapid ageing." Used first for mixed fabrics. Now the typical method, usually called direct printing. |
| Spirit Style | Fabric is pretreated with "spirits of tin salts." Simple, nonfast colors are mixed, printed, aged, rinsed in cold water, and dried. | Cheap and decorative effects only. Declined as the steam style became more widely used. |
| Raised Style | A chemical is printed. Fabric is then passed through a bath of a second chemical, which reacts with the first to produce the color. | Used extensively for mineral colors such as manganese bronze and iron buff. The illuminating color in a discharge print might also be developed by raising. |
| Discharge Style | A dyed fabric (back)ground is printed with a chemical that will destroy or remove the dye. Illuminated discharges are produced by including a dye in the discharge paste. A mordant in the madder style can also be discharged before the dyeing step. | Important for indigo and Turkey red ground colors which are difficult or impossible to print directly. Provides a good fit (registration) of details in the ground. |
| Resist or Reserve Style | The fabric is printed with a substance that prevents penetration/fixation of a dye or mordant. When dye is applied all over, it only fixes in the nonprint areas. Resists act by physical and/or chemical means. | Like discharge, important for indigo and gives good fit of details in the ground. Several variations of the madder style use resisted mordants. |
| Pigment Style | This method fixes an insoluble pigment to the surface of a fabric with a binder such as albumen. | Used for colors such as ultramarine blue which could not be applied and fixed by other methods. Paradoxically, also used for early synthetic dyes until better fixation methods were discovered. |

transatlantic commonalties are revealed by a U.S. edition of the same work some nine years later, this time with an added essay on coal tar colors.[15]

The consonance between European and U.S. publications of the period and the presence of recipes from both sides of the Atlantic in the notes of practical printers such as Dunster and Dalton demonstrate a ready interchange of knowledge in the industry as well as scorn for the ignorant by the knowledgeable.[16] Other valuable and practical printers' notebooks are available, particularly those with a connection to Rhode Island, and provide interesting views of what is presented in published texts.[17] O'Neill authored a two-volume work that is largely a review of the technical advances of the early nineteenth century seen through the patent literature.[18] Crookes wrote a book in 1882 that seems little more than a rehash of earlier works, while in 1887 Sansone produced a volume that includes most of the traditional methods and many of the new ones based on synthetic dyes.[19] While it came later, the work of Knecht and Fothergill has become a classic. Originally published in 1912, it goes into great detail and includes fabric swatches to illustrate the processes it describes. Even the fourth edition in 1952 includes exhaustive discussion of processes that must have been obsolete when the first edition was published.[20]

Indigo is perhaps the most famous natural dye. It provides a range of blues from light to dark with good fastness. Its early importance in commerce can be gauged from Isaac Newton's inclusion of indigo (distinct from blue) as one of the seven colors in the rainbow in his attempt to correlate colors with notes in the musical scale.[21] Indigo is unique among the natural dyes. In its normal state it is insoluble and has no substantivity. When it is chemically "reduced" in alkali it is converted to a pale yellow, soluble form. This has slight substantivity and will dye cotton immersed in such a dyebath. When the fabric is removed from the dyebath and exposed to air, the reverse chemical reaction, oxidation, reconverts it to its insoluble blue form, which is retained in the fiber. For darker colors, the limited substantivity means that the usual method of simply adding more dye to the bath is impractical. Instead, the sequence of immersion and oxidation was repeated until the required shade was built up. For much of the nineteenth century, indigo's use in printing was a specialized branch of the industry. Unless an establishment was equipped with a specialized indigo dyehouse, the typical calico printer had little use for it. Samuel Dunster includes a summary of work done in the indigo dyehouse in the years he was at Clay Print Works in Johnston, Rhode Island.[22] Beyond this, his notes include all aspects of printing with indigo.

*Indigo*

While other natural dyes were simply sold as chipped or ground plant material from which the color would be extracted, indigo came to the dyer and printer in an extracted form. The indigo plant contains about 2 percent of the coloring material. To extract the dye, the plant was fermented to reduce the dye to its soluble form: the extracted liquor was then aerated to oxidize the dye, which was collected as "indigo mud."[23] This paste was dried and cut into blocks for shipment and sale to the dyer or printer. The purity of dye in this form could still vary widely, however, and might range from 10 to 80 percent—with no simple, accurate way to determine the strength. Grit and woody material were common contaminants, and while this might not affect dyeing processes too much, in cases where indigo was printed directly, it made paste preparation tedious. Grinding for a week before printing was usual.[24] As with other print pastes, the preparation was often lengthy, involving boiling, cooling, and mixing. Straining was usually required to remove any material that might stick in the engravings of a cylinder, from whatever source.[25] Figure 40 shows the preparation of colors for printing.

Seventeenth-century dyers used a similar fermentation to reduce woad, but this required a high temperature that would melt the wax of a wax-resisted fabric. The introduction of indigo allowed a tepid temperature to be used in the fermentation so that wax-resisted fabrics could be dyed successfully.[26] The fermentation and dyeing were carried out in a *vat*, and this

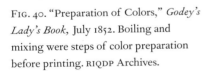

FIG. 40. "Preparation of Colors," *Godey's Lady's Book*, July 1852. Boiling and mixing were steps of color preparation before printing. RIQDP Archives.

became a term to refer to a chemically reduced dyebath. New inorganic chemicals provided alternative methods of reducing indigo for dyeing cotton. Copperas (ferrous sulfate) together with lime was most widely used from the 1740s, and the cooler temperature of the resulting vat made the work even easier. In the late nineteenth century, first the zinc/lime vat, and then sodium hydrosulfite (more properly called dithionite) were developed, rendering other methods obsolete. Hydrosulfite is still used today for dyeing and printing indigo and other vat dyes for which indigo is the prototype.

Using indigo dyebaths printers could take advantage of the dye's fastness and brightness to produce patterns using the discharge and resist techniques. In the *discharge style*, agents that destroy or allow the removal of the dye can be printed on a predyed fabric leaving behind a white pattern in a colored background *(ground)*. If the discharge paste contains color resistant to the destruction, a colored pattern—an illuminated discharge—is produced. For example, the paste might include a component of a raised-style color; the rinsing bath could then remove the discharge products and at the same time "raise" the replacement. The printing operation produces both the discharge and the illumination in a single step and thus the registration or "fit" of the design is uniformly good and is a feature of this style.

Indigo is easily discharged by a two-step acidic oxidation process, and two main variations of this were used in the nineteenth century to produce designs of white on blue. Sodium or potassium dichromate was usually used as the oxidizing agent after it became available during the 1820s.[27] The method used first involved padding the fabric with the dichromate; then printing a design in acid, and finally rinsing in chalk and water. Weak discharges might be used to get a pale blue instead of white, although such patterns more often were produced by a resist method. These discharge prints often included yellow or orange illuminating colors. A yellow figure could be produced on the indigo-dyed cloth by including a lead salt in the acid paste, which reacted with the dichromate to produce a chrome yellow: a later alkaline treatment could convert this to chrome orange. The discharge paste might include a mordant which would be fixed in the chalk rinse and allow for the production of color in a later dyebath. Similarly a white pattern on a green ground could be produced. Blue-dyed cloth was padded with dichromate and an aluminum mordant ("red liquor," discussed later under the madder style), then printed with acid. Both the indigo and the mordant were discharged in the acid print areas and removed in a neutral rinse. Later dyeing in a quercitron bath produced yellow in the blue unprinted areas to give the green.[28]

The second and later version of the oxidation discharge process for indigo printed a pattern in dichromate and achieved the discharge in a subsequent acid bath. Usually oxalic and sulfuric acids were used. Colored discharges were produced by including pigment colors (often chrome yellow) and an albumen binder in the print paste. The albumen was coagulated in the acid bath, fixing the pigment.

In the early twentieth century, discharge effects were achieved on indigo-dyed fabric by reduction rather than oxidation. One variation of this was the "Leucotrope" process in which the yellow discharge products of indigo were stabilized in either soluble or insoluble forms; the former would wash out leaving white, while the latter would remain to give a yellow-illuminated discharge.[29]

In the *resist style*, occasionally referred to as the *reserve style*, a substance is printed that prevents the penetration or fixation of the dye and/or mordant. Resists can act by forming a physical barrier or by chemically interfering with the fixation. When the fabric printed with such resists is immersed in a dyebath or printed over its entire surface, the originally printed areas do not take up dye, and remain uncolored. As with discharge, the print can be "illuminated" when the resist paste includes dye or a component that can be developed by later raising. The "fit" of colors, like that of the discharge style, is good.

Indian chintzes, such as that in Figure 41, include blue created by indigo-dyeing fabrics physically resisted with a wax paste.[30] The wax prevented the penetration of the dye, and the fabric in the printed areas remained white. When used to produce designs to European taste with small blue figures, the process was very painstaking because often more than 90 percent of the fabric was resisted.[31] The wax method was used in Europe to copy the Indian materials and relied, as discussed earlier, on the cooler dyeing vat of imported indigo. The wax resist method more efficiently produced textiles with small white designs in a blue ground, and a typical example is shown in Figure 42. The technique was largely superseded in England by the mid-eighteenth century but continued in Europe until the end of the century. Alternatives to wax were later used for resisting, and typical methods of the nineteenth century were based on both physical and chemical resists. The chemical resist derived from an oxidizing agent; copper sulfate or acetate, zinc sulfate, or lead sulfate were common. China clay or pipe clay provided the thickening and contributed the physical resist.[32]

In the simplest application of the resist method for indigo, a white pattern on a blue ground was obtained. Light and dark blue were obtained either by dipping in an indigo vat to a pale color, printing a resist, and then redipping; or; by printing the resist, dipping, removing the resist, and redipping. Other colors could be included by adding mordants or a mineral-

FIG. 41. Petticoat fragment, Indian, eighteenth century. Cotton top, back, and batting, 12½ x 19½ in. Quilted, 6 stitches per inch, in diamond pattern and in parallel rows along the hem to simulate cording, cotton twill tape facing. URI Historic Textile and Costume Collection (1953.11.01).

This fragment probably was once part of a quilted French petticoat. Indian calicoes came to southern France through the port of Marseilles beginning in the seventeenth century. In the next century, local women quilted them for petticoats. This fragment demonstrates the advanced knowledge of Indian printers in the eighteenth century. Through a complicated process involving mordants and resists, printers could produce a variety of brightly colored fabrics.

FIG. 42. Detail of indigo resist on cotton, ca. 1800. URI Historic Textile and Costume Collection (1956.13.15).

Indigo dye sometimes penetrated the resist, leaving traces of blue in the white pattern areas.

color precursor to the resist paste. Yellow or orange figures on a blue ground were particularly common and achieved by including lead salts in the resist paste. After dipping in the indigo and rinsing, the yellow was raised by passage through a dichromate bath. The pale blue with dark blue style could be modified to include a green if two resists were printed, one of them including a lead salt. A green color was produced on subsequent raising in a dichromate bath.

None of these resist methods for indigo was ideal, however. O'Neill describes "the expensive and clumsy system of resists which is only tolerated because of the want of a [direct printing] method which will yield the deepest shades."[33] Not until satisfactory direct printing was achieved in 1883 would this problem be solved.

Dark blue grounds with patterns of white, yellow, and orange were popular for most of the nineteenth century and into the twentieth. They could be produced by distinctly different methods and chemical processes. They were achieved in both the resist and discharge style, and the orange/yellow might be raised chrome yellow produced in situ, chrome yellow pigment and albumen, or a "Leucotrope" color. Figure 43 shows a sample card from S. H. Greene & Co. at Clyde Bleachery and Print Works in River Point, Rhode Island, which features indigo discharges. Figures 44 and 45 are details of the Star quilt (Fig. 39), which shows further examples of indigo-based resist and discharge work.

## DIRECT INDIGO PRINTING

Air is an oxidizing agent that reacts with reduced indigo and reprecipitates it in its insoluble form. Keeping air away from a fabric is easy when the fabric is submerged in a dyebath. In the past, once a dyebath was prepared, dyeing processes for indigo did not represent a great technical challenge. Printing indigo directly onto fabric was much more difficult. During both paste preparation and printing, the reduced indigo was exposed to air, and premature oxidation was hard to avoid. Indigo's value as a colorant ensured that, despite the difficulties, methods for printing it directly onto fabric were sought and used even when the results were inconsistent or uneven and dark shades were unobtainable.

Two methods of applying indigo directly to fabrics were developed in England in the eighteenth century and used well into the nineteenth century. Arsenic trisulfide, yellow orpiment, will keep indigo reduced longer than other reducing agents.[34] A paste of indigo thus reduced could be applied by brush to fill in blue details on a fabric previously printed with madder colors. This application was known as *penciling*, and indigo applied this way (and hence the print itself) was known as *pencil blue*. Floud dates its English introduction to 1740.[35] Prints achieved by penciling typically show poor registration of the blue details, and often reveal variations in the depth

# Washington
## Original
# Full Dyed Indigo

*As made in 1864*

S. H. Greene & Sons, Corp., Mfrs.                    Converse & Company, Agts.

Style 1014
Campus

1

2

3

of blue when two or more brush strokes overlap. Figure 46 is a typical print of madder colors with penciled blue details. The same penciling pastes were applied by block printing and later still by cylinder (roller) printing to add blue details to prints despite the uneven appearance that tended to result as the paste oxidized. In cylinder and block application it was still known as pencil blue, and Dunster has recipes showing this use in the 1850s.[36] In this way printers could achieve a combination of the madder colors with the blue of indigo and thus copy Indian chintzes that had been produced in a much more convoluted manner. Replacing the orpiment with granulated tin and glucose produced later refinements of pencil blue, although the problems of premature oxidation remained.[37]

The second method to apply indigo designs directly was known as china blue, presumably because of its resemblance to blues found on pottery.[38] In this method, indigo was printed onto the fabric in its unreduced form. Running the fabric through successive baths of lime and copperas (ferrous sulfate) achieved the necessary reduction to fix the dye. Such a sequence of dips is shown in Figure 47.[39] The dye was held in place during these steps by the precipitation of the thickening material in the first lime bath and later by the precipitation of calcium sulfate. While a sharp print could be obtained, the method could not achieve the darkest shades of indigo, and it could not be used on fabric printed with madder colors. Prints carried out this way are largely monochromatic blues; typical designs are of the toile-de-Jouy type. The pillar print fabric that forms much of the quilt of Figure 48 is typical of china blue printing. Dunster used this process in 1829, and a page from his notes is shown in Figure 49.[40]

FIG. 45. This detail of a Star quilt from the 1830s (Figure 39) illustrates indigo discharges and resists with chrome yellow illuminations, blue and yellow to make green, and a madder-style print with a rainbow in Prussian blue. The fabrics in this quilt are indeed a smorgasbord of all the significant printing techniques of the period. The back of this quilt is a pillar print, a neoclassical style incorporating pillars or columns festooned with garlands. The identical print in china blue can be seen in Figure 48.

FIG. 46. Whole-cloth quilt, 1770s. English block-printed cotton, cotton back, 65 x 75 in. Hand-quilted, 5 stitches per inch. Possibly made by Mrs. Waldron of Bristol, Rhode Island. Museum of Art, Rhode Island School of Design. Gift of Ms. Richard Colley (54.179). RIQDP #702.

Printed fabrics were precious in eighteenth-century Rhode Island. Nearly always imported, chintzes and calicoes graced colonial homes as window curtains, bed hangings, and bed covers. Sprigged floral designs like this one became fashionable for women's day dresses. Madder with pencil-blue details created the colors. According to a handwritten note attached to this quilt, the calico was "brought to this country before anything like that was made here." Originally a dress worn by a Mrs. Waldron of Bristol, the fabric was passed on as a quilt to her granddaughter Martha Bourne, who brought it to Barrington in 1820 when she married Ebenezer Smith. Martha eventually gave it to her own granddaughter, Ruth Colley, on the occasion of Ruth's marriage in 1882. It is actually a "quilt within a quilt," because a second quilted printed cotton is visible inside.

FIG. 47. "Indigo Vat," *Godey's Lady's Book*, July 1852. The label "indigo vat" is erroneous for this engraving, as it illustrates a step in the china blue process. Direct indigo printing in the china blue method involved running the printed fabric through successive baths of lime and copperas to reduce the indigo as illustrated. RIQDP Archives.

FIG. 48. (*Previous page*) Nine-Patch quilt, 1830s. Cotton top and back, 94½ x 88 in. Hand-pieced and hand-quilted in cross-hatch pattern, 7 stitches per inch. Maker unknown. Collection of Mildred Longo. RIQDP #658.

The numerous blue fabrics in this quilt represent the various methods for printing indigo in use at this time. The pillar print is an example of the china blue process. Other blues were printed in the pencil blue, resist, and discharge methods. The pillar print has a 21-inch repeat pattern and could have been either plate or cylinder printed.

FIG. 49. (*Right*) On this page from Samuel Dunster's *Print Dyes* 1 (1829), 109, the top two recipes are for mordants. The "sightening" mentioned in the "Old Chocolate" recipe was a small amount of dye added to the mordant paste so that the printer could see the paste on white cloth. In the "China Blue" recipe Dunster describes the extensive grinding of the color required before printing. The details of the dips to dissolve and reduce the indigo appear on the following page. Rhode Island Historical Society Library.

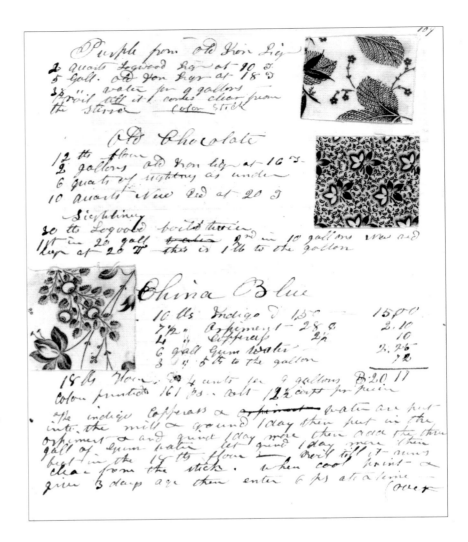

Efforts to improve the direct printing of indigo continued throughout the nineteenth century, and colorists tried many other methods in the years before stabilized hydrosulfite was available.[41] Successful direct printing of indigo came in 1883 with the glucose process. Fabric was pretreated with glucose (a reducing agent), and a paste of unreduced indigo and alkali was printed on it. The reaction to reduce and fix the indigo took place in later steaming. Finally a reliable method was available to produce dark blue indigo prints that were even and sharply defined. More modern methods using hydrosulfite are technically no better, simply more efficient and cheaper.

The lack of technical superiority of any one method of printing indigo resulted in the widespread use of all these various techniques. Examples of all of them can be found in nineteenth-century quilts.

The importance of indigo prompted intense chemical investigation. It was produced in the laboratory in 1877. Following analysis of its chemical structure in 1883, and work to find a satisfactory commercial process, successful production began in 1897.[42] Synthetic indigo was far more consistent in strength and was free of the sand and grit that plagued printers who used natural indigo.[43] Within fifteen years competition among synthetic indigo producers lowered the price of the dyestuff and the commercial growing of indigo soon ceased. Despite present trends to return to things natural, synthetic indigo will not have any serious competition from a revival of its natural predecessor.[44]

*The Madder Style*

The madder style was the most significant process for printing cotton with natural dyes. Dyers in the East used madder for centuries. Pliny observed it in Egypt almost 2,000 years ago.[45] The steps used by Indian printers in 1734 are described in a manuscript with accompanying samples which is now in the Musée National d'Histoire Naturelle in Paris.[46] Figure 41 is a fabric from a quilted petticoat produced at about the same time by the basic madder style along with wax-resisted indigo. Understandably the madder style excited the curiosity of those who saw it for the first time: colorless materials (mordants) were applied, and later a multicolored patterned fabric emerged from a dyebath. Once the technique was understood, however, it was adopted by the fledgling industry in the West. It remained the major method of achieving color in textile printing through the development of mechanized fabric production and the use of block and cylinder printing until synthetic alizarin allowed printers to achieve the same colors in the more flexible steam style. The principle of the madder style remained the same from the original process using naturally occurring minerals as mordants and madder root to mordants from the inorganic chemical industry and purified and synthetic versions of the dye.

The madder style involved the printing of a mordant on the fabric. The most common mordants used were iron or aluminum acetate. Tin salts were also used, though chiefly as adjuncts: chromium mordants came into use only with the introduction of synthetic alizarin.[47] Many other metals were examined as potential mordants, and although their compounds may have had some use in the printing industry, none achieved significant use as true mordants in the madder style. Mordants and the thickened pastes prepared from them had no color, but were referred to by the color that they would ultimately produce with madder. Thus a solution of aluminum acetate was known as red liquor and iron acetate solutions (depending on their strength) as black or purple liquors. This nomenclature persisted, even when a dye other than madder was to be used. Thus "red liquor" printed and later dyed in a bath of quercitron would produce a yellow design.

Few mordants came direct to the printers, who often would have to carry out the preparation for themselves. Iron would be dissolved in "pyroligneous" (acetic) acid to produce iron acetate, while the solution of aluminum acetate was produced by mixing solutions of aluminum sulfate with lead acetate. Lead sulfate precipitated, leaving aluminum acetate in solution. It is not clear what became of the large quantities of lead sulfate produced in this operation.

After printing the mordant, the fabric was carefully dried and then *aged* in moist conditions to fix the mordant on the fabric. During ageing the soluble metal salt decomposed to form an insoluble oxide or hydroxide. The chemistry involved was poorly understood: the fabric was simply hung and allowed to dry and age a few days. With the increase in production speed that came with cylinder printing, the slow drying or ageing processes proved insufficient to fix the mordant. The need for moisture in the ageing step was eventually understood, and ageing rooms were deliberately supplied with moisture by being placed near a river, or by having steam admitted.[48] Ageing was completed with a "dunging" process, a washing that until the late nineteenth century was usually performed with cow dung. This took the fixation a step further and removed thickening material and any unfixed mordant.

The mordanted fabric was then immersed in a dyebath, leading to its name of the *dyed style*. The fastest and widest range of colors were obtained with dyebaths of madder, and thus the method was more often referred to as the *madder style*. In the dyebath the dye bound to the mordant that was fixed in the printed areas of the cloth. Since the dye on its own had no substantivity for the fiber, it did not bind to the unprinted areas, so these remained uncolored. Any slight stain was removed in a later washing or *clearing* process. A wide range of shades would emerge from a given dyebath where different mordants, mixed mordants, and varying mordant concentrations had been printed. In a madder bath bright reds, pinks (from varying strengths of aluminum mordant), purples, and blacks (from iron) could be produced. "Madder chocolate" came from a mixture of iron and aluminum mordants. With quercitron added to the dyebath, mahogany browns and dull oranges could be produced. Quilts of the nineteenth century, particularly before 1870, are replete with fabrics in which the madder-style palette dominates. The Birtwistle dye book of 1858 shows work of the Allen Print Works in Rhode Island; the shades shown in Figure 50 are typical. Alternatively, as mentioned earlier, a completely different dye could be dyed on the mordanted fabric, although the range of colors would be less extensive and perhaps less fast. It was, of course, possible to run fabrics through the whole sequence of steps (printing, ageing, dunging, dyeing, and clearing) a second time using a different dye. In this way a yellow might be added to a madder print by printing an aluminum mordant and dyeing in a Persian berry bath.

The range of shades in madder style prints could be extended in several other ways. Catechu could be printed directly alongside the mordants. It resisted removal in the subsequent treatments and contributed a brown shade.[49] Lead salts could likewise be printed with the mordants and survive the dunging, dyeing, and clearing operations. Later a chrome yellow would be "raised" in a dichromate bath. These two colors were often referred to as "madder brown" and "madder yellow," respectively, terminology that is inaccurate but understandable. Other colors were included by raising iron buff and by printing bark liquors with tin to produce orange.[50]

Blues or greens were added to madder prints by putting blue on white or yellow areas respectively. The blue might be penciled indigo or Prussian blue. The latter could be applied using the raised style (by printing and ageing iron salts, then raising in a bath of prussiate) or the steam style (applying both components of Prussian blue in the same print paste and steaming). The details of the Star quilt (Figs. 44 and 45) include such prints.

The madder style survived for many years because the range of fast colors could not be achieved in any other way. Madder is a root in which the coloring matter, alizarin, is present as a glycoside derivative to the extent of about 2 percent. The alizarin could not easily be extracted from the root

FIG. 50. The recipes for these madder-style prints include Dutch madder, garancine, sumac (a tannic acid source), bark (quercitron), and wood (sappan, brazil). Madder yielded orange reds, purples, rich "chocolate" browns, and weak blacks. These colors constituted the madder-style palette. From George Birtwistle's "Dye Receipt Book," kept while he worked at Allen Print Works in 1858. American Museum of Textile History, Lowell, Massachusetts (1986.4).

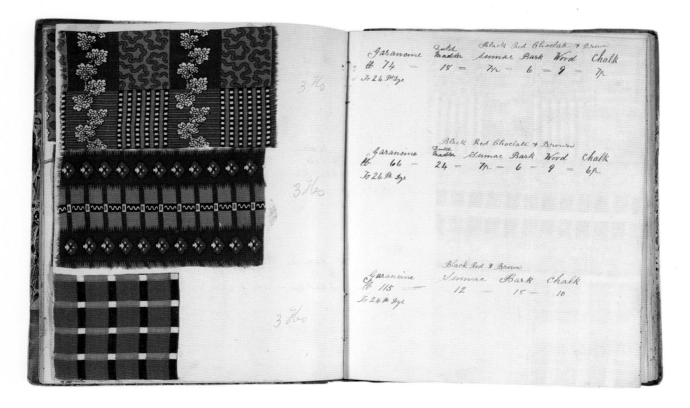

and purified the way that indigo was. Additionally, the low concentration and woody impurities made it impossible to produce a madder print paste which could be applied directly. Madder and related plants that contain alizarin have been known and used since ancient times. It was grown for the European industry in Holland, Turkey, France, and Italy, and recipes in the mid–nineteenth century usually refer to "French madder" or "Dutch madder" and so on.[51] In the 1830s "garancine," madder concentrated by treating it with heat and sulfuric acid, was introduced.[52] Additional color could be extracted from spent madder in the same way; this product was known as "garanceux." In 1852 "commercial alizarin" became available through a process of further refining garancine. In the late 1860s processes for the production of synthetic alizarin were developed. Travis gives a full account of this development and the commercial turmoil that resulted for the dye makers involved.[53] By the mid-1870s the new product with its advantages of high purity and consistency was becoming widely used. The freedom of this product from the woody material that characterized madder allowed calico printers to apply it directly to the fabric in a print paste using the steam style. In the same way several different dyes could be printed in the design in one operation. The new shades and printing processes associated with the introduction of synthetic dyes gave further impetus to the fading of the madder style into obsolescence.

DISCHARGES & RESISTS
WITH THE MADDER STYLE

Printers could also use discharge and resist variations of the madder style. In contrast to the usual understanding of these terms, the dye itself was not resisted or discharged; instead the mordant was. In either case, an acid, typically citric or tartaric, was the usual agent. The former was often obtained and used directly in the form of lime juice. For a resist, the cloth was printed with a design in acid, then padded or printed all over with a mordant. During ageing the mordant would not fix in the acid-printed areas, and on dyeing the print areas would remain white. For a discharge the steps were reversed: the cloth was padded with mordant, then dried and printed with an acid paste. After ageing, dunging removed the mordant from the print areas. Once again in the dyebath, the print areas would be undyed. While the two variations produced similar results, printers regarded the resist technique as easier.[54]

These simple methods could be extended to achieve complex patterns. Particularly popular over many years were patterns of white with light and dark shades of color. Most common are patterns in white, pink, and red, the so-called *double pinks*, but purple is also seen frequently. Figures 51 and 52 give examples of each from the Allen Print Works in Rhode Island. The most economical method of achieving such designs involved the use of covering and/or padding cylinders, and hence became known as the *cover and*

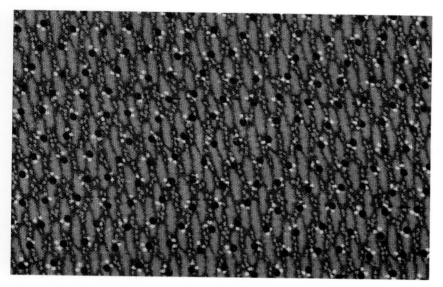

Fig. 51. Double pink fabric swatch, ca. 1880. Detail of salesman's sample card, Allen Print Works, Providence, Rhode Island. American Museum of Textile History, Lowell, Massachusetts (1428).

This madder print is typical of the cover and pad style. The white figure is an acid resist, the pale pink an "all-over" pad, and the dark pink is produced by a covering cylinder.

Fig. 52. Double purple fabric swatch, ca. 1880. Detail of salesman's sample card, Allen Print Works, Providence, Rhode Island. American Museum of Textile History. Lowell, Massachusetts (1420). This detail illustrates another cover and pad style. The two shades of purple came from dyeing with madder after printing with mordants of different strengths. Such colors were popular in the last quarter of the nineteenth century.

*pad style,* although it was simply a variation of the madder style.[55] The covering cylinder was engraved with a small-detailed design such as fine lines, or tiny flowers. The padding cylinder was engraved with either closely spaced fine diagonal lines or fine dots, the aim being to produce an even, all-over color. Thus a pattern was printed with an acid resist and dried. A dark shade of mordant was printed with a covering cylinder, followed by a pale shade of mordant printed with a padding cylinder. After the ageing, dunging, and dyeing steps, white and dark designs appeared on a light ground.

This method could be extended to multicolors by using the ability of tin crystals (tin chloride) to resist iron mordants while enhancing the red produced from an aluminum mordant (red liquor) in which they were mixed.

Thus, for example, an acid-resist print could be covered with a mixture of aluminum and tin salts, and then padded with iron salts. In the madder bath would emerge the white, acid-resisted pattern on a red (madder plus aluminum/tin, the iron cover producing no color because of the tin's resisting effect) and purple (madder plus iron in the areas unprinted with either resist or aluminum/tin) ground. A mixed cover of aluminum and iron would produce chocolate instead of the purple. The level of complexity could increase. For example, McCarthy includes a print of "Acid, black, chocolate, brown and two purples covered with purple."[56]

One advantage of the cover and pad style was its flexibility. The printer could print many yards of one design of acid resist, then subject it to a variety of covers and pads. Alternatively, a range of acid prints could be covered and padded with the same cylinders. Thus it is not uncommon in quilts to see the same design elements in a variety of these "cover and pad" fabrics.

### Turkey Red

Until the advent of synthetic dyes, the brightest and fastest red shades available on cotton were originally developed in the Levant and became widely known as Turkey red. For years the process was shrouded in mystery, and much money was paid for supposed recipes for this color.[57] As originally described, the process involved many steps carried out over a period of weeks or months.[58] Advances during the nineteenth century such as the introduction of modified madder and synthetic alizarin, Turkey red oil, and better bleaching methods allowed for the dyeing to be carried out in days instead of months. Some elements of mystery still surround this famous color, but modern science has identified the final product on the fabric as a 2:1 alizarin: aluminum complex anion with an associated calcium cation.[59]

There seems to be no clear definition of what is and is not Turkey red. To be "genuine" Turkey red, it must obviously be based on madder/alizarin with an aluminum mordant. Beyond this Turkey red may simply be defined by its brightness. It should probably be applied by dyeing and not by printing, since it is usually assumed that the true brightness of Turkey red could not be achieved by printing. The distinction, however, is a fine one: dyeing Turkey red uses oil as part of the mordanting process, while the red obtained by printing madder on an aluminum mordant does not. If oil is included in the preparation of the cloth before printing, it causes white areas in prints to be stained in the madder bath. In printed furnishing fabrics with no white areas, oil can be used and the bright shade of Turkey red can be closely approximated. It would be difficult to deny it the status of "genuine."[60] The dyeing of Turkey red typically resulted in poor penetration of the yarn or fabric, and later abrasion of the fabric in use might result in pale areas as the undyed core is exposed. This phenomenon has been used to identify Turkey red, though its reliability is uncertain.

The color was famous and became a byword for quality. Eventually the phrase became little more than advertising jargon. With the introduction of synthetic reds at the end of the nineteenth century, particularly of the azoic class, much simpler methods of achieving bright and fast reds were available, and many of these continued to be sold as "Turkey red." Even bright red direct dyes, packaged for the home dyer and having poor fastness to wet treatments, were labeled as "Turkey red."

Printers were only able to make use of true dyed Turkey red as a ground shade for discharge work, but they did so extensively.[61] Methods for such prints were known quite early, and there are extant examples.[62] The so-called Monteith method (ca. 1800–1810) was used to print bandannas. It involved lead plates with holes cut in the shape of the design. Fabric was clamped between layers of these plates, and a hypochlorite solution was poured over the assembly. The solution discharged the color as it flowed through the fabric exposed by the holes.[63] The later and more widely used method of discharging Turkey red involved printing an acid paste and passing the fabric into a bath of bleaching powder; where acid was printed, chlorine would be liberated and the color discharged. As with the discharges of indigo discussed earlier, Turkey red discharges could be illuminated with other colors instead of the discharged areas being left white. Blue could be achieved with Prussian blue dissolved in oxalic acid, printed with the acid, and precipitated in the hypochlorite bath. Yellow pastes included lead nitrate: the bleach bath precipitated the lead that was later converted into chrome yellow by raising in a bath of dichromate. Green was produced by combining the yellow and blue discharge, and black was produced by logwood and iron, usually simply overprinted on the red. The resulting color combination of white, yellow, blue, green, and black on a bright red ground, often called Turkey red calico, is well known and commonly seen in quilts. The detail of the Four Ts quilt (Fig. 53) contains two such discharge patterns. The color combination of this acid discharge process was popular enough that it was copied quite well after azoic colors were introduced in the late nineteenth century, by both discharge and resist technique.[64] An alternative method of discharging Turkey red grounds, developed in the late nineteenth century, used strong alkali. This lent itself to combination with the glucose process of direct indigo printing discussed earlier. The blue of indigo was faster than the Prussian blue of the acid discharge process, and the resulting print therefore had better fastness properties.

FIG. 53. This detail from a Four Ts quilt from 1870–80 (Figure 127) contains Turkey red discharge prints. The ground has a deep-red hue achieved with the long, involved Turkey red–dyeing process. The blue, yellow, green, and black colors could have been printed directly on the white discharged areas or added to the discharge paste.

*The Steam Style & the Spirit Style*

Printing colors directly onto fabric, as opposed to printing a mordant and achieving the color through a later dyeing, was originally used as a minor, supplemental technique for the madder style. It began to rise in importance with the development of the *steam style*. The ageing that fixed the mordants to the fabric in the madder style was accomplished by hanging the fabric in warm moist rooms. Around 1830 steaming processes were developed to speed the ageing: steam was fed into a chamber in which the fabric was hung. This was still a discontinuous or batch process: pieces of fabric were hung, and later removed. However, by 1850 continuous agers were developed that were little different from those in use today, with pieces joined end-to-end and run continuously through a steam chamber. The process became known as rapid ageing. The principle of applying steam to fabrics to age them led to the steam style.[65] Rather than the dye and mordant being applied separately, the two were mixed in the print paste before printing. The reaction of dye and mordant to produce an insoluble complex in the fiber took place in steam. Most or all of the components needed to achieve coloration were present in the print paste.

This was obviously a quicker and easier method of printing because it allowed for the use of many different dyes in a single printing operation. It is here that the full range of familiar natural dyes were found in printing: quercitron, brazilwood, peachwood, sappan wood, logwood, cochineal, Persian berries, and galls.[66] Between the 1830s and 1860s the steam style was used chiefly for *delaines*, a popular cotton-wool mixture, and other mixed fabrics, while the madder style continued to dominate for calico printing. In Charles Dalton's 1850–51 recipe book for delaines, the steam style is the only one used; and madder and indigo are notable by their absence.[67] Delaines are not unusual in quilts of the nineteenth century; the log cabin quilt of Figure 54 contains several examples. The steam style remained a minor technique for calico printing until concentrated madder extracts and synthetic alizarin became available after the 1860s and methods for direct indigo printing were developed toward the end of the century. Although no longer referred to as the steam style, it is now the major method for printing with dyes.

The steam style required somewhat different fabric preparation, and for delaines the fabric was prepared with sodium stannate. When the style was

FIG. 54. Log Cabin quilt, 1895. Wool, delaines, 84¼ x 74½ in. Stitching is related to top design, 5 stitches per inch. Made by Caroline Steere Farnum. Collection of Caroline F. Barlow. RIQDP #261.

Caroline Steere Farnum of Harmony, Rhode Island, made this quilt for her granddaughter Caroline Lewis. It contains six different examples of delaines, fabrics of cotton warps and wool wefts. The mixed fiber content made delaines difficult to print with traditional recipes for either cotton or wool. As a consequence, delaines were always printed in the steam style. By this time, the purple was most probably an aniline dye.

later applied to calico, an "oil prepare," a treatment with ricinoleic acid derived from castor oil, was usually used, perhaps with tin salts which brightened some shades.[68]

Obviously, mordants and dyes would eventually react together in a paste at room temperature, so it was important to mix them "as needed" to ensure good results. The mixing of a natural dye and mordant in a print paste requires a concentrated extract of the dye, free of wood and grit, that would not foul engravings or give uneven prints. Dyers and printers included rasping, grinding, and extraction in preparing their steam-style pastes; thus the colors used were referred to as "extract colors."[69]

The problems of printing indigo directly to obtain blues have been mentioned earlier. In the steam style printers generally used the mineral color Prussian blue despite its poor fastness to alkali. The brown color that results can be used as an identifying characteristic. When produced in the steam style rather than in the raised style, Prussian blue was more usually known as "steam blue." The full development of steam blue required a final run through an oxidizing bath. This bath might be of hypochlorite or of chrome, which would raise a chrome yellow and provide greens where blue and yellow were printed together.

The steam style produced colors which are reasonably fast to wet treatments. Colors could also be printed directly and developed by ageing at room temperature on fabrics that were then washed briefly in cold water before use. The resulting prints had poor fastness and were produced cheaply for the low-end market. The method was known as the *spirit style,* and the colors used were known as "spirit colors" since they involved the use of "spirits of tin salts" (tin oxychloride), either as a fabric preparation or as a component of the print paste.

*Printing Mineral Colors: The Raised Style*

In the *raised style* a chemical was printed on the fabric, and the color later developed or raised by passing the fabric through a bath of a second chemical that reacted with the first to produce the color. The full color of some natural dyes such as catechu is developed by a similar raising. The production of color is as rapid as that from the steam style, and the two methods could be combined in the same print. Once again, the details of the Star quilt (Figs. 44 and 45) include examples of these colors.

Mineral colors were very useful in the hundred years before synthetic dyes became available. They could be bright, cheap, and fast, and as a class formed a useful supplement to the natural dyes in use. A number of them have been mentioned earlier, such as chrome yellow as an illuminating color for indigo discharge and resist printing or as a supplement to the madder style. They might be used as pigments but most often were produced directly on the fabric by the raised style. Chrome yellow and orange (lead salts raised with dichromate to give lead chromate), Prussian blue (iron acetate with potassium ferricyanide), iron buff (iron acetate with alkali to give iron oxide), and manganese bronze (manganous chloride with alkali to give manganese dioxide) were the most widely used. A full list of mineral colors includes others of less frequent use, such as antimony sulfide, chromium arsenite, cadmium sulfide, arsenic trisulfide (orpiment), prussiate of copper, and copper arsenite (Scheele's green).[70] Chromium oxide as chrome green was also used occasionally.[71]

Discharge methods were available to produce designs with mineral or raised colors. The susceptibility of Prussian blue to alkali mentioned earlier afforded a means of discharging it to give an iron buff design: removing this with oxalic acid produced a white figure. Tin chloride discharges manganese bronze, and gives a white figure. The tin also acts as a mordant for berry yellow or as a component of Prussian blue, thus producing blue, green, and yellow figures on a brown ground.[72]

The great majority of the textile prints produced until recently used a technique in which the colorant (or its precursors) was soluble and penetrated individual fibers. Printers, however, have long contrived to make use of pigment colors. Pigments are insoluble and remain so during application. They require a binder to fix them to the surface of the fiber in the same way that paint is held on the surface of wood. The binder must be reasonably flexible and resist the treatments to which textiles are subjected. In the nineteenth century the most common binder was albumen from eggs or blood. Egg albumen was pale and expensive and used for pastel colors.[73] Blood albumen was cheaper, but its color restricted its use to dark shades. Other protein materials such as gluten (from wheat) and lactarine (from milk) were used.[74] Heat and acid coagulated the binder to a solid from which the color would not readily be removed. The pigment style was used particularly for ultramarine blue, a bright greenish blue pigment which was available synthetically from 1828.[75] The style was used for chrome yellow in discharge work as an alternative to developing the color in the raised style.[76] The pigment style was even used initially for printing the new synthetic dyes on cotton until tannin mordants became available. The simplicity of pigment printing with fixation by dry heat alone and the availability of bright fast pigments and synthetic binders that minimize the stiffening effect means that today more than half of all the fabric printed around the world is produced this way.

*The Pigment Style*

FIG. 55. (*Opposite*) Crazy quilt, 1885. Silk velvet, silk satin, painted and printed silk top, cotton back, 61 x 57 in. Hand-embroidered. Made by Frances Morriah Prentice Palmer (1828–1906). Collection of Richard and Cynthia Palmer. RIQDP #412.

The bright colors in this quilt were achieved with synthetic dyes. Crazy quilts incorporated odd-shaped pieces of fabrics including printed ribbons and other ephemera. This one has a souvenir playbill. Machine-made lace often edged crazy quilts. A century before, lace was handmade, making it too costly for most consumers. Rhode Island has a history of lace manufacturing; in 1949, over 60 percent of the lace mills in the United States operated in the state (Vittoria Rosatto, *Leavers Lace* [Providence: American Lace Manufacturers Association, 1949], 105).

Frances Prentice married John S. Palmer, a partner in the Providence firm of Palmer and Capron, which manufactured rolled gold plate and sterling gold rings. In his lifetime Mr. Palmer founded three insurance companies and served as president of two banks. A cloth strip on the back of the quilt is inscribed "Master John S. Palmer," probably the maker's grandson, born in 1881.

Synthetic dyes emerged from the early days of what is now referred to as organic chemistry, the chemistry of carbon compounds.[77] The raw material for many of these early experiments was coal tar, available in great supply as a by-product of the generation of coal gas used for lighting the Industrial Revolution. Synthetic dyes were known for many years as "coal tar dyes," reflecting their origin. Alternatively, since many were derived from aniline (in turn derived from coal tar), the term "aniline dyes" is often used. William Perkin created the first synthetic dye, mauve, accidentally in his attempt (now seen as hopelessly naive) to synthesize the natural drug quinine. His brilliance was in persevering with the investigation of what most would have discarded, the exploration of its commercial potential, and the invention of large-scale processes for the bulk preparation of this new color. Once the potential was demonstrated, other coal-tar dyes were soon developed. Most of these early synthetic dyes displayed very bright colors but poor fastness to light exposure. They had substantivity for wool and silk, but not for cotton. In calico printing they were initially treated as "pigments" and fixed with albumen. Later the use of a tannin mordant, a combination of tannic acid and antimony potassium tartrate, "tartar emetic," enabled these early dyes to be printed successfully on cotton, achieving very bright colors until well into the twentieth century. The crazy quilt of Figure 55 reveals the new bright colors available with synthetic dyes.

Over the course of the fifty years following Perkin's initial invention, most of the classes of dye that we recognize today were developed. The new dye industry also created synthetic alizarin and indigo, which soon replaced their natural counterparts. The synthesis and manufacture of dyes was the first manifestation of industrial organic chemistry. The companies that succeeded in this venture laid the foundations of future success in pharmaceuticals, herbicides, pesticides, and plastics. The largest chemical companies in the world today can trace their roots to preeminence in dye manufacture in the nineteenth century.

Aniline black, developed in the 1860s, was the only significant member of a class known as "oxidation dyes."[78] Aniline hydrochloride was printed with an oxidizing agent (usually a chlorate) and a catalyst (ammonium vanadate or copper sulfide, for example). It provided a much better black than iron with madder, galls, or logwood, so black is seen more frequently in late-nineteenth-century printed cottons than in those produced earlier. The development of aniline black on the fabric required oxidation under acid conditions, and it could thus readily be resisted or discharged with reducing agents or alkalis. When illuminated with the synthetic dyes or pigment colors, bright patterns on an intense black ground created a well-received new look.[79]

The other new synthetic dye classes for cotton were direct, sulfur, vat, and azoic dyes. Of these, vat and azoic dyes found the widest use in printing. The first example of an azoic dye was developed in 1880 and an analog, "Para red," soon became important in dyeing colors approximating Turkey red in brightness and fastness. The dye could be discharged with the hydrosulfite that was newly available for dyeing indigo, and the familiar appearance of Turkey red discharge prints was continued with azoic colors.

This led ultimately to the demise of Turkey red. Azoic dyes, also known as naphthol dyes or ice colors, could also be printed directly, leading to wider pattern possibilities.

Over the first years of the twentieth century, new vat dyes were developed. Applied with hydrosulfite in the same direct way as indigo, they were available in a full spectrum of colors and finally showed that synthetic dyes could be colorfast. Like azoic dyes they were widely used in printing, par-

*Down by the Old Mill Stream*

ticularly furnishing fabrics on which their excellent lightfastness was a particular advantage. They also found wide use as illuminating colors in hydrosulfite discharges.

The only new class of dye for cotton to be developed in the twentieth century is the reactive dyes. They combine the attributes of bright colors, a full gamut of shades, and good fastness properties. Since their introduction in 1956, they have become the dominant dye in textile printing. One quilt that embodies many of the developments of the nineteenth century is shown in Figure 56. In it can be seen direct-printed indigo, azoic red, and aniline black. It was produced in the 1890s by Mahala Peck (Fig. 57), a mother of fourteen. When she made it, she was in her nineties. The quilt makes a fitting end to this essay, which covers the changes in textile print coloration made mostly during Peck's lifetime.

FIG. 56. (*Opposite*) Nine-Patch variation quilt, 1890–1900. Cotton top and back, 84½ x 81½ in. Machine-pieced, tied. Made by Mahala Johnson Peck (1814–1909). Private collection. RIQDP #648.

Mahala Peck made this quilt in the twilight of her life judging by the technological advances exemplified in both the machine piecing and the fabrics themselves. By the 1880s, printers had begun to resolve the difficulties in printing strong blacks by using aniline black, an oxidation dye. The glucose process invented in 1883 finally allowed the direct printing of indigo to produce clear, sharp designs in deep blue. The new azoic dyes were just coming into use for red and other bright colors.

FIG. 57. Mahala Johnson Peck (1814–1909). Mahala and Charles Peck lived in the Christopher Rhodes house on Post Road in Pawtuxet, where they raised fourteen children. After Charles's death, Mahala stayed on in the house with two unmarried daughters, Emma and Jenny. When Emma and Jenny died in the 1930s, relatives found Mahala's quilts in the house. RIQDP Archives.

1. P. C. Floud, "The Origins of English Calico Printing," *Journal of the Society of Dyers and Colourists* 76 (1960): 275–81. This and two subsequent articles in the same volume ("The English Contribution to the Early History of Indigo Printing," 344–49, and "The English Contribution to the Development of Copper-Plate Printing," 425–34) provide a good background to what was presumably the major source of printed fabrics found in early U.S. quilts. He deals with similar subjects and extends his discussion to the nineteenth century in articles in *Ciba Review* (Peter Floud, "The British Calico-Printing Industry 1676–1840," *Ciba Review*, no. 1 (1961): 2–7, and "The English Contribution to the Chemistry of Calico Printing before Perkin," same volume, 8–14.)

2. Mattiebelle Gittinger, *Master Dyers to the World* (Washington, D.C.: Textile Museum, 1982), 26.

3. P. C. Floud, "The Origins of English Calico Printing," 278.

4. A. Verhecken, "Dyeing with Kermes Is Still Alive," *Journal of the Society of Dyers and Colourists* 105 (1989): 389; D. Cardon, "Kermes Is a Dying Dye," *Journal of the Society of Dyers and Colourists* 106 (1990): 191; Franco Brunello, *The Art of Dyeing in the History of Mankind,* trans. Bernard Hickey (Vicenza: Neri Pozza, 1973), 199. Brazilwood was the name given to the dyewood from the East Indian tree, Caesalpinia Sappan. Portuguese explorers named the region where they found a similar and valuable dye-wood, C. echinata, "Brazil." *The Shorter Oxford English Dictionary,* 3rd ed., s.v. "Brazil."

5. Sidney M. Edelstein, "The Dual Life of Edward Bancroft," *American Dyestuff Reporter* 43 (1954): 712. The story of Bancroft and this dye is covered in "Quercitron: A North American Dyestuff," elsewhere in this volume. Edelstein's article is included in his *Historical Notes on the Wet-Processing Industry* (New York: Dexter Chemical, 1972), a reprinted collection of thirty articles, chiefly from *American Dyestuff Reporter.* Edelstein founded the Sidney M. Edelstein Center for the History and Philosophy of Science, Technology, and Medicine at the Hebrew University of Jerusalem, which has become an abundant source of research in historic textile processing.

6. Charles O'Neill, *A Dictionary of Calico Printing and Dyeing* (London: Simpkin, Marshall, 1862), 14.

7. Louis Diserens, *The Chemical Technology of Dyeing and Printing,* vol. 2 (New York: Reinhold, 1951), 341–47; R. L. Harper, Jr. and R. L. Stone, "Cationic Cotton Plus Easy Care," *Textile Chemist and Colorist* 18, no. 11 (November 1986): 13.

8. John Penington, *Chemical and Economical Essays* (Philadelphia: no publisher listed, 1790.)

9. Elijah Bemis, *The Dyer's Companion,* 3rd ed. (New York: Dover Publications, 1973). Bemis wrote two editions of his book, in 1806 and 1815. This third edition includes a modern introduction and appendices by Rita J. Adrosko.

10. Edward Bancroft, *Experimental Researches Concerning the Philosophy of Permanent Colours and the Best Means of Producing Them* (London: T. Cadell and W. Davies, 1813).

11. William Partridge, *A Practical Treatise on Dying of Woollen Cotton and Skein Silk* (New York: H. Walker, 1823). Republished with notes by Pasold Research Fund, Edington, Wilts., U.K., 1973.

12. Cornelius Moloney, *The Practical Dyer* (Boston: Munroe and Francis, 1833). In his preface, Moloney suggests the industry strive no longer to "be tributary to foreign nations for these articles." The book lists testimonials to Moloney's skills, and subscribers to the work, including seven from Rhode Island. They are John McFail, Eli Brown, and George Thomson of Providence; and Royal Sibley, J. Dunnell, Barney Merry, and James Hudson of Pawtucket.

13. An Experienced Dyer, Assisted by Several Scientific Gentlemen, *A Practical Treatise on Dyeing and Calico-Printing* (New York: Harper & Brothers, 1846).

14. Charles O'Neill, *A Dictionary of Calico Printing and Dyeing* (London: Simpkin, Marshall, 1862).

15. Charles O'Neill, *A Dictionary of Calico Printing and Dyeing* (New York: H. C. Baird, 1869).

16. Samuel Dunster, a printer, spent much of his career in Johnston, R.I. He worked either as an employee or a consultant for many printers over the years 1828 to 1860 and kept careful records as he did so. Some eleven volumes of his notes are kept at the Rhode Island Historical Society Library in Providence, R.I. They include fabric swatches and the recipes used to produce them, plus copied recipes from other sources. He was familiar with almost all of the recognized printing methods of the time, and his notes include madder work, iron buff, pencil blue, china blue, and indigo resists. For researchers the works form a valuable and practical supplement to the texts of the time. They are usually referred to as "dye receipt books" or "dye swatch books," but such descriptions reveal neither the preponderance of textile printing, nor the level of commentary provided. "Practical Printer's Notes" might be a more appropriate description. Dunster includes several revealing asides about the ignorance of his employers or his rivals, and the ways in which they were persuaded to part with money for something worthless. He includes an "Invention" for a fast chemical black "to show how easily D. G. Scott was humbugged out of $50. . . . the fact was the man was 'fast' who sold it at that price." Samuel Dunster, *Print Dyes*, 11 vols., MSS 363, Rhode Island Historical Society Library, 6 (1859): 136. As late as 1860, Dunster added notes to volume 6, which he began while he was at Clay's Print Works in Johnston, R.I., in 1846. Charles Dalton, *Printer's Receipt Book* (1850–1851). This volume is in the archives of the American Association of Textile Chemists and Colorists, Research Triangle Park, N.C. The book has been described in Linda Welters and Martin Bide, "AATCC's Little Black Book: Printing Delaines in the 1850s," *Textile Chemist and Colorist* 27, no. 6 (June 1995): 17–23.

17. Daniel McCarthy (he is usually referred to in this way, although he signed himself "Dan. O'C. M'Carthy") was printer at Allen's Print Works in Providence, R.I. He maintained meticulous notes, recipes, and patterns during the period from 1845 through 1858. There are twelve volumes divided into *Miscellaneous Colours 1 and 2, Fancy Colours 1 and 2,* and *Madder Colours 1–8*; these are kept at the Rhode Island Historical Society Library, MSS 563. He was a contemporary of Dunster's and presumably worked with him at Allen's from 1848 to 1852. Like Dunster, his notes are revealing about the practical problems of the time and include regular reviews of "Dye House Operations" in which developments adopted in the plant are discussed. An illustration of the notes of another printer at Allen's, George Birtwistle, is Figure 50. Birtwistle's notes date from 1856 and 1858 and are kept at the American Textile History Museum in Lowell, Mass. Edmund Barnes worked earlier. His notes date from 1829 and begin at "Blackford Bridge, near Bury" (presumably England), move to "Dover N.H.," and the final page is from "Providence, R.I." The books are kept at the Cooper Hewitt Museum in New York City.

18. Charles O'Neill, *The Principles and Practice of Calico Printing, Bleaching And Dyeing etc.* 2 vols. (Manchester: Palmer and Howe, 1878).

19. William Crookes, *Dyeing and Tissue Printing* (London: George Bell and Sons, 1882). Antonio Sansone, *The Printing of Cotton Fabrics* (Manchester: Heywood and Son, 1887).

20. Edmund Knecht and James Best Fothergill, *The Principles and Practice of Textile Printing*, 4th ed. (London: Griffin, 1952).

21. Keith McLaren, "Newton's Indigo," *Colour Research and Application*, 10 (1985): 225.

22. Dunster, *Print Dyes 6* (1845–48): 36–65. The records include the number of carboys of oil of vitriol (sulfuric acid) used for the production of ferrous sulfate and names the bosses in charge of the dye house at various times during the period. In one case Dunster notes, "Jack pronounced the vats right on Tuesday night—I'm a little doubtful."

23. Sidney M. Edelstein, "Dyeing in the Confederacy," *American Dyestuff Reporter* 51 (1962): 36. Reprinted in *Historical Notes on the Wet-Processing Industry*, 116.

24. Knecht and Fothergill, *Textile Printing*, 345.

25. Ibid., part 4, 129–54.

26. Keith McLaren, *The Colour Science of Dyes and Pigments*, 2nd ed. (Bristol: Adam Hilger: 1986), 7. Many variations of the fermentation vat were developed, although woad (contributing some blue color as well as fermentation) and bran were common ingredients. Urine was the usual source of the alkalinity required. While printers abandoned it early, the use of the woad fermentation vat for dyeing wool, with its comparatively low pH that did not risk damage to the fiber, persisted into the twentieth century.

27. Partridge, *A Practical Treatise on Dying*, 239. Note 90 mentions that dichromate is absent from this book, and that it would shortly be introduced. Floud ("The English Contribution," 14) includes a discussion of some of the new techniques that were introduced in the 1820s as dichromate became available. Dichromate is also referred to as bichromate, and occasionally as simply "chrome," hence the process of "chroming" refers to a treatment with a solution of dichromate. Dichromate's importance also derived from its use as a component of the mineral color, chrome yellow.

28. An Experienced Dyer, *A Practical Treatise*, 564; O'Neill, *Dictionary of Calico Printing*, 107–10. Green colors in general were a challenge. Apart from some mineral colors such as chrome green or Scheele's green, there were no useful green dyes, and the production of green shades relied on a mixture of blue and yellow. With blue from indigo or Prussian blue, and yellow from quercitron, Persian berry, or chrome yellow, myriad methods were available to the printer.

29. Knecht and Fothergill, *Textile Printing*, 606.

30. Gittinger, *Master Dyers to the World*, 24–25. Gittinger illustrates the indigo resist process as practiced in India in 1734. The quilted fragment illustrated by Gittinger on page 179 was produced on the Coromandel Coast of India. It is strikingly similar to the fragment of Figure 41.

31. Floud, "The English Contribution," 346. The wax method was obsolete in England by the middle of the eighteenth century, largely replaced by the pencil and china blue methods discussed later. Floud refers to a description of the puzzlement in the early nineteenth century when a pile of flour, wax, and gum was excavated in England, until it was recalled that a print works formerly existed on the site. The wax resist seems to have survived longer in Europe, and Dunster includes a recipe for wax resist on silk. Dunster, *Print Dyes 1* (1829): 151.

32. An Experienced Dyer, *A Practical Treatise*, 533.

33. O'Neill, *Dictionary of Calico Printing*, 124.

34. McLaren, *The Colour Science of Dyes and Pigments*, 7. McLaren suggests that the discovery of orpiment's reducing properties derived from its use as a yellow pigment mixed with indigo to get green.

35. Floud, "The English Contribution," 346.

36. Dunster, *Print Dyes 8* (1848–52): 85. Among references throughout his notes to the use of the pencil blue technique, in an early example of recycling, Dunster describes using

old pencil blues in an indigo dyeing vat.

37. O'Neill, *Dictionary of Calico Printing*, 126. In his entry for indigo, O'Neill includes pencil blue recipes in which the reducing agent is tin or glucose.

38. Floud, "The English Contribution," 344.

39. Ibid., 347.

40. Dunster, *Print Dyes 1* (1829): 109.

41. O'Neill, *The Principles and Practice of Calico Printing*, vol. 2, 199. In a discussion of the methods tried, O'Neill describes a patent of 1846 that dealt with the enclosure of a print machine in a chamber filled with coal gas as a means to exclude air. Despite the money and effort expended, the results were uneven. McCarthy (*Madder Colours VIII*, 65–68) has notes on a Fast Blue, which seems to be a mixture of indigo developed by the china blue process and a raised Prussian blue. He comments that "this blue in every particular requires great care" and that oxidation must be avoided to prevent a "poor and impoverished appearance."

42. Anthony Travis, *The Rainbow Makers* (Bethlehem: Lehigh University Press, 1973), 223. Travis is currently Deputy Director of the Sidney M. Edelstein Center for the History and Philosophy of Science, Technology and Medicine at the Hebrew University of Jerusalem. Reference was made earlier to Edelstein's contributions to the history of textile processing.

43. Knecht and Fothergill, *Textile Printing*, 342.

44. Brian Glover, "Are Natural Colorants Good for Your Health? Are Synthetic Ones Better?" *Textile Chemist and Colorist* 27, no. 4 (April 1995): 17. Glover estimates that to dye the world's cotton with natural dyes to the same extent as is done with synthetic dyes would require about 30 percent of the world's agricultural land.

45. Brunello, *The Art of Dyeing*, 101.

46. Gittinger, *Master Dyers to the World*, 24–25.

47. Knecht and Fothergill, *Textile Printing*, 223.

48. O'Neill, *Dictionary of Calico Printing*, 7.

49. Knecht and Fothergill, *Textile Printing*, 307, 465; O'Neill, *Dictionary of Calico Printing*, 124. Catechu is an interesting colorant. Obtained from the exudate of a tree, it was first used in medicine, but by 1830 was cheap enough for use as a dye. Those who first used it mystified their rival printers who searched in vain for the new mordant for madder that they were convinced had been used to produce the new fast brown and fawn shades. McCarthy (*Madder Colours IV* [1854–55], 34) describes the unevenness of browns based on catechu and blames it on the "want of ageing and extreme cold weather."

50. McCarthy, *Miscellaneous Colours II* (1849–52), 99, *Madder Colours V* (1855), 6. The madder palette in this work is often extended with browns from catechu, iron buff colors, and oranges called "madder orange" by direct printing of bark with tin and aluminum salts. The presumably resulting yellow was converted to an orange in the succeeding madder dyebath. Dunster, *Print Dyes 6* (1846): 71, has a similarly named recipe.

51. Partridge, *A Practical Treatise on Dying*, 8. Partridge, writing before 1823, bemoans the fact that in the United States only one grade of madder is available. Later recipes of the nineteenth century usually distinguish, for example, between French and Dutch madder. McCarthy *Madder Colours V*, 5, includes a recipe in which French and Dutch madder are separate ingredients.

52. McCarthy, *Miscellaneous Colours II* (1852), 99, copies a recipe for the production of garancine. The use of garancine by Birtwistle is evident in Figure 50.

53. Travis, *The Rainbow Makers*, 191–203.

54. O'Neill, *Dictionary of Calico Printing*, 77.

55. Knecht and Fothergill, *Textile Printing*, 432, 472.

56. McCarthy, *Madder Colours III* (1852), 53.

57. Dunster, *Print Dyes 1* (1829–31): 26. He writes of a newspaper article about the payment of £5000 for a Smyrna Turkey red recipe. In the same volume, on page 146, he includes a written copy of a recipe, and underneath notes, "I don't believe a word of the above." In *Print Dyes 2* (1832): 24, he copies another recipe and next to one ingredient includes the comment "(what?)."

58. J. Merritt Matthews, *Application of Dyestuffs* (New York: John Wiley & Sons, 1920), 366.

59. P. F. Gordon and P. Gregory, *Organic Chemistry in Colour* (Berlin: Springer Verlag: 1987), 4.

60. Knecht and Fothergill, *Textile Printing*, 468.

61. Joyce Storey, "Turkey Red Prints," *Surface Design Journal* 20, no. 4 (Summer 1996): 7–8, 34–35, 38. Storey has studied and published widely on Turkey red printing.

62. Jane Tozer and Sarah Levitt, *Fabric of Society: A Century of People and Their Clothes, 1770–1870* (Powys, Wales: Laura Ashley, 1983), 29–30.

63. An Experienced Dyer, *A Practical Treatise*, 561; Knecht and Fothergill, *Textile Printing*, 50.

64. Knecht and Fothergill, *Textile Printing*, 646, 741.

65. Ibid., part V, 155–97. This section of the book describes both the ageing and steaming processes at length.

66. Rita Adrosko, *Natural Dyes in the United States* (Washington, D.C.: Smithsonian Institution Press, 1968); James Liles, "Dyes in American Quilts Prior to 1930 with Special Emphasis on Cotton and Linen," *Uncoverings 1984*, Sally Garoutte, ed. (San Francisco: American Quilt Study Group, 1985), 29–40. Adrosko gives a thorough review of the subject and includes recipes and an extensive bibliography.

67. Welters and Bide, "AATCC's Little Black Book," 17–23.

68. Knecht and Fothergill, *Textile Printing*, 240–47, 278.

69. Sansone, *The Printing of Cotton Fabrics*, 70.

70. An Experienced Dyer, *A Practical Treatise*, 136.

71. O'Neill, *Dictionary of Calico Printing*, 52; McCarthy, *Fancy Colours I* (1855), 18, 108. Several examples of "sage" are included in the notes, produced by reducing dichromate with sugar, and raising the resulting chromic salt in alkali. Confusingly, the later reference is to a color produced by a combination of Prussian blue and chrome yellow as "chrome green."

72. An Experienced Dyer, *A Practical Treatise*, 564. Dunster, (*Print Dyes 2* [1832]: 46) has discharges of manganese bronze to give patterns of white, blue, and green in the brown ground.

73. McCarthy, *Miscellaneous Colours II*, 4, has a recipe for printing ultramarine blue which includes "the whites of 70 eggs."

74. Welters and Bide, "AATCC's Little Black Book," 21. In England Dalton was given recipes for printing ultramarine blue with binders of gluten and lactarine. Note the similarity between the binders and the materials used for animalizing cotton.

75. Anthony Butler and Rosslyn Gash, "A Higher Shade of Blue," *Chemistry in Britain* 29 (1993): 952.

76. Knecht and Fothergill, *Textile Printing*, 584.

77. The introduction and development of synthetic dyes and their relation to natural dyes has been widely written on. Good general references cited earlier include Gordon and Gregory's *Organic Chemistry in Colour*, Travis's *The Rainbow Makers*, and McLaren's *Colour Science of Dyes and Pigments*. Several articles in the November 1992 seventy-fifth anniversary issue of *American Dyestuff Reporter* also provide background on the synthetic dye industry.

78. Anthony Travis, "From Manchester to Massachusetts via Mulhouse: The Transatlantic Voyage of Aniline Black," *Technology and Culture* 35, no. 1 (January 1994): 70–99. The importance of the color may be gauged from the extensive research to improve it, and the extent of litigation associated with the use of patented methods.

79. Knecht and Fothergill, *Textile Printing*, 321.

*Printed Textiles
in Rhode
Island Quilts*

# Technology Reflected

MARGARET T. ORDOÑEZ

PAINTED AND PRINTED COTTONS FROM INDIA BECAME A HIGHLY DESIRABLE commodity in the western world in the seventeenth and eighteenth centuries.[1] Known as calicoes or chintzes, these exotic riches from the Far East symbolized wealth for those who hung them in their houses or wore gowns made of their yardages. Their popularity forced the French and British governments to protect domestic textile industries by prohibiting their importation, use, and production, but seventy-five years of prohibitions did not diminish the desire for the forbidden prints.[2] The best promotion scheme in the world could not have created a market more eager for a product than the one that had developed for printed cottons by the mid–eighteenth century.

Consumers in New England showed no less interest than their European counterparts for the new textiles. Merchants strove to supply the expanding American market. Rhode Island merchants imported fashionable cottons from England, West India, and China. The April 1759 *Newport Mercury* advertisements by "Simon Pease, jun." proclaimed the arrival of the latest shipments of "callico" and "chints" from London via Boston.[3] The next month he promoted new-fashioned "Furniture for Beds," meaning fabrics suitable for bed valances, curtains, and covers.[4] In 1762 Gideon, John, and Edward Waton described the calicoes they offered for sale as "2 purple," "single purple 3 colours," and "china blue."[5]

Beginning early in the eighteenth century, New England entrepreneurs tried producing calicoes despite Britain's discouraging such production in its colony. These efforts and the developments that followed are the basis for this essay, which explores the production and consumption of painted and printed cotton fabrics in Rhode Island during the eighteenth and nineteenth centuries. Two inspirations for this exploration are Rhode Island quilters who used the fabrics available to them, and the cotton fabrics themselves which reveal much about the technology and fashions of their time.

Starting as early as 1712, printers around Boston, Massachusetts, promoted their calico-printing businesses. Florence Pettit located advertisements for fourteen textile printing firms in New England between 1712 and 1776. One of the ads in 1713 promoted products printed by "James Franklin and wife."[6] James was Benjamin Franklin's elder brother and a printer of the *Boston Gazette,* one of the earliest colonial papers. James Franklin also advertised in 1720 that he printed "Linens, Calicoes, Silks &c. in good Figures, very lively, and durable colors, and without the offensive smell which commonly attends the Linens printed here."[7] After trouble with the Massachusetts authorities, Franklin moved his business to Newport, where it continued to prosper.

*Eighteenth-Century Printers*

These New England firms did not retain the notoriety achieved by Philadelphia printers who opened businesses in 1774 and 1775. The most famous of the Philadelphia printers was John Hewson, befriended and encouraged by Benjamin Franklin. Hewson's block-printed cotton squares and isolated motifs became centers for quilts. At least a dozen examples of Hewson's fine work are extant, eight in quilts.[8] He retired in 1810, and his son, John, Jr., continued printing cottons for fifteen years. Their business weathered a number of difficult periods for the American textile industry plus numerous changes in fashion.[9]

As Americans established their independence, printers in Rhode Island joined those who would compete for a share of the calico market. The climate of the market in the 1780s did not spell easy success for calico printers. Trade that had opened with India and China after the Revolutionary War supplied large quantities of muslins, calicoes, and other cottons. British manufacturers sought to drive the Indian goods from the market by supplying cotton fabrics in unlimited quantity with easy credit. Dealers imported plain Indian cotton for American printers but brought in greater quantities of already printed cottons for consumers.[10] Vigorously enforced statutes enacted by Parliament in 1774 controlled exportation of machinery and equipment that could be used for woolen, cotton, linen, or silk manufacturing. Then in 1782 additional statutes covered "any blocks, plates, engines, tools, or utensils used in, or which are proper for the preparing or finishing of the calico, cotton, muslin, or linen printing machines."[11] These factors became a major obstacle to the successful establishment of cotton manufacturing in the United States as the following Rhode Island examples illustrate.

A manuscript written by Anthony Arnold described a nineteenth-century printing operation in Rhode Island. In 1780 Jeremiah Eddy and a painter named Alverson began printing cloth with oil colors in a shop near Stone Pond.[12] Arnold described the process of cutting motifs in wood blocks and printing: "Jeremiah Eddy cut the tipes [types] on the end of small pieces of hard wood and put on the paint on the tipes with a brush, stamping the cloth by hand in small flowers to please the eye."[13] Alverson quit due to ill health, and a second partnership with Col. Benjamin Hopper lasted into the spring of 1781. At that time Eddy met "a German . . . from the british servis who had worked in the printing business and he gave the said Eddy knowledge of Printing with water colors, he then cut larger tipes in blocks and pieces of boards of hard wood and printed running vines and large flowers and he printed hundreds of various figures, the women brought in their sheets made of Tow and lining taken from their beads, and had them printed and made into gounds."[14] Reduced prices for calicoes resulting from increased supply no doubt influenced Eddy's decision to close his business in late 1781 or early 1782.

The German who had come to Providence probably was Herman Vandausen, a recent immigrant to East Greenwich, Rhode Island. He had learned about printing cottons in Mulhouse, France where calico printing had been legalized in 1745.[15] John Brown, a successful Providence merchant, declined to help Vandausen start up a cotton printing business because of the high financial risk. Nevertheless, Vandausen opened a printing shop, cutting wood blocks and printing homespun linen cloth that local women wove and bleached.[16]

These early calico printers with their carved wooden blocks provided a valuable service: "A calico, or as it was then called a chintz dress, was at that time a rare and costly article, and ranked as high in the scale of fashion as the silks and velvets do now. As there was little or none of the calico in the shops for sale, every family made their own cloth, and then carried it to the printing establishment to be printed, each person selecting their own pattern and colors. The patterns were very neat and pretty, and the colors remarkably brillliant."[17] A single example of cloth reportedly printed by Vandausen survives in a private collection.[18] Its leaves and small blossoms on trailing vines were block printed in dark brown on linen fabric.

The story that has been passed down about Vandausen is similar to the one Arnold recorded about Eddy. One phrase in the Arnold manuscript, "and he [Vandausen] gave the said Eddy knowledge of Printing with water colors, he then cut larger tipes in blocks," is ambiguous as to whom the latter "he" identifies. This becomes a problem in attributing ownership to the three carved wooden blocks in Figure 58. Rhode Island Historical Society donor records attribute the blocks to Vandausen although Keith be-

FIG. 58. The 1780s wood blocks for printing calico were hand carved either by Herman Vandausen or Jeremiah Eddy, early Rhode Island calico printers. Rhode Island Historical Society.

lieved them more likely to be Jeremiah Eddy's.[19] Either way, they represent individual motifs that could be arranged in a variety of patterns.

In the 1790s competition from imports and lack of funds forced Vandausen to join the textile printing firm of Zachariah Allen.[20] Allen, "an enterprising merchant, a firm patriot," founded Allendale Insurance, a firm that insured textile factories.[21]

Three other men invested in calico printing in Providence during the postrevolutionary period. By 1794 Messrs. Schaub, Tissot, and Dubosque began a business using wooden blocks to print homespun linens and cloth imported from Calcutta. Bishop reported that Dubosque had learned the techniques in Alsace; Pettit identified all three as French-trained printers. The group set up their business in a chocolate mill; the practice of retooling mill buildings for different manufacturing continued throughout the Industrial Revolution. The firm used a friction-calendering machine that employed flint to produce a surface on the fabric that was smooth enough for printing.[22] Later in 1797 Peter Schaub and Robert Newell, also of Providence, printed calicoes.[23] Evidence of any Rhode Island printing firm's continuing into the next century remains to be discovered.

Indian printers used wooden blocks and brushes to create colorful designs on cotton fabrics for export. They also had mastered a multistep application of wax resist on cloth to protect pattern areas during dyeing. Using mordanted dyes and ambient-temperature indigo baths made their products

WOOD-BLOCK PRINTING

unique in seventeenth-century Europe. Western printers tried to copy the Indian methods of dyeing and printing, but marketing strategies and western tastes altered the use of colors and motifs. Indian designs reflected European influence as early as 1662 when directors of the British East India Company supplied Indian manufacturers with patterns that would sell well in Europe.[24] The resulting fantastic flowers, exotic birds, flowering trees, and meandering vines on light-colored grounds appeared in western silk embroideries, crewel work, and block-printed cottons particularly for bed hangings, valances, coverlets, and quilts.

Block printing involved a carved wooden block, even application of print paste to the block's raised surface, and transfer of the paste to a fabric, as pictured in Figure 59. The print paste could contain a mordant, discharge, resist or china-blue indigo as discussed in the previous essay. A 9 to 12–inch by 4 to 7–inch block had all or part of a design carved in relief with a handle on the opposite side. A printer obtained print paste for the block by pressing it down on a woolen cloth stretched over a wooden drum containing thick varnish that provided a somewhat elastic surface. This set-up was called a "sieve," and a "tearer," often a child, had the responsibility of evenly covering the wool cloth with paste. Pins at the corners of the blocks guided the printer in placing the block in a position so that it fit the other parts of the design. The cloth to be printed lay on a long table padded with a blanket, so the printer could push the block down onto the fabric and then strike it with a mallet to transfer the print paste completely. If a pattern had more

FIG. 59. This engraving shows the general layout of a printing room. The printers are stamping the cloth with blocks. The print paste is supplied by the sieve, the box on the table between the printers. From *Godey's Lady's Book*, July 1852. RIQDP Archives.

than one color, additional blocks filled in other parts of the design. To print a cloth measuring 30 inches wide and 28 yards long with 9-inch by 5-inch blocks in three colors required 672 applications of each block, obviously a very labor-intensive process.[25]

Alterations of the blocks varied over the years. Felt pounded into portions of the raised wooden surface held print paste more evenly than the wood. Metal strips hammered into the surface allowed the printer to produce designs with fine lines. Likewise, metal pins inserted into the wood made fine dots on the surface of the cloth. Rows of small white dots create patterns and outline features in the motifs in Figure 60. This is an eighteenth-century whole-cloth quilt with an Indian-inspired arabesque arrangement of blossoms and leaves that grow from diagonally-running vines. Colored with two shades of blue on a white ground, this fabric looks like a direct china-blue print but may be a blue-resist print. Both of these methods are discussed in the previous essay.

Many indigo resists have white designs on a blue ground because the paste or wax protected the pattern not the ground from being dyed. The fabric in Figure 60 is different; it has blue designs on a white ground.[26] The same fabric is in a New Jersey quilt at the Shelburne Museum in Vermont and in a bed flounce owned by a Rhode Island woman. After examining both of these, Pettit concluded that resist paste probably was painted around the motifs with a brush.[27] Tracings on Mylar of motifs in the Rhode Island quilt reveal a high consistency of designs from one repeat to the next that would not be possible with a brush. Obviously these objects merit further examination. The china-blue process pictured in Figure 47 would have been possible as early as the 1740s and was suitable for wood blocks and copper plates.[28] Could the china-blue direct printing be responsible for the design in this quilt's top? How the fabric in the quilts and bed flounce was printed is just part of the mystery. Where did it originate? Is it English or American? Who printed it? How did the fabric or blocks get to New Jersey and Rhode Island?

One of the steps toward modern textile printing involved engraving a flat copper plate to print cloth instead of paper. Printers decorated fabrics with copper plates in Ireland and England in the 1750s and at three sites in France during the next decade. Other European factories further perfected the technique in the 1770s.[29] One of these was a famous printing shop opened by Christophe-Philippe Oberkampf in 1760 at Jouy, France. Originally printing with wood blocks, Oberkampf's "toiles de Jouy" gained a reputation for the best printed fabrics available. He insisted on skilled staff, excellent engravings, good water, fast dyes, fashionable designs, fine cottons, and good preparation of the cloth.[30]

FIG. 60. (*Overleaf*) Whole-cloth quilt, late eighteenth century. Cotton top, linen back, wool batting, 95¾ x 92½ in. Hand-seamed and hand-quilted in diamond pattern, 6 stitches per inch. Maker unknown. Rhode Island Historical Society (1994.15.1). RIQDP #510.

The Indian-inspired design was either printed with the china blue technique or with a paste resist before dyeing in indigo. Previous use of the eighteenth-century fabric in this whole-cloth quilt is indicated by the faded sections. The high value of printed cotton cloth, imported or domestic, helped ensure its continued use. The backing is a blue and white hand-woven check of hand-spun linen, known as furniture check.

ENGRAVED-COPPER PRINTING

Oberkampf believed that "successful textile printing depends above all on the preparation of the cloth."[31] The multistep preparation included removing sizing from the Indian cotton cloths by washing and beating, reducing the fuzz on the fabric surface by singeing with a hot copper plate, bleaching six to seven days to minimize the effect of an off-white ground on colors, washing between steps, and finally calendering with wooden rollers to smooth the fabric's surface.[32] All this was necessary to prepare fabric for printing.

In 1770 Oberkampf began using copper plates in addition to wood blocks. Production increased from 3,600 block-printed pieces in 1761 to 22,800 pieces in 1775 with block and plate printing. Printing with the hand-engraved copper plates involved applying print paste that contained a mordant to a plate's surface, wiping off the excess with a blade leaving paste only in the incised areas, and pressing the fabric against the "inked" plate with two large rollers. Printers at Jouy used the rolling press pictured in Figure 61 to print monochromatic designs on cotton. They applied additional colors with small blocks or with brushes in a process called penciling.[33] After printing the mordants, dyers used the appropriate methods to dye fabrics as discussed in the previous essay.

Copper-plate printing offered a number of advantages over wood-block printing. Perhaps the most significant improvement was the fineness of line that engraving copper made possible. Block printing produced fine lines only with metal strips driven into a wood base. However, moisture often caused wood blocks to crack and warp. Using copper plates avoided those problems, although chemicals in the print paste could corrode and pit the metal. One limitation of engraved-copper surfaces occurred in printing

FIG. 61. This scene of plate printing from 1783 is from *Les travaux de la manufacture*, a copper-plate-printed cotton that pictured many activities of the Oberkampf's factory at Jouy. The designer was John Baptiste Huet. The Metropolitan Museum of Art, Rogers Fund, 1927 (27.44.3).

FIG. 62. (*Opposite*) Medallion quilt, ca.
1800. Cotton top, new cotton back, 90 x
87 in. Hand-pieced and hand-quilted in
crosshatch pattern, 6 stitches per inch.
Maker unknown. Western Rhode Island
Civic Historical Society, Paine House,
Coventry. RIQDP# 802.

This quilt is a compendium of block
prints and copper-plate prints. The plate-
printed border surrounds only three sides
of the quilt. The inadequate amount of
the plate print and its multiple piecing
suggest that a limited amount of the
precious fabric was available. Originally
quilted, it received a new tied-on backing
at some point in its history.

areas of solid color. Print paste did not spread evenly in large, carved-out
sections. To produce shaded and solid-colored areas in motifs, engravers
cut fine, adjacent lines to hold the paste. After printing, the print paste ran
into the thin unprinted lines just enough to produce a solid appearance
although hatching can be detected in many engraved-copper prints. Wood
blocks created a textured, grainy appearance in solid areas that metal could
not reproduce. Printers combined both methods of printing to produce
polychrome designs.

The most easily recognizable copper-plate print style is monochromatic, most often red, sometimes sepia or purple, and more rarely green or
china blue. Typically finely etched lines created isolated scenes on a white
ground. Scenes' themes varied from allegorical, bucolic, and fanciful to
commemorative, patriotic, and historic. This unique style came from a variety of French and English workshops but today is promoted as "toiles de
Jouy" patterns for furnishings and wallpapers.[34] American attempts at
copper-plate printing in the eighteenth century were almost nonexistent;
certainly none became a notable or lasting success.

The fabrics in Figure 62 represent both copper-plate and block printing.
The brown-on-white border of the medallion quilt (ca. 1800) was printed
with a copper plate. When the length of a pattern is greater than twenty to
twenty-two inches, as with these finely-etched classical scenes, copper-plate
printing is probable. The size of repeated motifs on plate prints often was
greater than with wood-block or cylinder prints which will be discussed
later. A full-size plate typically measured from thirty-six to forty inches in
height and covered the entire width of the fabric.[35]

This brown-on-white furnishings print probably dates from after 1797
when designers placed increased emphasis on classical and mythological
subjects. Monuments like the one in Figure 62 appear as early as the 1760s
in English prints with people in contemporary dress; the substitution of
classical costume occurs near the end of the century. Oberkampf wrote in
1799 that "interior decoration is now completely governed by the Antique.
Printed calico fabrics will be used in boudoirs if they have these motifs."[36]

Changes in style, such as minimizing the amount of open ground between scenes, accompanied other alterations that diminished the quality of
the designs. Designers squeezed scenes close together, sometimes using
ornamented geometric designs to frame motifs and devices such as swags
to fill in spaces. These changes reflect not only new fashions but also improved methods of engraving and possibly cylinder printing, with elements
pushed together to fit them into a limited repeat length. The golden days of
copper-plate printing were past. Cylinder printing decreased production
time too much for plate printing to be a viable business in the early nine-

teenth century although advertisements for "copperplates" and "copper-plate furniture chintzes" still appeared in Providence newspapers in the 1830s.[37]

Most of the fabric squares and triangles inside the plate-printed border in Figure 62 are block prints, some very finely done. Stripes, stylized plant motifs, and meandering flowering vines are on dark brown grounds, a popular style in the late eighteenth century. Others show where blue was penciled over blocked-on yellow to yield bright green. A few indigo-resist or discharge prints, probably dress fabrics, have small white or red geometric patterns on blue grounds. Isolated sprigs of flowers printed on light grounds are very typical of earlier eighteenth-century woven-silk patterns. Printed stripes, also fashionable in turn-of-the-century woven silks, appear in several designs.

Continuous straight lines and complex designs required careful placement (registration) of wood blocks and copper plates. Printing by these two methods was very labor intensive and slow. Each block or plate had to be re-inked after each use. Proper registration slowed the process; in addition, printers had to apply blocks to alternate spaces and wait until the print paste had dried to fill in the areas between them. Plates required that the fabric be advanced after each impression in a stop-and-go operation. Obviously printers needed a better method to speed production.

The solution was using a cylinder that could be continuously supplied with print paste rather than flat surfaces of wood or copper. Efforts to design such a machine began as early as 1701 using wooden rollers. Eventually in the 1780s engraved copper cylinders competed with wood rollers, and by the late 1790s improvements resulted in equipment that successfully printed calicoes with an engraved cylinder.[38] Printing with wooden rollers carved in relief continued. This method, called surface printing, often failed to print evenly along the edges of the designs, but its use continued into the nineteenth and early twentieth centuries.[39]

The circumference of the copper cylinders limited the length of a repeat, but the continuous design eliminated registration problems that occurred where the edge of a block or plate met the adjacent printed pattern. Samuel Widmer, Oberkampf's nephew, marveled at the early cylinder-print production of 5,000 meters a day that equaled the output of forty-two individual printers with precision that was better "than anything done by hand."[40]

The first equipment had only one engraved cylinder that printed one color; blocks filled in other colors. As technology and expertise improved in the next century, an increasing number of cylinders printed at the same time, each with an engraving of a different portion of the pattern. The machine pictured in Figure 63 shows a cylinder that pressed against a large, padded drum which carried the print cloth under the engraved cylinders. Originally this cylinder rotated through the paste trough, but later improvements incorporated a second cylinder that supplied print paste from the trough. A sharp-edged blade called the "color doctor" removed excess paste from the surface of the roller, leaving coloring matter only in the incised

FIG. 63. Cylinder printing machines had one or more engraved cylinders mounted at intervals around a large, padded drum. Each cylinder applied print paste for one color in the design. From *Godey's Lady's Book*, July 1852. RIQDP Archives.

areas of the design, just as in copper-plate printing. Another blade, the "lint doctor," cleaned lint from the engraved cylinder after it came in contact with the print cloth on the padded roller.[41] This new method of printing operates in virtually the same way today after two hundred years although screen printing, a twentieth-century innovation, is rapidly replacing cylinder printing.

In Rhode Island cotton yarn and fabric production became well-established industries, expanding and contracting as economic conditions varied. Improvements in equipment and facilities increased production. In 1814, for example, the second steam engine in the capital was installed by the Providence Dyeing, Bleaching & Callendering Company at a cost of $17,000.[42] That year several Rhode Island manufacturers installed power looms in their factories, diminishing the need for hand looms.

Growth was not a constant, however. In 1817 economic troubles caused a number of banks to fail; many companies, particularly the cotton manufacturers of Rhode Island and other parts of New England, suspended operations entirely despite a high demand for cotton. This resulted in reductions in the labor force and sales of mills and property at "a fraction of the original cost."[43]

Imports continued to be a threat to industrial growth. In 1820 low-quality fabrics of cotton, silk, and wool were manufactured in East India and Europe especially for cheap exports. Their "high finish" concealed their "flimsy texture."[44] An optimistic spirit prevailed in Rhode Island, however, and the state's industrial base grew. The region gained a reputation for industrial growth. In proportion to its population, Rhode Island had more manufacturers than any other state. Providence entrepreneurs such as Almy, Brown, and Slater owned approximately one hundred cotton manufactories in Rhode Island and nearby Massachusetts and Connecticut by 1823.[45]

At the beginning of the 1820s, Taunton Manufacturing Company in Massachusetts and Dover Manufacturing Company in New Hampshire added print works to their facilities. A new company, Merrimack Manufacturing Company in Lowell, Massachusetts, opened soon afterward and began printing calicoes in 1822.[46] Other cotton firms soon opened printing facilities to compete with the stream of imports. Bishop reported increased popularity of calicoes in 1823, favorably compared domestic prints with foreign ones, and accused foreign manufacturers of counterfeiting American cottons. He wrote about "American Calicoes, or chintzes, of seven or eight colors, fast and brilliant as any imported."[47] The early cylinder printing equipment usually had only one cylinder; fabrics with seven or eight colors meant that printers added colors to a cylinder print with wood blocks or, more likely, used blocks entirely.

Rhode Island printers did not lag far behind others in setting up block-printing works.[48] Cotton print cloth came from their own or nearby mills. In 1824 William Sprague included calico printing at his Cranston cotton manufactory, which he had opened in 1808.[49] Figure 64 shows the Cranston plant, which Sprague converted to bleaching, dyeing and printing. William's sons, Amasa and William III, owned the firm when this cloth label was printed.

At least three other firms began calico printing within the next two years in Pawtucket and Apponaug.[50] The quality of the fabrics met with local approval. A writer for the *Pawtucket Chronicle* stated that "the domestic calicoes we are happy to say, meet the approbation of the ladies in preference, owing to the superior strength of their texture, and the permanency of their colors."[51] William Sprague won ten dollars "For the best piece of Calico" at the Rhode Island Cattle Show and Exhibition of Manufacturers in 1826.[52]

Simon Henry Greene and Edward Pike opened a Warwick shop for bleaching and printing cottons in 1828. See the S. H. Greene & Sons salesman's sample card in Figure 43. The new industry had spread throughout northeastern Rhode Island on rivers near Providence. In 1830 William M. Cook opened a printing shop in Coventry, the first to be located in midwestern Rhode Island. Two other new Providence businesses opened that year, Royal Sibley and Philip Allen & Sons.[53] Of the early printers, Sprague, Bliss, Greene, Pike, Sibley, and Allen would supply numerous yards of calico to consumers for many years.

Rapid growth, more power looms, and lack of overseas outlets for exports resulted in an oversupply of cotton fabrics. Coupled with a general recession in 1828–29, the cotton yarn and fabric industry once again was in trouble. As before with economic depressions, some cotton manufactures "went down in the general wreck of business." A number of analysts have

FIG. 64. A. & W. Sprague cloth label. William Sprague II built a cotton mill in Cranston in 1808 and added a print works in 1824. His sons Amasa and William III expanded the operation after his death in 1836, making it one of the most significant textile operations in Rhode Island. The company controlled nine mill villages by midcentury but went under in the Panic of 1873. This Cranston operation eventually became Cranston Print Works. Courtesy of Rhode Island Historical Society.

concluded that calico printing came to the rescue of those New England manufacturers whose sales had decreased. New product lines of dress goods, interior furnishing fabrics, and fancy goods stimulated buying, revitalizing the cotton industry and providing employment for increasing numbers of workers.[54] Samuel Slater's biographer stated that: "Before the commencement of the printing business, the cotton manufacture was considered in a precarious condition; so that no one ventured on the finer fabrics, but since calico printing has been established, the cotton manufactures in the United States may safely be considered as built on a permanent basis."[55] The industry survived and prospered because calico printers had established a viable market for inexpensive cottons that soon would be produced more efficiently than ever before with cylinder-printed calicoes. For the rest of the century, however, economic conditions remained "a race between the powers of expansion and the forces of check."[56]

After 1830 established cotton mills adjusted the widths of their looms to the measurements needed for printing, and new print works opened. Rhode Island printers began to install equipment for cylinder printing. William Sprague, Greene & Pike Bleachery, Philip Allen, Compton Mills (Benjamin Cozzens and Ed Carrington, Warwick, 1832), and Franklin Printworks (Royal Sibley, Providence, 1833) were among the first print works to have single-color machines. Other companies gradually switched to cylinder printing as the Banigan family history illustrates. Peter Banigan, his wife, five sons, and two daughters emigrated to the United States from Ireland in 1832, settling in Pawtucket in 1837. Peter and his sons worked at Pawtucket's new Jacob Dunnell print works "where several of the latter became expert block printers, and when machine printing was introduced they also learned that art."[57]

At least three additional companies opened printing shops in the thirties along with a growing support industry.[58] In 1832 the Phenix Iron Foundry began to manufacture machinery for the calico printers.[59] Bleaching establishments had been part of the industry since the turn of the century, and now they catered to calico printers.[60] Engravers also contracted with calico printing firms.[61]

From the 1770s to the 1820s engravers incised designs into the surface of copper plates and cylinders by hand, a costly procedure that required more time than designing patterns, preparing fabric, or printing calicoes. New die-and-mill technology perfected in the 1820s increased the speed of transferring designs to copper cylinders, reducing costs of printed cottons significantly while producing consistency in repeating patterns.[62] An engraver transferred a pattern to a small cylinder made of untempered steel. He cut the design into the soft metal surface; after tempering, the hardened steel cylinder is called a "die." Then he pressed the die against a second soft steel cylinder, a "mill," to reproduce the pattern in relief on the mill's surface. After tempering the mill, the engraver repeatedly pressed it across a copper cylinder to indent the surface with the pattern. The greatest cost in producing engraved copper cylinders was making the mill, which could be incorporated in other designs or reused whenever cylinders had to be replaced.[63]

Incised patterns on copper surfaces also could be achieved by etching. Engravers cut through a layer of acid-resistant varnish covering a copper cylinder. An acid bath etched the exposed areas of the pattern creating a more accurate and rapid reproduction of the original design than engraving.[64] Equipment that most accurately reproduced patterns in the varnish was a pantograph engraving machine which used a diamond-tipped tracer to cut the repeated designs. After improvements in the pantograph system in 1856, much of the engraving occurred at the calico print works, forcing a number of engraving firms out of business.[65]

Innovations in engraving and etching contributed to a change in the way that engravers achieved shading in their patterns. The use of parallel and cross hatching decreased as calico-print engravers used dotted shading in naturalistic floral designs. The new shading effects accompanied increased use of finely patterned grounds which had been undecorated in earlier years except for carefully spaced dots. For multicolored designs printers used both a cylinder and blocks. "It is still found necessary to execute parts of the patterns in fine goods with blocks, after the ground-work has been laid on by the cylinders; because different parts of the pattern, executed with different colours, cannot be made so exactly to fall into and fit with the other parts, by the cylinder as by the block."[66] Developments in pantograph equipment for etching cylinders improved the registration of multiple cylinders after midcentury.

A union or mule machine combined surface printing with wooden rollers and copper-cylinder printing to produce prints that could have both fine and rough designs.[67] Union printing and cylinder printing can appear similar, especially since the difference in runny print paste from a copper cylinder and uneven edges of surface printing is difficult to identify.

Examples of printers' experimentation during the late twenties and thirties are in Figure 65, a quilt with fabrics that belong to the early days of printing in Rhode Island. This quilt belonged to the Allen family; men from two generations of the family worked at Hope Mill in Scituate. The quilt is a very good document of printers' trying to work out successful color combinations called colorways.[68] With widely spaced, small, thistle-like flowers, six different colorways appear on these fabrics, some more successful than others. The printers tried six different grounds: plain red or brown printed by padding cylinders and covers of black, blue green, blue, or red

small dots. The flower contained three parts—stem, body of the blossom, and spiked petals—each printed separately.

Some trials succeeded; some did not. A flower of dark and light red on a dotted red ground produced an attractive monochromatic design, but parts of that red-colored flower disappeared on a plain red ground. The unpieced alternating blocks in the quilt have the flower printed with a black stem and two shades of red blossom covered with brown that the printer probably called "drab." Pieces of this fabric have "scrimps" where folds prevented the padding cylinder from printing the brown ground evenly, broad streaks where the print paste was unevenly applied to the cylinder, and the scalloped edge of the padding cylinder's engraved surface silhouetted against uncovered white fabric. In this little quilt the quiltmaker, possibly Isabella Allen, used experimental prints probably from a local mill; a number of Scituate manufactures printed calicoes.

The other fabrics in this quilt illustrate a variety of patterns and techniques representative of the first third of the nineteenth century. They include: geometric flowers on a honeycomb ground; imitation ikat and twill stripes; small paisleys on a busy stripe; monochromatic leaves on a closely dotted surface; tedious alternating solid and dotted lines, probably a die-and-mill engraving; delicate geometric motifs; heavy black outlines around simple designs, possibly union prints; block and cylinder printing together; and a limited amount of shading with dots inside designs.

This simple drab-colored quilt incorporates the kinds of fabrics that inspired this essay. The amount of effort and time that designers, printers, and dyers expended to create a product for an appreciative, yet sometimes quixotic market is an untold story few people recognize when they view a quilt.

Bishop related one manufacturer's attitude about producing a marketable product. Governor James Smith of Providence began cotton factories in Willimantic, Connecticut, and Woonsocket in 1838, invested in several mills in Scituate, and purchased "the well-known Providence Steam Mill." Writing about Smith's successes, Bishop said: "Since then his investments in Cotton manufacturing have steadily increased, and his earlier enterprises have grown into prominent notice, employing hundreds of looms and including the various operations of dyeing and printing, thus adapting his fabrics for the most extended sale. He had early recognized the principle that adverse fluctuations were least felt by those manufacturers who fitted their fabrics for distribution among the largest number of consumers."[69]

Despite local support for domestic products, the fabrics that printing manufactories offered consumers from the late 1830s to midcentury, however, often did not equal the quality of earlier imported calicoes. Many imported prints during this time period were no better. Was consumer demand in a developing market or the changing technology responsible for the "deterioration in design and colour, found in printed cottons produced increasingly by mechanical means for a mass market?"[70] Hefford proposed this explanation for design in English prints: "A search for new forms led to hectic, indiscriminate patterning, striving for difference and falling between ugly novelties and perversions of old forms. In attempting to find new combinations, even the colours ceased to be pleasing."[71]

These observations also describe New England products as evidenced

FIG. 65. (*Opposite*) Sixteen-Patch quilt, ca. 1830s. Cotton top, back, and filling, 60 x 59 in. Hand-pieced and hand-quilted in outline pattern, 5–6 stitches per inch. Probably made by Isabella Maria Flag Merrill Allen (1805–1891). URI Historic Costume and Textile Collection (1954.39.186). RIQDP #126.

This quilt belonged to a family associated with textile mills in Scituate, Rhode Island. It contains examples of printers' experiments in six different colorways for a single pattern, suggesting its fabrics came from a local mill. Its brown color, possibly from quercitron, revived the "drab style" fashionable at the beginning of the century.

FIG. 66. (*Opposite*) Four-Patch quilt, 1830–50. Cotton top and back, 108 x 99½ in. Hand-pieced and hand-quilted in squares, 6–7 stitches per inch. Descended in the Walcott family, Slater Mill Historic Site, Pawtucket, Rhode Island (65.009). RIQDP #669.

From 1830 to 1851, the Walcott family owned Walcott Mills on the Blackstone River across from Slater Mill in Pawtucket. Mary-Louise Walcott of Greenville, Rhode Island, owned this and other quilts that contain good-quality, busy-patterned calicoes. This one represents the most successful attempt at combining many printed fabrics. It and two of the other quilts share several identical prints.

by quilts of the period and extant samples such as those in Dunster's and McCarthy's record books. Successfully combining the busy prints and heavy colors of the latter thirties and the forties in a quilt required a good sense of design. Like the printers' efforts with the little flower in the Allen quilt, quilters' combinations succeeded well in some quilts and less in others.

The quilt in Figure 66 is a successful example. The unidentified quilter in the Walcott family had access to an amazingly large assortment of good quality fabrics that represent the decades before midcentury. The Walcotts owned a textile mill in Pawtucket from 1830 to 1851, so they had connections with local producers of calico.[72] They also could afford to buy fabrics on the market. The two cylinder-printed side borders frame light and dark prints that represent the best of the work from this time. Blocks, finely etched or engraved cylinders, and union machines produced the discharged or re-sisted indigo, madder-style, and raised prints.

All the pieces in the quilt are printed. The small, detailed patterns dom-inate, producing a busy surface when seen at close range. Viewed further away the piecing pattern creates competing vertical, horizontal, and diago-nal lines. The light and dark colors hold all of these opposing features to-gether. The division of colors into light and dark is reflected in early store advertisements of new goods: "A Hansome assortment of seasonable Dry Goods consisting of fashionable dark and light Prints."[73] Another announce-ment promoted "Rich dark chintzes—comprising a large assortment of very desirable patterns, just received by T. M. Cory, 16 Arcade."[74]

Distinguishing light and dark values of the prints was important to dy-ers, also. McCarthy's "Receipt" books in which he recorded recipes, data, and results of experiments contained separate annual reports on light and dark prints; titles such as "Dye House Operations. 1852–53 Light-Work" began annual reports; "Dark Work" followed later in the book.[75]

The strong contrast of light and dark work in Figure 67 creates a dis-tinctive 1840s quilt for a four-poster bed. Two unusual fabrics in the quilt are patriotic prints with American flags, visible in Figure 68. One of them includes cannons with the flags; the other very similar one with slightly smaller-scale designs also has little soldiers. The choice of such a fabric probably reflects the quilter's husband's band, founded as the Providence Brass Band in 1825 and reorganized as the American Brass Band after 1837. Joseph Carpenter Greene was still directing the band in the early 1860s when he led the band as it paraded the First Rhode Island Regiment into the battle at Bull Run.[76] The American Band is still active today, one of the oldest bands in the country.

Another notable fabric in the quilt is a complicated rainbow print in Fig-ure 68. Rainbow or fondue prints have parallel bands of color that gradual-ly change from light to dark. Varying concentrations of a mordant or a

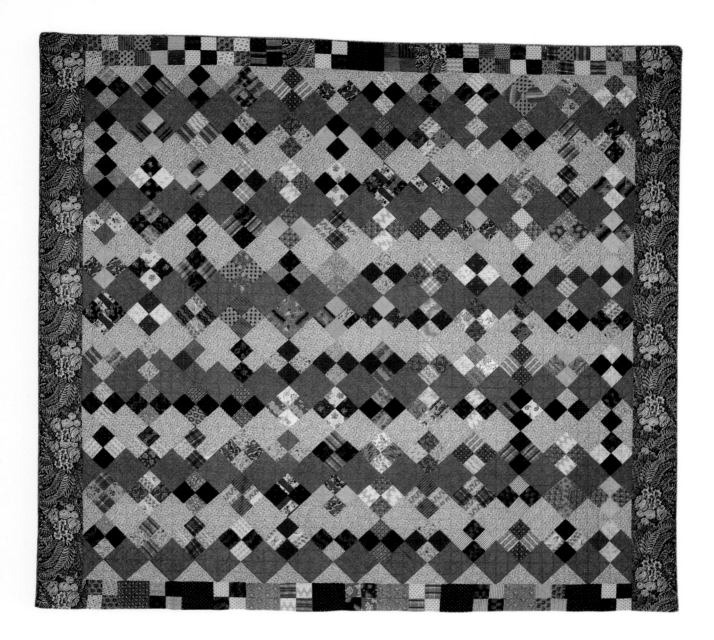

chemical for a raised color produced a monochromatic rainbow, and different mordants or chemicals created a polychromatic one.[77] Rainbow prints were particularly popular from 1820 to 1860. Printers produced rainbows with blocks, cylinders, union machines, and a Perrotine—a continuous printing machine that used three wooden blocks. Figure 68 has a Prussian blue rainbow separated from a brown rainbow by a strip of imitation ikat. The rainbows are not continuous; multicolored bands cut across the rainbows but not the ikat strip. The 1840s printer who produced this complex print did not have a simple job, but much experimental work on rainbow prints occurred in the 1820s.[78]

McCarthy and Dunster both included rainbow prints in their recipe books. In 1845–46 McCarthy made the rainbows in orange, chocolate, purple, and pink.[79] During those same years while he was working in Johnston, Rhode Island, for Clay Printworks, Dunster printed three shades of "Dahlia or spirit purple (logwood)" and three shades of blue and chocolate with "rollers," probably meaning engraved or etched cylinders. In 1846 Dunster also printed a rainbow with at least five sections in blue and chocolate.[80] He experimented with a six-inch-wide rainbow that year but did not get an even blending; then he used the rainbow as a ground and covered it with an all-over pattern.[81]

*Down by the Old Mill Stream*

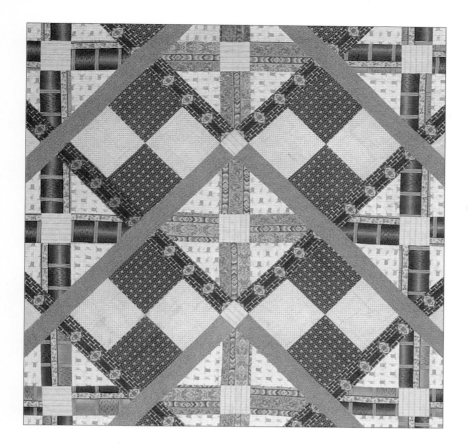

FIG. 67. (*Opposite*) Four-Patch, Album Patch quilt, 1840s. Cotton top and back, 91½ x 98 in. Hand-pieced and hand-quilted in interlocking circles, 5–6 stitches per inch. Made by Mrs. Joseph C. Greene. Cranston Historical Society. RIQDP #555.

Mrs. Greene pieced and quilted this patriotic quilt for her son, Liberty. Her husband was the first leader of Providence's American Brass Band, one of the oldest continually functioning bands in the United States. Liberty used the quilt until the 1920s, when he was in his eighties.

FIG. 68. Detail of Figure 67. Significant fabrics in this Four-Patch, Album-Patch quilt from the 1840s (Figure 67) include two early object prints and a well-executed rainbow print. The rainbow fabric is a steam-style print because it combines madder colors and Prussian blue.

Philip Allen printers continued to print rainbows in the 1850s. McCarthy experimented with printing acid on cotton in different concentrations, thus resisting varying amounts of dyeing to produce a rainbow.[82] His record book had pages of rainbow prints on cotton in 1854–55. Both he and Dunster also saved samples of green rainbow patterns printed on delaines, mixtures of cotton and wool that presented problems to dyers because of the different affinities of the two fibers for dyes.[83]

Many of McCarthy's rainbow samples show how printers used the cylinders that were available at the time in different combinations. He experimented with printing a five-colored leaf on a stripe and also on a rainbow with a large-scale crackle design in the ground.[84] This five-colored leaf represents another stage in solving registration problems in cylinder printing that significantly diminished the amount of block printing needed. Some of the 1845–46 printing samples in McCarthy's madder recipe book are printed with four cylinders and one block.[85]

Technological advances such as combining mineral dyes with madder as discussed in the previous essay increased production in print shops and dye houses but required increased experimentation to produce marketable cloth. The rainbow in Figure 68 is a good example of successfully using steam

FIG. 69. (*Opposite*) Christian Cross signature quilt, 1847. Cotton top and back, 94 x 87 in. Hand-pieced and hand-quilted, 6–7 stitches per inch. Made for a Hopkinton, Rhode Island, minister and his wife. Babcock-Smith House, Westerly, Rhode Island. RIQDP #612.

This dated quilt is a valuable record of 1840s prints. The three most significant ones are the four rainbow prints, the steam style color combinations, and the Turkey red calico sashing.

style on mineral dyes and madder. Many samples of four-cylinder steam-style prints make up Dunster's 1846 report. The same close scrutiny of output with reports of successes or failures of using steam to speed up ageing is evident in that year's report.[86] Product development, good record-keeping, and close attention to costs were obviously part of Philip Allen's successful production.

Many steam style colors, some possibly printed with a union machine, are in the fabrics of the 1847 signature quilt in Figure 69. Patterns in some of the chocolate and Prussian blue prints have unevenly printed edges. Four different prints with these colors include a brown and three blue rainbows; the blending of shades in the brown rainbow is not very subtle. Another print has rather weak-looking stripes in two shades of blue printed over a red, black, and white plaid, so some of the pieces in this quilt could have been unsuccessful mill trials from local print shops. Of course, the brown rainbow and this weak stripe might have been purchased. A large number of poor-quality prints reached the market in the first half of the nineteenth century.

Another feature of some fabrics in this quilt that could reflect poor-quality work is dark, heavy outlines around motifs. These heavy outlines could disguise misregistration of blocks and cylinders or bleeding of print paste into unprinted areas. They are common in quilts from 1830 to 1860. Dunster included 1830 samples from Sprague in Cranston that had heavy dark outlines encircling motifs. His 1844 samples, probably from Clay Printworks in Johnston, had a number of examples in which the print paste ran into the next color.[87] Schoeser and Rufey claim that the dark outlines in the forties reflected the designer's desire to copy authentic late-eighteenth- and early-nineteenth-century patterns rather than to cover flaws.[88] Most likely, both scenarios represent reasons for the frequency of occurrence of the heavy outlines.

Similar reasoning might explain unprinted white halos around motifs. Designers could have put halos around motifs for emphasis or room for migration of cylinder-printed or blocked-on colors. Whichever the reason, halos appeared in printed cottons during the 1830-to-1860 period but occurred less frequently than the wide, dark outlines. Both are visible in the fabrics in the Christian Cross quilt in Figure 69. Dunster's 1846 recipe book had good examples of halos.[89]

The Turkey red calico sashing in this quilt is a perfect example of printers' applying discharging chemicals in paste printed on a previously dyed fabric as discussed in the previous essay. The tiny three-color pattern on a Turkey red dress-weight cotton was available through most of the nineteenth century. The sashing surrounds squares placed in an on-point arrangement with no border, typical characteristics of Rhode Island quilts

*Down by the Old Mill Stream*

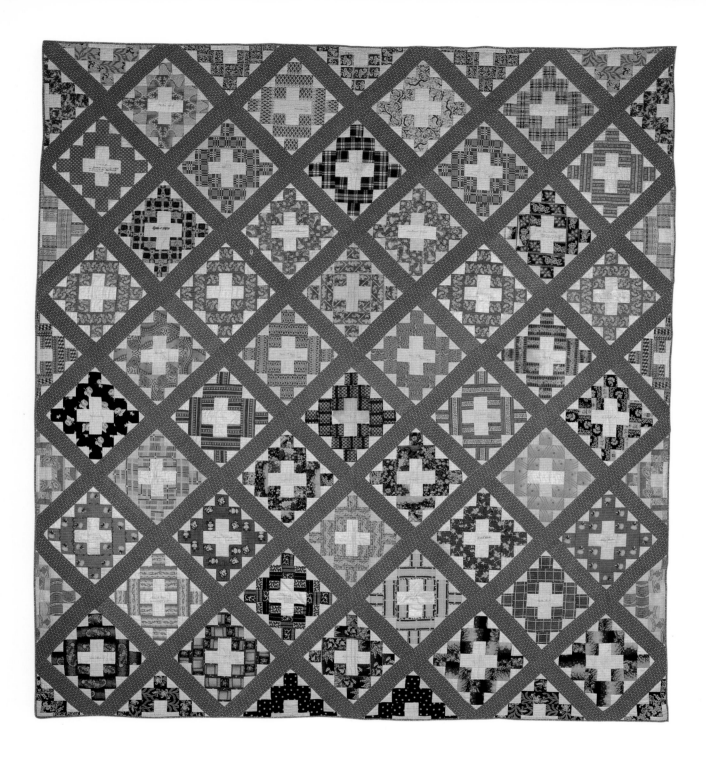

before 1860. The quilting pattern is related to the piecing design of the top, and the binding is cut on grain, both features typical in early quilts from the state.

The backing of the quilt is a good-quality cylinder print with dark blue blocked on the design. Fabrics with block-printed blue designs, probably indigo, appear on the quilt top as well. Block printing continued into the twentieth century, but cylinder printing was responsible for making the industry viable (Fig. 70).

Calico printing in the United States was successfully established by mid-century. In June 1850 Rhode Island industries supplied 40 percent of the calicoes made in the country.[90] An expanding transportation system, improved communication, and developing markets resulted in distribution of manufactured goods throughout the country.[91] The demand for printed and colored cotton fabric continued to expand, but domestic production provided only one-third or less of the calicoes marketed. Merchants imported nineteen million dollars' worth of these fabrics in 1856.[92] The next year exports of domestically manufactured printed and colored cotton equaled only 10.2 percent of the quantity imported.

With stiff competition, manufacturers had to maintain the product characteristics—color range, colorfastness, durability, and design—demanded by their market. The quality of the fabric, design, and execution shown by samples in Dunster's books from 1844 to 1848 while he worked for Clay Printworks in Johnston were noticeably lower than Philip Allen and Sons examples from 1848 to 1852. Of particular note is the difference in design; Allen prints were much more sophisticated than those from Clay.

Efforts to maintain cost efficiency as well as quality at acceptable levels are evident in the dyers' record books. Working with dyes from natural

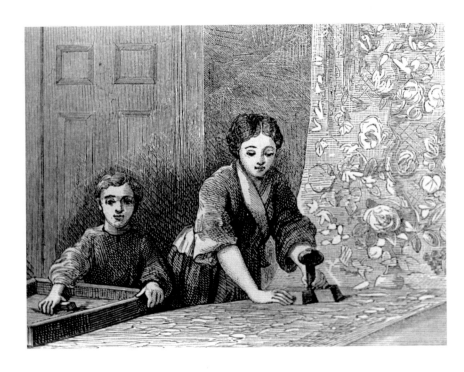

FIG. 70. In block printing, the wood was carved so that the design stood out from the base of the block. The child to the left applied print paste to the blocks from a sieve. Block printing continued until the end of the century for certain designs despite the rapid advancements in cylinder printing. From William Crookes, *A Practical Handbook of Dyeing and Calico-Printing* (London: Longman's, Green, 1874), Plate V. RIQDP Archives.

sources guaranteed variation in products. Dunster used "bark" (quercitron) in a recipe to get yellow and instead got drab. He made a note that "The Bark was bad I never could make green or yellow with it."[93] Later he had trouble with indigo when white or light blue specks appeared on the indigo-dyed surfaces. He decided that "little specks of sediment" were adhering to the cloth and that "Gently moving the frame up and down when being entered and also when being taken out of vat so as to wash them off will cure the evil."[94]

Experimentation with innovations and new recipes was constant. In 1854 McCarthy wrote that he was trying garancine in short and long dyeing procedures. He saw no difference in the product but "vast differences" in the time and labor required, commenting that he "can turn out one-half more work in the same time."[95] He tried "silicate of soda" which was being marketed as "dunging salts" on samples of cloth so that the dye house could "dispence with dung, but none of them gave satisfaction."[96] They had to continue using dung but did not stop experimenting to find ways to make the dunging baths more effective.

Occasionally the dyers wrote about equipment failures and their concern about the effect of the chemicals on the cylinder surfaces and the doctor blades. Dunster reported that he had changed from muriate of tin to tin chromate because the former was too "severe on the docters [sic] and color too I think."[97] McCarthy recorded similar problems with nitrate of copper "eating and blackening the copper rollers." He changed to muriate of copper and placed samples of brown fabrics that he had used in the experiments in his recipe book.[98] These records of processes and recipes confirm that nineteenth-century printers and dyers had much more than a rudimentary knowledge of chemistry. They continually worked to produce an acceptable product as economically as possible.

Frequently McCarthy and Dunster recorded the cost of dyeing procedures and treatments such as bleaching. Their lists of costs for chemicals, freight, labor, fuel, engraving, and general expenses provide invaluable detail about the workings of the printing shops and dye houses. The recipes and printed samples also record the progress being made in the industry.

By 1860 the printing industry required no major changes in equipment and technology. Cylinder printing continued as the workhorse of the industry into the twentieth century. Advances in dye chemistry provided new colors every decade after 1856. From the producers' viewpoint a very competitive market existed. Sustaining and increasing sales depended on offering new designs each season. Consumers responded by increasing their use of printed

*Consumers' Choice: Prints after 1860*

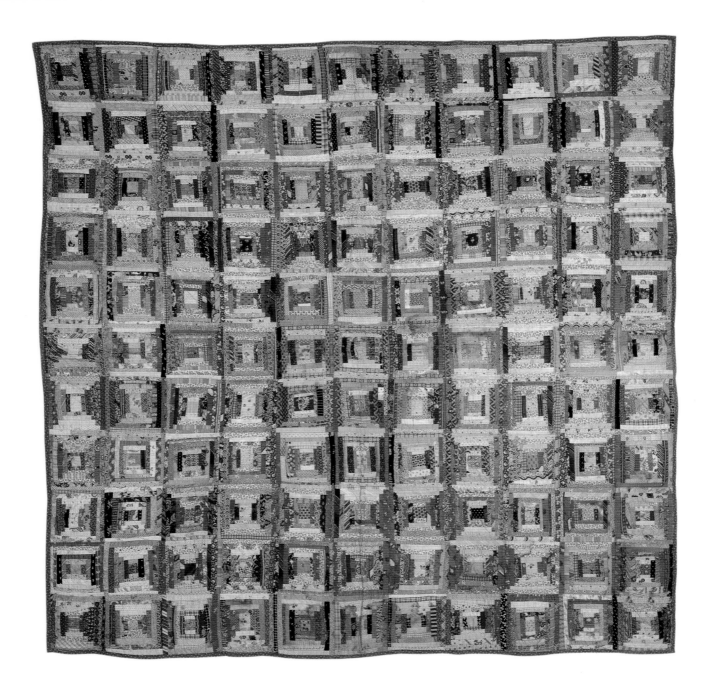

cottons in dresses with wide skirts and in home furnishings. Quilts reflected the wide range of fabrics available on the market better than ever before because they contained an increasingly large number of small sized pieces of fabric.

The Log Cabin was one quilt pattern made with many small pieces that gained in popularity during the seventies. The quilt in Figure 71 is a variation of that pattern, Courthouse Steps. Made by Marenza Hill Nye (Fig. 72) in the 1870s, the quilt has many samples of multishade monochromatic dress prints. It reflects manufacturers' efforts to improve the quality of design in printed cottons in the 1860s and 1870s. Few busy die-and-mill grounds compete with the main motifs; many grounds are colored and plain. Black outlines frame design elements rather than fill in space around motifs as was typical before 1860. Some of the patterns are still busy designs with competing elements, but others exhibit a simplicity not seen since the beginning of the century. The plaids may be an inexpensive copy of woven designs or represent a Scottish influence based on Queen Victoria's frequent trips to Balmoral.[99]

A few of the designs such as a repetitive leaf motif could reflect Japanese influence, which began in the sixties and continued through the eighties.[100] A red and tan color scheme of the same time period appears on a number of fabrics in this quilt.[101] Used for both interior textiles and apparel fabrics, this combination of colors often occurs, especially in prints influenced by paisley shawls.

FIG. 71. (*Opposite*) Courthouse Steps quilt (variation of Log Cabin), 1870s. Cotton top and back, 65 x 65 in. Hand-pieced and hand-quilted in outline stitch, 5 stitches per inch. Made by Marenza Hill Nye (1851–1931). Collection of Bertha T. Nye. RIQDP #442.

Rhode Island was no different than other states in the popularity of Log Cabin quilts and their many variations. The fabrics exhibit a change in design from overly busy die-and-mill grounds to simple grounds. This was one of at least ten quilts made by Marenza Hill Nye of Foster.

FIG. 72. The wife of a stone mason who built stone walls, Marenza Hill Nye (1851–1931; here ca. 1928) raised five children. Marenza's quilting frame is still used by daughter-in-law Bertha Nye who lives in the house where Marenza was born and lived for almost 80 years. RIQDP Archives.

FIG. 73. (*Overleaf*) Album Patch quilt, late 1880s. Cotton top, back, and ties, 91 x 67 in. Machine-pieced, tied. Made by Abby Newell Crawford (1871–?). Collection of Martha Crawford. RIQDP #865.

Abby Newell of Pawtucket used a printed fabric in the center of her borderless Album Patch quilt. Around midcentury this quilt pattern placed on point probably would have been used for a signature quilt, but it contains no signature. Noteworthy fabrics in this quilt are shawl or robe prints and furnishing prints with large-scale motifs and chinoiserie-inspired designs.

Prints with paisley designs have as long a life as the double pinks. Quilters included them in Rhode Island quilts from the 1830s to the end of the century, long after the fashion for paisley shawls had ended, in the 1870s. In fact, shawl designs continue to thrive in printed cottons. Figure 73 is a late 1880s quilt with a typical shawl print that could have been used in women's wrappers or dresses and men's at-home jackets or robes. Montgomery Ward sold "robe prints for comforters" in 1876.[102] Larger in scale than the dress prints in this Album Patch quilt, the shawl prints exhibit the earlier red and brown color scheme with black added.

Several printed cottons in this quilt represent fabrics for interior furnishings rather than apparel. One of these large-scale designs represents another often-repeated theme called "chinoiserie." Many eighteenth-century woven silks and later toile-de-Jouy type prints featured European-interpreted Chinese people, landscape, and architecture. Printed chinoiserie designs appear occasionally throughout the nineteenth century and are carefully positioned in this quilt.

The variety of printed patterns available to consumers continued to expand. Consumer demand spurred foreign and domestic mills to produce ever-novel designs. Many American print works produced more than one thousand new designs each year. The last two quilts in this essay are superb examples of the quantity of different designs.

The Flying Geese pattern was a showcase for a variety of fabrics even before midcentury, but the small scale of the triangles making the quilt in Figure 74 provided ample opportunity to display the wide range of fabrics available by the late 1880s. Red, brown and black are the most frequently seen colors in the pieces. Few secondary or tertiary colors occur despite their availability at this time. Polka dots abound: small and large, light on dark, and dark on light. Also present in limited number are object or conversation prints.

The fabrics in the quilt have recurring motifs from earlier times. These include robe prints, a lace pattern, and several patterns called double pink or double purple. Printers produced these monochromatic, small figure prints in the madder style throughout the century. Since this style prevailed so long, it does not help date a particular fabric, but close analysis reveals the number of shades present in the design and provides a clue to the complexity of the print. Most often more than two shades of color make up the design. Printers often referred to these as "3 reds" or "5 purples."[103] See typical examples in Figures 51 and 52.

Strip quilts likewise provided opportunity to use many fabrics. The late 1890s quilt in Figure 75 includes some of the new indigo blues that were available in this decade. Quilts such as this one are excellent documents of innovations in dye manufacture, discussed in the previous essay. This quilt

FIG. 74. (*Overleaf*) Flying Geese quilt, 1887. Cotton top and back, 84½ x 69½ in. Hand-pieced and hand-quilted in diagonal pattern, 6–7 stitches per inch. Made by Margaret Dempsey. Collection of Judith Spencer. RIQDP #370.

Out of the abundance of inexpensive printed cottons grew patchwork designs like this one, with its hundreds of different calicoes. A label, feather-stitched in yellow yarn to the back of this quilt, reads, "Margaret Dempsey from her grand mother Margaret Dempsey 1887 given for her name." The younger Margaret married the owner of Mackie Worsted Mill in Centerdale, Rhode Island. The elder Margaret's great-great-granddaughter is the current owner of this quilt.

FIG. 75. (*Page 153*) Herringbone strip quilt, late 1890s. Cotton top and back, 88½ x 83½ in. Hand-pieced, tied. Made by Nancy Carpenter Hixson (1844–1927). Collection of Mrs. Joseph A. Carpenter. RIQDP #96.

Nancy Carpenter Hixson of Cumberland, Rhode Island, was from an early New England family. The Carpenters came to the New World on the third ship after the Mayflower and later moved to Rhode Island. Nancy used a mixture of old and new print designs in this strip quilt. Shirting fabrics with small one- and two-color designs are prominent. Her granddaughter now owns the quilt.

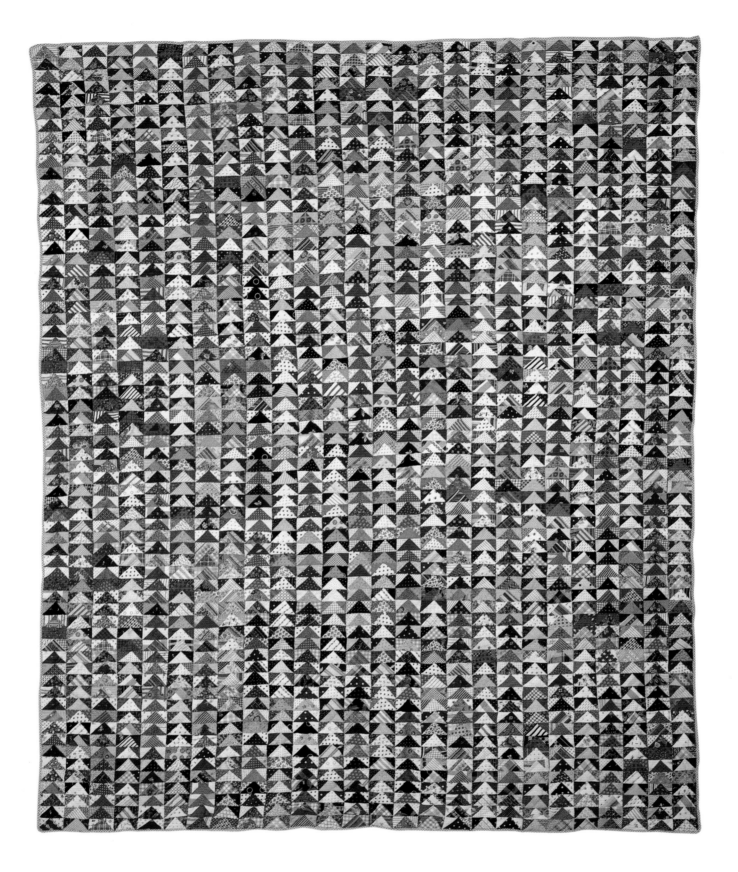

also displays many different shirting fabrics printed with one or two colors; these reflect shirt fashions at the turn of the century. New England printing firms had developed a good market for fine plain goods including a "better class of shirtings."[104]

All the quilt fabrics in this book represent stages of development in the textile industry starting in the eighteenth century in western Europe and

America. Advancements in technology, equipment, dyes, and chemicals constantly changed calico production in Rhode Island and elsewhere. Consumer demand for new designs and colors accelerated as the industry grew. These Rhode Island quilts reflect each of the milestones faced by the printing industry.

*Notes*

1. Kathryn Berenson, *Quilts of Provence: The Art and Craft of French Quiltmaking* (New York: Henry Holt, 1996), 38–39, 43–45. This is a good account of the French people's desire for imported patterned cottons that they called *indiennes*. Specifically, calicoes from Calicut were plain or painted and printed cotton fabrics. Indian textile workers produced chintzes by a combination of mordant printing and indigo-resist dyeing. Often writers have used both "calico" and "chintz" to describe printed cottons. Kax Wilson, *A History of Textiles* (Boulder, Colo.: Westview Press, 1979), 96–97, 245–46.

2. Josette Brédif, *Printed French Fabrics: Toiles de Jouy* (New York: Rizzoli, 1989), 208–10, 245–46.

3. *Newport Mercury*, April 10, 1759. The next year Thomas and Benjamin Forsey advertised "China callicoes" and "a large and neat assortment of English and West-India Goods," in the *Newport Mercury*, April 22, 1760.

4. *Newport Mercury*, April 17, 1759; May 8, 1759; Pease used his house as his sales base. The Thames Street store of Christopher Champlin also stocked figured calicoes and chintz, "some suitable for bed furniture." *Newport Mercury*, July 3, 1759.

5. *Newport Mercury*, October 26, 1762.

6. Florence H. Pettit, "The Printed Textiles of Eighteenth-Century America," in *Imported and Domestic Textiles in Eighteenth-Century America: Irene Emery Roundtable on Museum Textiles, 1975 Proceedings*, Patricia L. Fiske, ed. (Washington, D.C.: Textile Museum, 1975), 34.

7. Jeannette Turner Bowker, "American Cylinder Printed Calicoes: A Search for and an Evaluation of Calicoes Printed before 1850" (master's thesis, University of Rhode Island, 1974), 30.

8. Patsy Orlofsky and Myron Orlofsky, *Quilts in America* (New York: Abbeville Press, 1974), 57–63.

9. Florence M. Montgomery, *Printed Textiles: English and American Cottons and Linens, 1700–1850* (New York: Viking Press, 1970), 92–98; Mary Schoeser and Celia Rufey, *English and American Textiles from 1790 to the Present* (New York: Thames & Hudson, 1989), 45.

10. John Leander Bishop, *A History of American Manufactures from 1608 to 1860*, 3 vols. (Philadelphia: Edward Young, 1868; reprint, New York: Augustus M. Kelley, 1966), 1:411, 2:55.

11. Ibid., 2:396–97.

12. D. Graeme Keith, "Cotton Printing" in *Concise Encyclopedia of American Antiques*, Helen Comstock, ed. (New York: Hawthorn Books, 1958), 1:299. Also discussed in Florence H. Pettit, *America's Printed and Painted Fabrics, 1600–1900* (New York: Hastings House, 1970), 179.

13. Keith, "Cotton Printing," 299. A "type" was "a small rectangular block, usually of metal or wood, having on its upper end a raised letter, figure, or other character, for use in printing." *Oxford English Dictionary*, 2nd ed., s.v. "type."

14. Ibid.

15. Brédif, *Printed French Fabrics*, 208.

16. Cole incorporated extracts from "Judge Staple's 'Annals of Providence'" and referred to Vandausen as "Dawson." Staple described the spinning and bleaching processes that villagers used to prepare the fabric that Vandausen printed. J. R. Cole, *History of Washington and Kent Counties, Rhode Island* (New York: W. W. Preston, 1889), 1120. Also see Pettit, *America's Printed and Painted Fabrics*, 178. Bishop reported that Vandausen used Indian cotton print cloth. Bishop, *American Manufactures*, 1:404.

17. Cole, *History of Washington and Kent Counties*, 1120–21. Judge Staple included the explanation that printing on linen produced more brilliant colors than on cotton. One's perspective on this argument might relate to if a person owned a flax-producing farm or a store that profited from selling printed cottons.

18. Photograph of the textile sewn into what Bowker calls a "pot holder" is in Bowker, "American Cylinder Printed Calicoes," 33. This textile belonged to the late Marian Fry of East Greenwich, a noted local historian; three Fry family quilts are illustrated in this book.

19. Pettit, *America's Printed and Painted Fabrics*, 179. Wood blocks could be single motifs like these or much larger. Since positioning a block on a fabric was done by hand, size was limited.

20. Pettit, *America's Printed and Painted Fabrics*, 178; *Biographical Cyclopedia of Representative Men of Rhode Island* (Providence: National Biographical Publishing Co., 1881), 259.

21. John E. Sterling, "Rhode Island Historical Cemeteries," cemetery database at the Rhode Island Historical Society Library, Providence, R.I. Further information on the Vandausen-Allen business is not available, but Allen's sons, Crawford and Philip, owned nineteenth-century calico-printing businesses, and their company continued in Providence until at least 1908. Diane L. Fagan Affleck, *Just New From the Mills: Printed Cottons in America* (North Andover, Mass.: Museum of American Textile History, 1987), 76.

22. Bishop, *American Manufactures*, 2:59–60; Pettit, *America's Printed and Painted Fabrics*, 180. Judge Staple's "Annals of Providence" description of this business is cited in Cole, *History of Washington and Kent Counties*, 1120.

23. Pettit, *America's Printed and Painted Fabrics*, 180. In 1800 Schaub continued in another business related to calico printing, the manufacture of paper hangings. Keith, "Cotton Printing," 299.

24. Berenson, *Quilts of Provence*, 39.

25. C. T. Hinckley, "Everyday Actualities, No. II: Calico-Printing," *Godey's Lady's Book* (July 1852): 6. Hinckley's footnote to the "block-printing" scene in Figure 59 stated that the printers were applying a discharge to the fabric, which would already have been dyed with indigo or printed with mordants for madder-style printing. The bottle attached to the sieve supplied the discharge rather than a tearer. Hinckley did not explain who spread the discharge evenly over the sieve.

26. Over one hundred similar fabrics are extant and have gained much attention in the twentieth century: *Antiques Magazine* (November 1931) cited in Jean Ray Laury, *Ho for California! Pioneer Women and Their Quilts* (New York: E. P. Dutton, 1990), 23, 151; in 1958 by Keith, "Cotton Printing," 299–300; in 1970 by Montgomery, *Printed Textiles*, 194–211; and extensively by Pettit in *America's Indigo Blues: Resist-printed and Dyed Textiles of the Eighteenth Century* (New York: Hastings House, 1974), and in 1975, Pettit, *Printed Textiles*, 44–55.

27. Pettit, *America's Indigo Blues*, 202–3. The Shelburne quilt (#1952-581) is Figure 203

in Montgomery, *Printed Textiles*, 207. Montgomery stated that it and three others pictured nearby are similar to English prints from the third quarter of the eighteenth century.

28. P. C. Floud, "The English Contribution to the Early History of Indigo Printing" in *Journal of the Society of Dyers and Colourists* 76, no. 6 (June 1960): 347–48; Gösta Sandberg, *Indigo Textiles: Technique and History* (Asheville, N.C.: Lark Books, 1989), 141.

29. Brédif, *Printed French Fabrics*, 52; Francis Nixon receives credit for the invention of copper-plate textile printing in 1752 at the Drumcondra Printworks near Dublin, Ireland. Christa C. Mayer Thurman, *Textiles in the Art Institute of Chicago* (Chicago: Art Institute of Chicago, 1992), 94.

30. Brédif, *Printed French Fabrics*, 28, 30.

31. Ibid., 46.

32. Ibid., 46, 62.

33. Ibid., 72–73. Wood-block prints far outnumbered copper-plate prints at Jouy. Ibid., 128.

34. Examples of English copper-plate prints are in Wendy Hefford, *The Victoria and Albert Museum's Textile Collection: Design for Printed Textiles in England from 1750 to 1850* (New York: Canopy Books, 1992). Other copper-plate prints copied eighteenth-century woven-silk designs. Textiles with symmetrical rococo floral motifs and fancy stripes are in Hefford, *Printed Textiles in England*, Plates 15, 28–31.

35. Brédif, *Printed French Fabrics*, 52. A number of extant eighteenth-century prints from Jouy have fabric widths around 36 inches (92–94 cm) although those for special purposes such as shawl borders and handkerchiefs were less. The width of the indigo-printed fabric in Figure 60 is about 36 inches; getting an exact measurement is difficult since the low-thread-count fabric distorts easily, and lines of quilting stitches prevent the fabric from lying flat.

36. Ibid., 141. Even the platelike pictorial scenes that enjoyed a brief resurgence in the 1820s appear overcrowded, stunted in height, and lacking artistic merit. Peter Floud, "Pictorial Prints of the 1820s," *Antiques* 71 (November 1957): 455–59, cited in Hefford, *Printed Textiles in England*, 13.

37. *Providence Daily Journal*, January 1, 1835. "Copperplate chintzes" could refer to a design style rather than a printing technique.

38. Brédif, *Printed French Fabrics*, 58. In 1785 at Livesey Hargreaves & Co., Thomas Bell introduced cylinder-printing equipment that he had patented two years earlier. A similar machine built at Jouy was not satisfactory; use of the technique waited until after the French Revolution to be tried again in 1797, this time with success.

39. Montgomery, *Printed Textiles*, 291. Two colorful surface roller prints from 1921 and 1922 are in Schoeser and Rufey, *English and American Textiles*, 186–87. The roughness of the print was appropriate for the stylized and abstract designs on cretonne, a sturdy cotton or linen fabric for draperies and upholstery.

40. Brédif, *Printed French Fabrics*, 58.

41. George S. White, *Memoir of Samuel Slater, The Father of American Manufactures* (Philadelphia: 1836), 396. The former blade was called the "lint doctor," the latter the "color doctor."

42. A large part of Whitney & Hoppin's cost was for transportation from Philadelphia. The first steam engine in Providence had been installed in 1812 at Prov. Wollen Manufacturing Company. Bishop, *American Manufactures*, 2:181, 207.

43. Ibid., 235–36, 251.

44. Ibid., 256.

45. Ibid., 284; the largest cotton factory in Rhode Island was Coventry Manufacturing Company. In 1826 Rhode Island manufacturing villages in order by size were Pawtucket, Slatersville, and Pawtuxet-Kent County, ranking third, sixth, and eighth, respectively, in New England. Ibid., 309.

46. Affleck, *Just New From the Mills*, 11. Dover Manufacturing Company would become Cocheco Manufacturing Company and the employer of Samuel Dunster from 1828 to 1832 and 1852 to 1860. Eleven volumes of his recipe books provide invaluable information about printing over a thirty-year period. They are discussed in the previous essay and later in this one. Samuel Dunster, *Print Dyes*, 11 vols., MSS 363, Rhode Island Historical Society Library. Bishop credits the 1822 Lowell company as being the first calico printing firm, but Affleck explained that even though Merrimack was the first to plan a print works, the other two existing companies actually began printing before Merrimack. Bishop, *American Manufactures*, 2:275.

47. Bishop, *American Manufactures*, 2:284, 279. One reason he cited for the superiority of domestic calicoes was the high quality of the cotton used for printing in comparison to similar English prints on "inferior Bengal or Surat cotton."

48. Some early nineteenth-century dyers no doubt block-printed calicoes, but records are sketchy or nonexistent. Pettit listed Benjamin and Barney Merry of Pawtucket as calico printers in 1805. Pettit, *Printed and Painted Fabrics*, 237. Grieve reported that "Barney Merry, the pioneer dyer and bleacher, built his homestead next adjoining Mr. Slater's house on the south." Robert Grieve, *Illustrated History of Pawtucket* (Pawtucket: Pawtucket Gazette and Chronicle, 1897), 137.

49. Pettit, *Printed and Painted Fabrics*, 201–6. By his death in 1836 Sprague owned six other mills in various locations; he had laid the foundation for vast manufacturing interests that expanded throughout New England until the business ran into financial troubles during the depression in 1873. Cotton manufacturers B. B. and R. Knight acquired the Cranston facility in 1888, and the resulting Cranston Print Works Company still prints fabrics today.

50. Shinkwin & Bliss, Pawtucket, 1825; Apponaug Printworks, 1825; Pawtucket Calico Company, 1826. Calico printers are listed in: Bowker, "American Cylinder Printed Calicoes," 78; Louise E. Majorey, "Printed Textiles in Southern New England: 1823–1860" (master's thesis, University of Rhode Island, 1987), 74; Pettit, *Printed and Painted Fabrics*, 237–38. Bishop, *American Manufactures*, is perhaps the best nineteenth-century source of information on calico-printing firms in Rhode Island and New England.

51. Reprinted article in the *New England Farmer*, December 8, 1826.

52. "Reports of the Rhode Island Agricultural Society," in *New England Farmer*, October 27, 1826. The Rhode Island Society for the Encouragement of Domestic Industry established a $12,000 fund in 1823 so that the interest from the fund could support the premiums awarded to category winners. Bishop, *American Manufactures*, 2:285. The 1826 event was the seventh exhibition to be held. *New England Farmer*, October 20, 1826.

53. Royal Sibley formed a partnership, Sibley & Kelley, in 1833 and named the company Franklin Print Works. Crawford Allen bought it in 1836. Crawford and Philip Allen followed their father Zachariah, the eighteenth-century printer, in textile production while their famous brother Zachariah invented and manufactured equipment. Brothers Philip and Zachariah both served the state as governor. Crawford had dyeing and printing businesses in Arkwright (a historically named village in Coventry), Providence, and Pawtucket. A large number of extant samples from Philip Allen & Sons show style and technological changes during the early decades of printing in Rhode Island. Dunster, mentioned in

note 46, included 1830s Philip Allen & Sons Printwork prints in his sample books while he was working at Cocheco. Likewise, when he worked for Allen from 1848 to 1852, he detailed procedures with accompanying fabric samples in his books as did Daniel McCarthy in his twelve volumes of Allen production from 1845 to 1858; MSS 563, Rhode Island Historical Society Library. The American Museum of Textile History in Lowell, Mass., owns an 1858 recipe book kept by Allen printer George Birtwistle and numerous sample cards. The Connecticut Historical Society in Hartford has merchants' sample cards for 1850 and 1860 from the Allen print works.

54. Majorey, "Printed Textiles," 14; Pettit, *Printed and Painted Fabrics*, 184; Caroline F. Ware, *The Early New England Cotton Manufacture: A Study in Industrial Beginnings* (New York: Russell and Russell, 1966), 94; *History of the State of Rhode Island* (Philadelphia: Hoag, Wade and Company, 1878), 234.

55. White, *Memoir of Samuel Slater*, 403.

56. Victor S. Clark, *History of Manufactures in the United States, 1607–1860*, 2 vols. (New York: McGraw-Hill, 1929), 1:547; Ware, *Early New England Cotton Manufacture*, 95, 98.

57. Grieve, *History of Pawtucket*, 242. Designations for printers sometimes specified block or machine printing. Although James Dunlop was listed as a "calico printer" in the city directory, his obituary stated that he was "a machine printer . . . at the Dunnell Print Works for many years." *Pawtucket and Central Falls Directory, 1869–70*, 73; *Pawtucket Gazette and Chronicle*, September 3, 1886.

58. William M. Cook, Coventry, 1830; Pimbley's Bleaching & Print Works, Pawtucket, 1836; Crawford Allen, Pawtucket, 1836.

59. Cole, *History of Washington and Kent Counties*, 1125.

60. "The Providence Manufacturing Co. will receive cotton goods to bleach at their bleachery. They also singe and bleach printing cloth for madder colors." *Providence Daily Journal*, January 1, 1835.

61. Charles Payne emigrated from England as a child with his parents. He served an apprenticeship as an engraver for calico printers with Samuel Lord before opening his own business. In 1849 he and Jude Taylor established the engraving firm of Payne & Taylor in Pawtucket. *Representative Men and Old Families of Rhode Island*, vol. 2 (Chicago: J. H. Beers, 1908), 878. James Warburton served his apprenticeship in England before coming to Rhode Island in 1847 as an engraver in calico printing, working "with Jude Taylor and other well-known Pawtucket engravers." Obituary in *Pawtucket Gazette and Chronicle*, July 22, 1898.

62. Engraver Joseph Lockett of Manchester is credited with developing engraving and etching for calico printing starting in 1808 with equipment invented to engrave bank notes. White, *Memoir of Samuel Slater*, 397. Designs probably engraved by Lockett in the mid-1820s are in Hefford, *Printed Textiles in England*, 129.

63. Ibid., 396–97. When a hand-engraved copper surface became so worn that the pattern had to be re-engraved, the time-consuming process had to be repeated with the certainty that the second engraving would not match the first one exactly. Brédif, *Printed French Fabrics*, 175, n. 128.

64. White, *Memoir of Samuel Slater*, 398.

65. Payne & Taylor closed their engraving business after the introduction of the "pentograph" engraving machinery and began making hair cloth in 1863; this manufacture continued into the twentieth century. *Representative Men*, 878.

66. White, *Memoir of Samuel Slater*, 398.

67. Ibid., 399; James Burton was responsible for this invention which actually worked in 1805.

68. One of the Goddard, Brown, and Ives projects of the early 1840s, Hope Mill first made sheeting in narrow (thirty-six or thirty-eight inches) and double widths (sixty-four inches). The parent company also developed Lonsdale Mill and Blackstone Mill. Samuel G. Allen, the husband of the probable quiltmaker, bought machinery in Liverpool for Hope Mill and later became mill superintendent as did his Quaker son-in-law, Richard Greene Howland. "Alice Merrill Howland, Donor File," University of Rhode Island Historic Textile and Costume Collection, Kingston, R.I. Alice, Richard's daughter, contributed a significant collection of textiles and clothing from the three generations of her family to the URI Collection. The founders of Wamsutta Company, New Bedford's first mill, used Hope Mill as their model in 1847–48. Ware, *Early New England Cotton Manufacture*, 108.

69. "Index to Representative Manufacturers," s.v. "Hon. James Y. Smith, Providence, Rhode Island," in Bishop, *American Manufactures*, 2:529. Of eleven profiles in his "Index," Bishop included three men from Rhode Island and five from Massachusetts, indicative of the strong manufacturing base in southern New England.

70. Hefford, *Printed Textiles in England*, 15.

71. Ibid.

72. Grieve, *Illustrated History of Pawtucket*, 140. The Walcott Manufacturing Company produced cotton cloth on the east side of the Blackstone River in Pawtucket, across from Slater Mill.

73. *Providence Daily Journal & General Advertiser*, January 28, 1830.

74. *Providence Daily Journal*, January 1, 1835. Many sources from the eighteenth century and afterward used "chintz" and "calico" interchangeably.

75. McCarthy, *Madder Colours* 3 (1852–54), 99, 110.

76. *Providence Journal*, March 26, 1956; Providence *Evening Bulletin*, July 11, 1975.

77. Hefford, *Printed Textiles in England*, 31, 154; Plates 176, 177, 178, 181, 210—textiles from Lancashire, 1824–26.

78. Montgomery, *Printed Textiles*, 306.

79. McCarthy, *Madder Colours* 1 (1845–49), 62–64.

80. Dunster, *Print Dyes*, 4 (1845): 158; 5 (1846), 5; 5: 8.

81. Ibid., 5: 6.

82. McCarthy, *Madder Colours* 3, 51.

83. McCarthy, *Madder Colours* 4 (1854): 30–33; Dunster, *Print Dyes*, 10 (1855): 9. In mid-1852 Dunster moved back to Dover, N.H., to Cocheco Manufacturing Company where he had started in 1828. He continued his record keeping through 1858.

84. McCarthy, *Madder Colours* 1, 46.

85. Ibid., 45–46.

86. Dunster, *Print Dyes*, 5:19–66; he was working at Clay Printworks in Johnston, R.I., at this time.

87. Dunster, *Print Dyes*, 2:60, 4:86.

88. Schoeser and Rufey, *English and American Textiles*, 88. Dunster was working in New Hampshire at the time, but New England printers often included samples from England and from other American mills in their record books. Dunster, *Print Dyes*, 2:60.

89. Dunster, *Print Dyes*, 5:27–29.

90. Bishop, *American Manufactures*, 2:453. Forty-two textile printers in the United States produced calicoes worth $3,922,505 in 1850. Another report estimated that the state had

seventeen dyers and calico printers by midcentury. Pettit, *America's Printed and Painted Fabrics*, 180.

91. A Rhode Island merchant's 1858 order book contains about 200 samples of printed cottons, names of printers and mills, style numbers, lengths of pieces, and notes. Some of the patterns came in as many as nine colorways. Swatchbook, Winterthur Library, Winterthur Museum and Gardens, Winterthur, Del.

92. The value of printed and colored cotton imports to the United States in 1854, 1855, and 1856 was approximately $17 million, $12.5 million, and $19 million, respectively. Printed and colored cotton accounted for 50, 58, and 63 percent of the cotton imported those three years. J. Smith Homans and J. Smith Homans, Jr., eds., *Cyclopedia of Commerce and Commercial Navigation*, 474 (New York: Harper and Brothers, 1858).

93. Dunster, *Print Dyes*, 5:31, sample #236.

94. Ibid., 6:24.

95. McCarthy, *Madder Colours* 3, 195.

96. Ibid.

97. Dunster, *Print Dyes*, 8: 17.

98. McCarthy, *Madder Colours* 2, 43.

99. Linda Parry, *The Victoria and Albert Museum's Textile Collection: British Textiles from 1850 to 1900* (New York: Canopy Books, 1993), 10.

100. Schoeser and Rufey, *English and American Textiles*, 119, 128; Parry, *British Textiles from 1850 to 1900*, 12.

101. Schoeser and Rufey, *English and American Textiles*, 104. This source credits this new color scheme to the introduction of "Manchester brown," an azo dye used on silk interior fabrics after 1865.

102. Barbara Brackman, *Clues in the Calico: A Guide to Identifying and Dating Antique Quilts* (McLean, Va.: EPM Publications, 1989), 88.

103. In 1852 McCarthy had included "lightwork" samples printed with a six-cylinder machine. He assigned most of them a general name such as "5 pinks covered in pink." The sixth roller printed on an acid that resisted the dye, creating white spots in the "five-pinks" designs. McCarthy, *Madder Colours III*, 51.

104. Clark, *History of Manufactures*, 2:408.

# Social Connectedness

CATHERINE A. CERNY

QUILTS & THE STORIES ASSOCIATED WITH THEM CALL TO MIND PERSONS
and events from the past. The relationships that bind individuals to society
are complex, bridging family and community life and crossing generation-
al experiences. Memories speak to social relationships, whether existing
solely in the past, reinforcing those of the present, or establishing connections between past and present. At the same time, the stories associated with
quilts lend a perspective on daily life and, in particular, women's contribution to establishing and sustaining close, emotionally bound, interpersonal
relationships. Whether based on the experiences with the quiltmaker or
passed down through generations of owners, the memories contribute to
an understanding of connectedness that has sustained social life in Rhode
Island. Social connectedness refers to the condition or quality of being linked
together as a group or community at one moment and over time.[1] This subject has become a persistent theme in the study of American quiltmaking.[2]

Nineteenth- and early-twentieth-century writers often romanticized the
making and use of quilts, drawing on the images of quiltmaking as metaphor for social connectedness.[3] Contemporary research has sought to un-
cover the foundations of these stories and provide a more accurate account
of women's history.[4] Knowledge about the influence of sentiments in shap-
ing the stories, however, can lead to better understanding of the social significance of the stories, especially as quilts reflect the emotional nature of
women's lives. Because of this knowledge, documentation of quilts and
quiltmakers yields a unique perspective on women's history.

In the case of Rhode Island quiltmaking, the memories associated with
extant quilts not only distinguish the quiltmaker but also mark a heritage
bequeathed to subsequent generations of owners. With most quiltmakers
and owners being women, the quilt represents a unique type of genealogy

Mary Mayette Murphy made this quilt with her daughter Alice in 1931. She had come to North Providence to help during Alice's pregnancy. Alice had settled in Rhode Island in 1922 upon her marriage to John Arbour, a machinist. Mary and Alice made the quilt for the present owner, Alice's daughter, who was five years old at the time.

through which women have gained recognition, both individually and collectively, for their participation in family and community life. Owners' responses on the interview portion of the Rhode Island Quilt Documentation Project show that sentiments associated with quilts preserved by Rhode Island families, collectors, and curators reflect attachments to family, community, and nation and mark a particular heritage of social connectedness. Where complete biographies are unavailable, oral histories augmented by personal documents (e.g., letters, diaries, journals) can advance knowledge of the day-to-day routine of women's lives.[5] Synthesis of this knowledge is beginning to identify everyday mechanisms by which female quiltmakers have achieved empowerment within families and communities.[6] Identifying personalities and activities of daily life lends character to family lineage and women's history.

An examination of the social context of Rhode Island quilts necessitates attention to the relationship between the quiltmaker and the people who contributed to or participated in the quiltmaking, the people for whom the quilts were made, the people who subsequently owned the quilts, and the present and future owners. The story behind the making of a pair of quilts by Mary Mayette Murphy (1864–1955) and her daughter Alice Ann Murphy Arbour (1890–1980) and their use by Mary Murphy's granddaughter and great-granddaughter demonstrates how the quilts memorialize customary practices within a household and preserve these remembrances for subsequent generations.

The Double Irish Chain quilt (Fig. 76) was machine-pieced and hand-quilted in 1931 when Mary Mayette Murphy (Fig. 77) came from Arnprior, Canada, to visit her pregnant daughter (Fig. 78) in North Providence, Rhode Island. Alice had moved from Ontario in 1922 upon her marriage to John Arbour, first employed as a machinist for Brown and Sharpe in Providence. John Arbour later owned his own business. Mary and Alice made the quilt for Alice's daughter Mary, the present owner, who was five years old at the time. The owner remembers crawling under this quilt on her hands and knees as it was stretched on a quilting frame that filled the entire kitchen. She notes that "a sense of family and continuance has always been fostered in me by the possession of this quilt which actually was made purposely to be in my future when its makers would no longer be with me."[7] Mary's memories of her family while the quilt was being made juxtapose past and present and join the three generations of women. The commemorative value of the quilt is compounded as the present owner also associates the Double Irish Chain quilt pattern with her Irish grandfather.

Mary Murphy and Alice Arbour made a second quilt, a Dresden Plate, for the baby born February 9, 1932. This quilt is now owned by Mary Murphy's great-granddaughter, thus linking four generations of Murphy women.

Fig. 77. (*Left*) Mary Mayette Murphy (1864–1955) lived in Arnprior, Canada. Of French Canadian heritage, she married an Irishman. She initiated quilting projects during her visits to Rhode Island to see her daughter Alice. RIQDP Archives.

Fig. 78. (*Right*) Alice Murphy Arbour (1890–1980) and her mother, Mary, made the Double Irish Chain quilt in Figure 76 for Alice's daughter Mary. They made a Dresden Plate and a second Double Irish Chain for Alice's other daughters. RIQDP Archives.

The great-granddaughter notes that the quilt was "made for my grandmother by her mother and herself. Given to me by my mother in 1991 for use in my home."[8] Like her mother, the current owner recognizes the quilt as "a remembrance of my roots, my great grandmother, my grandmother, and mother—especially of the makers who found a way through quiltmaking to give me an inheritance of comfort, love and pride which is always with me."[9]

Throughout the nineteenth century and into the middle of the twentieth century, identity for most women was defined within the domestic setting. Often the role of wife and mother overshadowed recollection of a quiltmaker's personality for all but immediate acquaintances. Yet, the individuality of a quilt distinguishes each quiltmaker. Closer viewing of a common pattern (e.g., Dresden Plate) reveals unique combinations of fabric and color, and stimulates, in turn, memories of the quiltmaker. The two Murphy quilts spark memories of great-grandmother Mary Murphy: she was "very lively, quick, and very efficient. Whenever she visited from Canada she always initiated a project of some sort and all would soon be busily involved. She was always ready for fun and loved to play jokes so that we were on guard and once completely awed my sister and I by using her sewing skills to fashion an outfit for a dead mouse caught in a trap then placing that well-dressed mouse under my *father's* (a real authority figure) napkin at supper—in a match box."[10]

Quiltmaking has been an occupation both inclusive and exclusive of men. We generally assume women drafted the designs, assembled the quilts, and selected the persons to receive them. Yet, quilts formed the basis of shared experiences between wife and husband, mother and son, grandmother and grandson. While women made the majority of the quilts, they might receive assistance from husbands (e.g., a man would build a quilting frame) or sons. One Block Island quiltmaker guided her young son in his attempt to stitch quilt pieces and then stored the quilt until she gave it to him as a gift at his wedding.[11] Women placed quilts in the cribs of baby boys and on the beds of sons and included quilts among possessions inherited by grandsons. At the same time, communities of women (e.g., church groups, sewing societies) applied shared interests toward civic obligations. Together with men, quiltmakers worked in concert to support church, grange, or other town activities. Women pieced fund-raising quilts; men purchased chances to win raffle quilts. Yet in each instance, recognition of women's enterprise by men rarely extended beyond the family and community.

Owners' feelings toward their quilts are sensitized to the interplay between both generative and day-to-day dimensions of family life. The generative dimension, marked by births and weddings, highlights a continuity of values and traditions across generations of family. The day-to-day dimension describes particular personalities, accomplishments, and events. Traditionally quilts have focused on women, who through their daily activities insured continuity of family beyond their immediate generation and, thereby, enhanced one's experience of kinship.[12] Today, quilts do not simply remind us of the persons who have given us life but also acknowledge the sum of women's experience, in the past largely shaped by family life.

A woman's lineage was multifaceted, initially consisting of an inheritance from her parents, yet supplanted by the traditions of her husband. Just as births, marriages, and deaths were rites of passage that underscored the life experience, a woman's marriage and the birth of her children revealed a connection of self with one's descendants. A quilt traced heritage from mother to daughter to granddaughter. For women who never had children or did not marry, quilts provided a means by which they could be remembered by extended family or friends. This generative aspect of women's experience is detailed through processes of quilt gift giving and inheritance.

A wedding highlighted the complex, sometimes uncertain nature of female heritage. With her departure from her parents' home and entrance into her husband's household, a woman assumed new responsibilities, including care of husband and children. A wedding quilt simultaneously represented enduring relationships that had already been established and those that were anticipated. It reminded the new bride of her former life and announced her entry into a new family and community. Often a mother made

FIG. 79. (*Opposite*) Friendship Star quilt, 1857–58. Cotton top and back, 95 x 87 in. Hand-pieced and hand-quilted, 8 stitches per inch. Made by friends of Emeline Gallup Smith (1818–1886). Babcock-Smith House, Westerly, Rhode Island. RIQDP #607.

In the mid–nineteenth century when a bride moved away from her home and community, quilts became a reminder of her life before marriage and of the friends and family she left behind. Emeline Gallup married Orlando Smith in 1845 and moved to Westerly, Rhode Island, from her natal home in Ledyard, Connecticut. Her hometown friends contributed signed blocks for this quilt.

a quilt on the occasion of a daughter's wedding, or a grandmother in anticipation of a grandchild's wedding.

During the nineteenth century, friends and relatives within the bride's home community contributed quilt blocks and/or signed their names to make wedding quilts. The addition of hometown names and messages memorialized quilts as treasures of one's youth. A mother might convey an important message to her daughter on the occasion of her wedding. Susan Manton's signature quilt, given on her wedding in 1856, included such a note: "Perseverance and Industry accomplishes much for my daughter Susan, Mother."[13]

Friendship quilts maintained bonds between women even after the marriage. Emeline Gallup left Ledyard, Connecticut, to marry Orlando Smith on April 10, 1845. Orlando and Emeline bought the old Babcock farm in 1848 and founded Westerly Granite on the property. A decade later, Emeline and her old friends in Ledyard, Lebanon, Preston, and Norwich contributed blocks for a Friendship Star quilt (Fig. 79). Each signed her name in the center of her block; some added a date or a place name. Emeline added "Westerly, RI" to her signature (Fig. 80).[14] Today, the tradition of friendship quilts commemorates the diffuse yet enduring nature of women's relationships, especially those bridging the transition from adolescence to married life. Simultaneously, quilts characterize constancy in women's culture and enable contemporary owners to empathize with the experiences of their ancestors.

The birth of a child signaled a woman's investment in her husband's lineage. The emotional effect of a quilt is understood through the owner's memories. As seen with the Murphy quilts, a grandmother's and mother's cooperation eventually linked four generations of women. Most frequently, a mother made a quilt in anticipation of her child's birth. Although a child might soon outgrow its use, a quilt did not lose sentimental value. The affection first established between quiltmaker and child qualified the experiences of later owners or users of the quilt in diverse ways. A mother's gift of a son's baby quilt to the daughter-in-law, for example, might strengthen the affection between the two women. "Sammy's quilt," begun in 1937 when Florence Luther Chaplin was pregnant with Sammy and finished in 1939, was given to Sam's wife during the 1970s. Florence liked her daughter-in-law and felt that she would care for the quilt. In turn, the daughter-in-law recalls that Florence taught her all she knew.[15]

In contrast to wedding quilts, owners' memories of quilts made for children focus on the reciprocal affections between generations. In this context, the quilts remind us of the value of family unity by channeling interactions at moments of celebration or tragedy. The quilt becomes a conduit for venting emotions. For instance, a Sunbonnet Sue–Overall Sam quilt, which hung

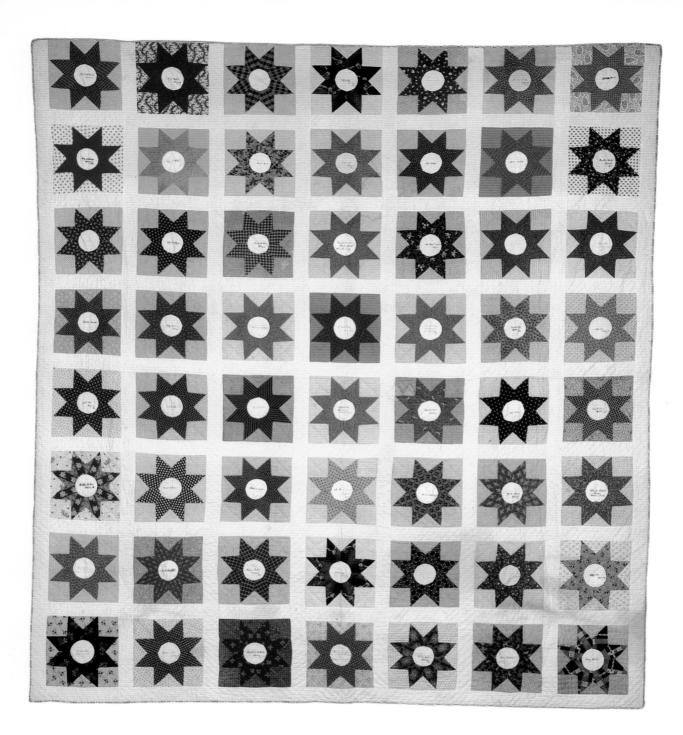

in the quiltmaker's room in the rest home, was made as she awaited the birth of her first child decades earlier. The child did not survive, and the quilt was not finished until 1989 with the help of her daughter and a friend. The quiltmaker, who had Alzheimer's disease, would look at the quilt and smile. Sewing was one of the last things she could do, and her daughter feels that the quilt was therapy for her.[16]

FIG. 80. Signature block of friendship quilt presented to Emeline Smith. Emeline signed her block "Emeline Smith, Westerly, R.I." RIQDP Archives.

FIG. 81. (*Opposite*) Churn Dash quilt, ca. 1890s. Cotton top and back, 89 x 79½ in. Hand-pieced, tied. Made by Lois Albee Hayward Slade (1835–1907). Collection of Prince Family. RIQDP #22.

Lois Slade, who lived on Almy Street in Providence, made a quilt for each of her four grandchildren to be presented to them when they married. This quilt was made for Benjamin Howard Slade, who was just twelve years old when Lois died. Before her death, Lois had arranged for Howard and his bride to receive the quilt, which came by mail. He married Bessie Allen on October 18, 1921. He had not known that the quilt existed before receiving it.

Among Rhode Island quiltmakers, grandmothers were especially prolific in their quiltmaking. Whether made for weddings, birthdays, or other occasions (e.g., a child's first bed), the quilts marked the important occasions as grandchildren matured. Grandmothers could speak about the importance of family life in child development without having to address the daily routines and pressures of child rearing. Aunts, great-aunts, and godmothers similarly championed family connectedness by making a quilt or insuring a child's inheritance of a family quilt. In each instance, the quilt envisioned the value of familial support possible through the nurturing of personal relationships. When grandmothers made quilts for each grandchild, for example, the quilts gave form to kindred ties among cousins, founded through connectedness to the quiltmaker. Lois Albee Hayward Slade, the owner's great-great-grandmother, made the Churn Dash quilt shown in Figure 81 as a gift to be presented at the marriage of her grandson in the late 1800s. The quilt was one of four that the quilter made for her grandchildren.[17] As reminders of both the grandmother and of cousins, the quilt may lessen feelings of separation and fragmentation as descendants become widely separated geographically. The practice of making wedding

quilts for each grandchild, male or female, allowed men access to a perspective on family heritage usually restricted to women. As we have seen, quiltmaking ascribes importance to a social connectedness that underscores female lineage; men can become partners to this enterprise.

Most owners in the RIQDP database inherited family quilts through several generations. The quilts were passed down from one quiltmaker, from several quiltmakers within a family line, or from quiltmakers of both the husband's and wife's families. In some cases, quilts were passed from mother to daughter, from grandmother to granddaughter, or from aunt to niece. In other cases, quilts crossed matrilineage, inherited initially by a daughter and then by a sister-in-law. On occasion men were quilt owners. A quilt might be won by a husband at a church raffle, be given to a son or grandson upon his wedding, or be one of many quilts distributed to children or grandchildren upon the death of the quiltmaker. During the RIQDP, a number of men came alone or with their wives to documentation days, showing interest in and appreciation of family quilts. More often however, it was the wife who provided the history and demonstrated safekeeping of a husband's quilt. The tendency to associate women with quilts underscores a presumption about the centrality of women's disposition toward nurturing the household. Yet more than this, through caring for quilts, women can express feelings about the joys and hardships of being female.

Owners recognized quilts as important family possessions and, on occasion, lost quilts were found. One quilt owner remembers her mother removing quilts made by her grandmother Marie Louise Valance Pierel from a trunk and showing them to her nine children. After her mother died in 1955, the husband remarried, and the quilts were lost. The family believed that the quilts were given away by the second wife. Subsequently, one of the quilts was found in the possession of the second wife's son. The quilt was presented to the current owner at a family reunion, a Fourth of July family picnic during the mid-1970s.[18]

Memories of the past coupled with present experience anticipated future family connections. Preservation of quilts endorsed a grandmother's concern for her grandchild's fate. Many Rhode Island families had unfinished quilts within their collections. These included pieced blocks and quilt tops. The reasons the quilts remained unfinished were not known. A quiltmaker may have disliked quilting or lost interest in finishing the quilt. She may have been distracted by a pressing family emergency or have died. In a few instances, leaving the quilt unfinished appeared to be deliberate. Hosannna Doyle Michaud and Marie Reine Tougas, mother and daughter, made an appliqué quilt top with the intention that it be completed by the granddaughter, great-granddaughter, and great-great-granddaughter. The quilt, unfinished, is currently owned by Marie's daughter.[19] Perhaps the original quiltmakers saw this as an opportunity to entice their descendants into a practice that lent special meaning to their lives.

Owners preserved quilts by completing the quilt or restoring worn quilts thereby safeguarding a family legacy for the next generation. A Log Cabin quilt, thought to have come to the United States from England when the owner's husband's grandmother was a child, was restored and finished in 1991 with the addition of batting and backing, and then quilted by hand. The owner planned to give the quilt to her daughter, also a quilter, at her marriage or for her first home.[20]

A number of the quilt owners shared their ancestors' interest in quilt-making. Barbara Barber's Tree of Life quilt (Fig. 82) made in 1993, was inspired by the late eighteenth-century *broderie perse* technique. The energy of her great-grandmother, also a quiltmaker, is recalled in the contemporary quiltmaker's work. Barber took over three years to make the quilt, completing the appliqué in 412 hours and the quilting in 683.5 hours.[21] Memories of her great-grandmother, Katie Gleason Waite (Fig. 83), are stimulated as Barber views the sketchbook (Fig. 84) her grand-grandmother kept for trips to the family's summer home in Riverside and the crazy quilt (Fig. 85) she made.[22] Barber's mother had stored the crazy quilt in a trunk only to be brought out and seen when she was very good. In this case the quilt had been inherited by men in the Waite family. The owner is acting as caretaker until she gives it to her son.

Social connectedness for each individual, while established by quilt ownership, is personalized through memories of the quiltmaker. For Rhode Island respondents, many of these memories are drawn from childhood experiences with the quilt and tied to a grandmother. Owners recall sleeping under a grandmother's pieced quilt as children or finding quilts in trunks or attics. When one owner cleaned out her mother's house, she found a scrap quilt that had been packed in a box for forty years. The quilt had been used on the pine spool bed in her grandmother's summer house in Massachusetts. The owner felt very close to the grandmother (1870–1947), who was remembered for being feisty and the backbone of the family despite her five-foot height.[23]

The fabrics in quilts spark many memories. Owners' memories not only recall affection for the quiltmaker but indicate an appreciation for family heritage. Mothers, grandmothers, and aunts collected fabrics from old garments. Notes attached to quilts identified the source of fabric: "Wishing you a very happy Christmas and hoping you will like the present which I send, as it contains many pieces of your mother's dresses."[24] The fabrics represented the person through allusions to her actions. A quilt can become a testament of the quiltmaker's life: "This quilt was made by mother during the last winter of her life (1903–1904) as a remembrance for Elizabeth to have when she should grow up. The plaid silk lining was from one of mother's wedding dresses. Married 3rd 1859—died May 17, 1909."[25] The quiltmaker was Mary Gertrude Way; Elizabeth was her daughter and the mother of the present owner. Ownership of the quilt not only marks the

FIG. 82. (*Overleaf*) Tree of Life quilt, 1993. Cotton top and back, 63 x 54½ in. Hand-appliquéd and hand-quilted, 14 stitches per inch. Made by Barbara W. Barber (1945–). Collection of Barbara W. Barber.

Barbara Barber is a contemporary quiltmaker, teacher, and author from Westerly, Rhode Island. She made this quilt in the *broderie perse* technique, which involves appliquéing cut-out motifs from printed textiles onto solid-colored background fabrics. Although antique quilts in this technique exist, none from Rhode Island are known.

FIG. 83. Barbara Barber's great-grand-mother, Katie Gleason Waite (1839–1912), made numerous quilts (see Fig. 85), which have been an inspiration to Barbara's quiltmaking. RIQDP Archives.

FIG. 84. (*Below*) Katie Waite lived in Orange, Massachusetts, with her husband, James, and son Loren. James was a partner in the firm Hunt and Waite, which invested in fulling mills and the manufacture of textile machinery. The family owned a summer home in Riverside, Rhode Island, where Katie enjoyed needlework and sketching, as evident in this page from her sketchbook entitled "Bound to get to Newport in season for the races, Aug. 6, 1886." RIQDP Archives.

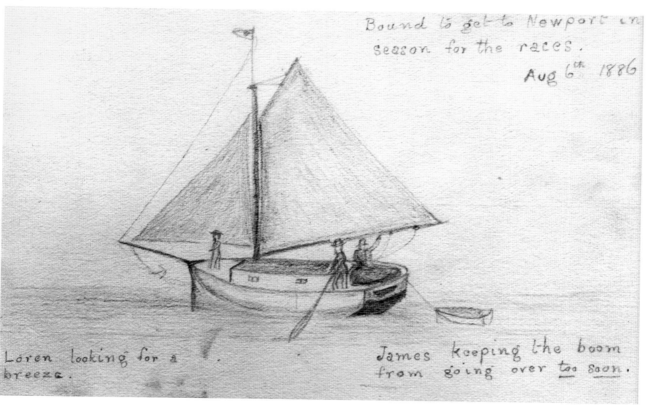

relationship between grandmother and grandchild but provides a personal connection with family continuity and history.

Strong attachments to quilts may be understood through memories of quiltmakers involved in the customary activities of daily life. One owner remembered going to Grandma's with her mother to do laundry on Mondays. Another remembered her grandmother sitting in a chair outside, waving her cane at a diving blue jay; her mother remembered pushing a needle into a quilt to help tie it when she was child. Quilt owners admired the personalities of the quiltmakers, including being easygoing, having a sense of humor, being willing to break with tradition, and being assertive. One owner recognized qualities of the quiltmaker in herself. Quilts evidenced for children the interrelationship of social connectedness and individual recognition. Quiltmakers embodied an integration of individuality and female identity through both their lives and their work. While descendants drew upon the stories of the previous generations, contemporary owners interpret the stories to reflect the circumstances of the times and their own lives.

Owners' memories also reflect the public character of women's lives. Female accomplishments flourished both within and beyond the family. Creativity found expression in ways other than quiltmaking. Rhode Island quiltmakers were skilled gardeners, canners, cooks, and seamstresses. They spun, wove, knitted, embroidered, crocheted, and sewed. They were accomplished horsewomen, cardplayers, and pianists. Anna Elizabeth Tarbox Briggs (1859–1940) wrote poetry and quoted verses to children. She kept a scrapbook of quotes and anecdotes, in addition to quilting with her sister Weltha Tarbox and with members of the Earnest Workers in her Baptist church (Fig. 86). She spun the yarn used in her knitting and crocheting.[26] The women who made quilts worked as teachers, nurses, milliners, dressmakers, jewelry factory workers, housekeepers, restaurant owners, farmers, and postal clerks. Like the women in Figure 87, they worked at Rhode Island textile mills (e.g., Esmond and Harris Mills, B. B. & R. Knight, Fruit of the Loom, and Cranston Print Works) and used fabrics, either free for the taking or purchased as seconds. For one owner, a purchased quilt gained added signifi-

FIG. 85. (*Opposite*) Crazy quilt, 1885. Silk satin, velvet, damask, and brocade pieces, silk embroidery, painted motifs, 57¼ x 70 in. Hand-pieced, prequilted backing. Made by Catherine (Katie) Parnelia Gleason Waite (1839–1912). Collection of Barbara W. Barber. RIQDP #203.

The "crazy patchwork" style first appeared in the 1880s, reflecting interest in Japonism and the Arts and Crafts Movement. Crazy quilts incorporated fancy fabrics, commemorative ribbons, and painted motifs attached to a foundation fabric with decorative embroidery stitches. As an example of Victorian home decor, this quilt is particularly appropriate as it includes a miniature portrait of Queen Victoria and musical notes for "Home Sweet Home."

FIG. 86. Basket quilt, late nineteenth century. Cotton top and back, 91 x 86 in. Hand-pieced and hand-quilted, 8 stitches per inch. Made by Anna Elizabeth Tarbox Briggs (1859–1940). Family collection. RIQDP #46.

Anna Tarbox of East Greenwich worked in textile mills as a weaver prior to her marriage to Alvin Briggs in 1891. Having learned to quilt from her mother Polly, she made at least five quilts. Anna purchased her fabrics from local mills in West Warwick and Crompton (East Greenwich). She participated in quilting bees with the Earnest Workers at the Six Principle Baptist Church.

cance as she questioned whether the fabric in the Rhode Island quilt had come from the Fruit of the Loom Mill in Pontiac. Her grandfather and other family members had worked at the mill.[27] The use of mill fabrics in their quilts documented a balancing of personal needs, employment obligations, and domestic responsibilities not always apparent in women's quiltmaking.

The activity of quiltmaking was particularly amenable toward promoting a kinship among women; the affinity understood through familial experience readily qualified as a camaraderie among women. E. Marie Evelyn Green Herlein liked to experiment with different patterns and colors. She designed and pieced quilts by herself, but her mother helped with their assembling and quilting early in her life, and later friends helped.[28] The nature of such sisterhood was evidenced in the gift, inheritance, or purchase of a quilt. Yet, emotional attachments often are demonstrated indirectly, as in a quilt made for and/or given to a friend's child. Eight-year-old Avis Bearse (Fig. 88) received a quilt embroidered with farm animals (Fig.

FIG. 87. This silver gelatin print captured millworkers in front of the Centerville Manufacturing Company in Centerville (Hopkinton), Rhode Island, in the 1860s. About half the factory workers are women. They are dressed in the fashions of their day—including hoop skirts and voluminous bishop sleeves, neither of which would have been safe to wear when working near textile machinery. Rhode Island Historical Society.

*Down by the Old Mill Stream*

FIG. 88. The quilt in Figure 89 was made for Avis Bearse Simmons (pictured here as a child, ca. 1930) by Marion Corp, her grandmother's friend in Providence, who had no children of her own. RIQDP Archives.

89) when she was bedridden for a year due to illness. Marion Corp, her grandmother's friend and the quiltmaker, had no children of her own and made the quilt especially for her.[29] As with family quilts, representative fabrics accentuated the degree of an owner's affection toward a friend. The quilt became an accessible substitute for the friendship, a reminder of a close relationship, often no longer possible. For instance, another owner purchased a Chinese Lantern quilt when her friend Charlotte Haupt, the quiltmaker, sold her home to enter the Methodist Retirement Center in East Providence. The fabrics in the quilt come from the quiltmaker's dresses and aprons. The quilt's new owner continued to visit her in the nursing home.[30]

*Essays on Culture, Technology, & Quilts*     177

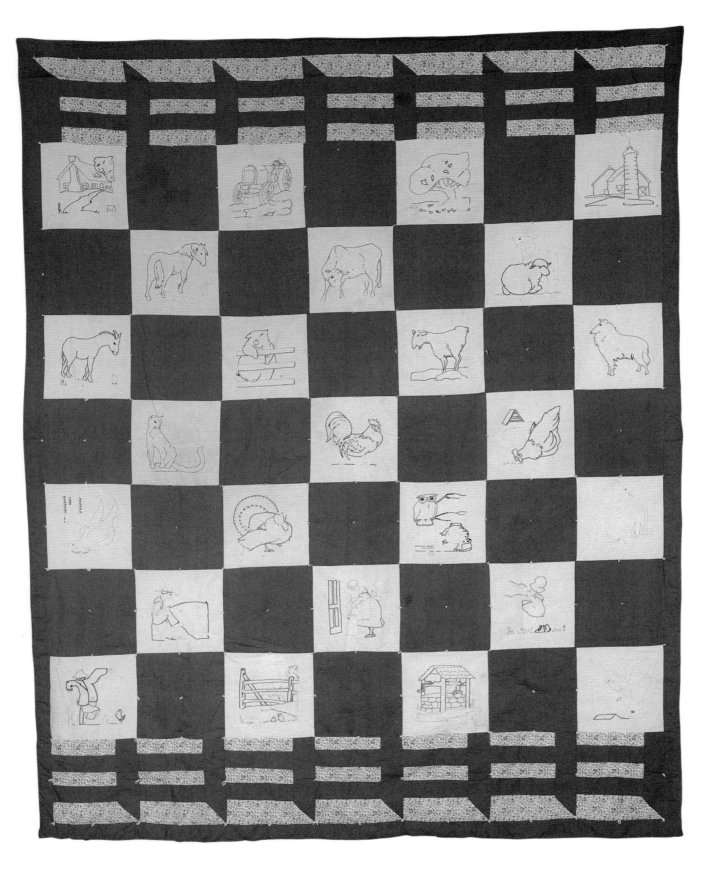

Neighboring women used their shared interest in quiltmaking to enhance close relationships within the community. In the early twentieth century, Lillian M. Champlin and her mother, Catherine R. Chace, met with other Block Island women for all-day quilting bees. The quilts were tied in the dining room of their West Hillcrest house.[31] The informal gatherings afforded women opportunities to expand their interests beyond quiltmaking. Through mutual support and cooperation, they adapted new skills to their respective individual styles.

During their gatherings in the late 1800s, another group of friends, who lived on the hill in Kingston, applied china painting and embroidery to decorate an 1890–91 crazy quilt (Fig. 90) with floral motifs.[32] Each block was made by a different woman. The appreciation of these women toward each other was reflected in a saying on one block: "A stitch for a Friend."[33] One of the women, Mary Ida Slocum Champlin (Fig. 91), assembled the blocks and preserved the top. A Cumberland quilt contains signatures and dates with the verse, "It is said that friendship is the medicine for all misfortunes should they assail the remedy be near at hand."[34]

Quiltmaking has allowed women to call upon their experiences of family and community to distinguish a female identity whose essence was founded on values of continuity and unity. This is especially true in Rhode Island where some families have resided in the state since early colonial times and, in a few cases, have lived at the same homestead. Family legacies have become intimately intertwined with community and state history. For the immigrant, families adapted traditions to the new conditions. In both instances, family integrity depended on achieving acceptance within the community and integration into its economic life. Sometimes only extant quilts record these connections: a quilt made jointly by women of a church to raise funds or the use of fabric seconds from the mill where the quiltmaker or her husband was employed. The diverse relationships the quiltmaker formed through her actions within the community extended the image of the woman as nurturer and caregiver into the public domain.

The presence of fund-raising and friendship quilts in Rhode Island collections documents the active involvement of quiltmakers in social clubs, churches, and granges. Through their collective efforts, women contributed to the vitality of their communities. At the same time, many women gained recognition for leadership or other accomplishments. In 1882, the ladies' group of the Rocky Hill Social Club in East Greenwich recorded one thousand and thirty names on their fund-raising Sawtooth quilt (Fig. 92). Each name represented a monetary value of ten cents, contributed by friends and neighbors toward funding a new Baptist chapel. An account of this project and thanks to contributors were documented on the quilt's border: "We thank, in behalf of the members of the social, all who have aided us in

FIG. 89. (*Opposite*) Farm Animals quilt, 1933. Cotton top and back, blanket filler, cotton embroidery, 76 x 60 in. Machine-pieced and tied. Made by Marion Corp. Collection of Avis Bearse Simmons. RIQDP #369.

Eight-year-old Avis Bearse of Warwick received this quilt during an illness. Early children's quilts were scaled-down versions of adult quilts, but by the 1880s quilt designs with special appeal to children appeared in periodicals. Motifs such as animals, people, and toys were embroidered or appliquéd on quilt tops. Sunbonnet Sue and Overall Sam were favorite patterns for children's quilts between 1925 and 1950.

FIG. 90. (*Opposite*) Crazy quilt top, 1890–91. Silk satin, velvet, plaid, damask, and brocade fabrics, silk embroidery, painted motifs, 58½ x 43 in. Made by friends from Kingston, Rhode Island. Collection of Mrs. Ralph T. Vale. RIQDP #188.

Twelve friends made this quilt top, each reportedly contributing a different block. One block contains the words "A Stitch for a Friend." A velvet-covered album with photographs of many of the friends survives.

FIG. 91. Mary Ida Slocum Champlin feeding chickens at her home on North Road in Kingston, ca. 1905. Mary was one of the friends who contributed blocks to the quilt top in Figure 90. She saved the top but never finished it. RIQDP Archives.

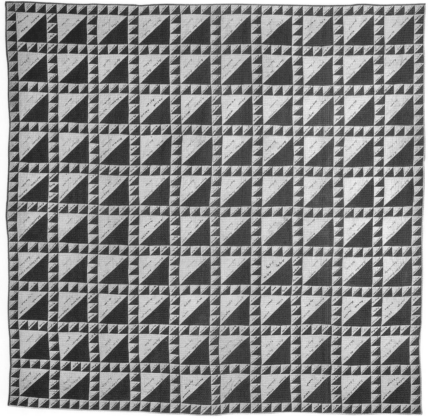

FIG. 92. Sawtooth quilt, 1882. Cotton top and back, 88½ x 87 in. Hand-pieced and hand-quilted in outline pattern, 8 stitches per inch. Made by the Ladies of the Rocky Hill Social Club. William L. Henry family collection. RIQDP #60.

The ladies of the Rocky Hill Social Club made this quilt as a fundraiser for construction of a Baptist chapel in East Greenwich. They had been holding Sunday school in the district schoolhouse. A total of 1030 Rhode Island names appear on the quilt, each representing a contribution of ten cents. The quilt was completed on November 1, 1882. The chapel, an unpretentious 30 x 40 ft. structure, was dedicated in October 21, 1883. It was razed in 1958 to make way for the Kent County Freeway.

FIG. 93. (*Opposite*) Album Patch signature quilt, inscribed "Frenchtown Sewing Society, 1874." Cotton top and back, 92½ x 77 in. Hand- and machine-pieced, hand-quilted, 4 stitches per inch. Made by Mary Reynolds Greene Fry (1817–1897) and friends. Private collection. RIQDP #47.

This quilt, said to be a church fund-raiser, commemorates the Frenchtown Sewing Society founded May 28, 1874. Mary Reynolds Greene Fry (who signed her name "Mrs. Joseph Fry") was treasurer from 1875 to 1878. Frenchtown, a hamlet in East Greenwich, was settled in the seventeenth century by French Huguenots, many of whom had experience working in the French silk industry.

this our first attempt at raising money. Mrs. William Bennett, Mrs. Henry Wood, and Mrs. L. F. Shippee, the committee on the quilt."[35] Evelyn Brayton won another Sawtooth quilt for selling the most squares and thus winning the most votes. The quilt was a fund-raiser for the Oaklawn Baptist Church.[36] Similarly, women used their quiltmaking to show appreciation to church leaders. Reverend Spoffard Dodge Jewett and his wife Abigail brought with them a friendship quilt made by the women in their West Chester, Connecticut, congregation when they transferred to Providence in 1848.[37]

Family memories offer further insight on women's involvement in the civic affairs of the United States. Rhode Island quilt owners and museum registrars alike noted connections between the quiltmaker and the first settlers, town founders, civic leaders, and soldiers in the Civil War. To a limited extent, women's participation in religious and civic affairs spawned political involvement. The Album Patch signature quilt (Fig. 93), made by the Frenchtown Sewing Society in the late nineteenth century, was one of many used in church fund-raising. Recognition given to officers of the Society included treasurer Mary Reynolds Greene Fry (Fig. 94), grandmother of Marion Fry.[38] The legacy of community involvement was passed from grandmother to grandchild. Marion Fry served as Town Council president of East Greenwich and of the East Greenwich Preservation Society and was a proud owner of many family quilts.[39]

While the quiltmakers, like many of us, principally were observers of history, they nevertheless experienced historical events and recorded their observations. This participation was reflected directly or indirectly in women's quiltmaking. The crazy quilt made by Ruth Spooner Grant, for instance, commemorated the owner's great-great-grandmother's walk from Swansea, Massachusetts, to Providence, Rhode Island, when she was fifteen, to see Abraham Lincoln.[40] More directly, Rhode Island quilts demonstrated a family's continued allegiance to the nation and its achievements. Several quiltmakers incorporated ribbons printed with dates, platitudes, and references to revolutionary leaders (e.g., "1776 . . . 1876 . . . George Washington . . . The Father of Our Country . . . The First in Peace . . . The First in War . . . The First in the Hearts of his Countrymen")[41] in their commemoration of the United States centennial. Some quiltmakers incorporated commemorative fabrics into their quilts. For others, patriotism was an expression of more individual experiences. Alice Barrett's medallion quilt (Fig. 95) featured flags from different countries, obtained as premiums from tobacco cans. The quiltmaker (Fig. 96) and her husband James, a textile worker in England, emigrated to the United States and settled in Johnston. The flag of her adopted country occupies the most prominent position in the quilt.[42] Just as family quilts signaled the owners' connectedness to family heritage, they established the family as participants in American history.

FIG. 94. Mary Reynolds Greene Fry (and unknown child) is seated in front of her East Greenwich home. The original home burned down in 1793; this house was built in 1794–95. RIQDP Archives.

To date, the Rhode Island Quilt Documentation Project has provided brief glimpses of women's lives in Rhode Island. Nonetheless, from these memories we gain insights about the values that have structured quilt-makers' views of family and community. Quiltmaking promotes the contiguity between family and women. First, quiltmaking celebrates family heritage and women's culture. It preserves a sense of unity in family life, which is continually subject to change due to births, marriages, and deaths, by highlighting the meaning of women's actions and thus underscoring the timelessness of women's experience. Second, quiltmaking helps women sort out the ambiguities of female identity by defining a community within which women could negotiate an individuality. Quilts traditionally have concerned

FIG. 95. (*Page 185*) Medallion Flag quilt, ca. 1912. Cotton, 69 x 36 in. Hand- and machine-pieced, cotton feather-stitch embroidery. Made by Alice Henshell Barrett (1864–1945). Collection of June Barrett Langevin. RIQDP #233.

Patriotism has been a frequent theme in quiltmaking since the early nineteenth century. Both the 1876 Centennial and the 1976 Bicentennial were marked by the popularity of patriotic quilts. Commemorative fabrics or patterns often included eagles or flag imagery. This medallion-style quilt contains flags from many countries. Fabrics originally were premiums in tobacco cans. The U.S. flags in this quilt contain forty-eight stars, which dates it to 1912, when Arizona became the forty-eighth state in the Union.

FIG. 96. Alice Henshell Barrett (1864–1945) and her husband, James, a textile worker in England, emigrated to the United States and settled in Johnston, Rhode Island, where they raised six children. In this photograph Alice holds her grandson, Robert Ronne. RIQDP Archives.

women and facilitated a woman's acceptance by other women, initially at her birth into her father's family and later through marriage to her husband. They bring recognition to the women who created traditions, and comment on the circumstances that shaped their lives. They mark the importance of a sisterhood that bridges identity across family, community, and nation.

For contemporary owners, a quilt is a powerful metaphor for characterizing social connectedness as an emotionally based kinship between individuals within family and community. An owner's memories concern the quiltmaker's connectedness to a woman's heritage through affiliations with family and community. At the same time, the memories pertain to the owner's connectedness to a family and community history through affiliation

with the quiltmaker. This history, however, is unlike that documented in history books. Rather it is a history shaped by women largely within the domestic setting. Owners' sentiments toward their quilts give a unique perspective on the role of women in preserving the unity and continuity of social life.

*Notes*

1. *Oxford English Dictionary*, 2nd ed., s.v. "connectedness."

2. See Patricia Mainardi, *Quilts: The Great American Art* (San Pedro, Calif.: Miles, 1978); Pat Ferrero, Elaine Hedges, and Julie Silber, *Hearts and Hands: The Influence of Women and Quilts on American Society* (San Francisco: Quilt Digest, 1987); Elaine Showalter, "Common Threads," in *Sister's Choice: Tradition and Change in American Women's Writing* (Oxford: Oxford University Press, 1991), 145–75; Cheryl B. Torsney and Judy Elsley, eds., *Quilt Culture: Tracing the Pattern* (Columbia: University of Missouri Press, 1994); John Forrest and Deborah Blincoe, *The Natural History of the Traditional Quilt* (Austin: University of Texas Press, 1995).

3. Catherine A. Cerny, "Cultural Foundations of Aesthetic Appreciation: Use of Trope in Structuring Quiltmaking Sentiment," in *Aesthetics of Textiles and Clothing: Advancing Multi-Disciplinary Perspectives*, Marilyn R. DeLong and Ann Marie Fiori, eds. (Monument, Colo.: International Textile and Apparel Association, 1994), 152–62.

4. See Virginia Gunn, "From Myth to Maturity: The Evolution of Quilt Scholarship," in *Uncoverings 1992*, Laurel Horton, ed. (San Francisco: American Quilt Study Group, 1993), 192–205. As an example of this scholarship, see Laurel Horton, ed., *Quiltmaking in America: Beyond the Myths* (Nashville, Tenn.: Rutledge Hill Press, 1994); Jacqueline Marx Atkins, *Shared Threads: Quilting Together—Past and Present* (New York: Viking Studio Books, 1994).

5. See Ricky Clark, "The Needlework of an American Lady: Social History in Quilts," in *In the Heart of Pennsylvania: Symposium Papers*, Jeannette Lasansky, ed. (Lewisburg, Pa.: Oral Traditions Project of the Union County Historical Society, 1986), 65–75; Ruth Haislip Roverson, ed., *North Carolina Quilts* (Chapel Hill: University of North Carolina Press), 1988; Ricky Clark, "Ruth Finley and the Colonial Revival Era," in *Uncoverings 1995*, Virginia Gunn, ed. (San Francisco: American Quilt Study Group, 1995), 33–65.

6. See Ricky Clark, "Sisters, Saints, and Sewing Societies: Quiltmakers' Communities," in *Quilts in Community: Ohio's Traditions*, Ricky Clark, George W. Knepper, and Ellice Ronsheim, eds. (Nashville, Tenn.: Rutledge Hill Press, 1991), 118–56.

7. RIQDP Archives, University of Rhode Island Library Special Collections, Kingston, R.I., RIQDP #4.

8. RIQDP Archives, #3.

9. RIQDP Archives, #3.

10. RIQDP Archives, #3 and #4.

11. RIQDP Archives, #494.

12. Kinship refers to relationships among members of a family, within and across generations. The sentiments associated with kinship can be extended to characterize the feelings one has for a community and nation. For example, when a person feels kinship with a neighbor, she feels a "close connection" or a connectedness with the person.

13. RIQDP Archives, #59.

14. RIQDP Archives, #607.

15. RIQDP Archives, #57.

16. RIQDP Archives, #324.

17. RIQDP Archives, #22.

18. RIQDP Archives, #449.

19. RIQDP Archives, #175.

20. RIQDP Archives, #280.

21. Cloth label on back of quilt.

22. RIQDP Archives, #203.

23. RIQDP Archives, #23.

24. RIQDP Archives, #228.

25. RIQDP Archives, #231.

26. RIQDP Archives, #46.

27. RIQDP Archives, #435.

28. RIQDP Archives, #450 and #451.

29. RIQDP Archives, #369.

30. RIQDP Archives, #283.

31. RIQDP Archives, #575.

32. RIQDP Archives, #188.

33. RIQDP Archives, #188.

34. RIQDP Archives, #98.

35. RIQDP Archives, #60.

36. RIQDP Archives, #547.

37. Documentation from accession records of 1962.29.1, Rhode Island Historical Society, Providence, R.I. (RIQDP #514).

38. RIQDP Archives, #47.

39. "Marion L. Fry, East Greenwich historian, former Town Council president, dies at 82," *The Providence Journal-Bulletin*, January 21, 1995, A6.

40. RIQDP Archives, #5.

41. RIQDP Archives, #671.

42. RIQDP Archives, #233.

# Part Two

*Stitches through Time:*
*A Selection*
*of Rhode Island Quilts*

# Toile Quilt

KATHLEEN A. MCAREAVEY

ACCORDING TO FAMILY TRADITION, THIS SIMPLE ONE-PATCH QUILT was made from fabrics once used as bed hangings. The copper-plate prints, known as toiles, are typical of fabrics manufactured in England and France from 1760 to 1810. These were popular bed and window hangings.

Examination of this quilt revealed much more than was at first apparent. Many squares had been repaired by overlays of new fabric. Originally the quilt was pieced with square blocks of three different cotton prints: (1) a brown copper-plate print, (2) a red copper-plate print, and (3) a lightweight floral printed in the indienne style that is no longer visible. When the delicate indienne wore out, a second red toile of the same design as the first was applied on top of the indienne pieces and those sections overquilted. As is typical of early quilts, the middle layer was a wool homespun blanket, and the backing was pieced homespun linen.

Enlarged photographs of the toile blocks, put together like a jigsaw puzzle, provided enough of an image to identify it as a copper-plate print from Nantes, France, ca. 1788–1793.[1]

*Note*

1. Henri Clouzot, *Painted and Printed Fabrics, The History of the Manufactory at Jouy and Other Ateliers in France, 1760–1815* (New York: The Metropolitan Museum of Art, 1927), Plate 68.

FIG. 97. One-Patch quilt, late eighteenth century. Cotton top, linen back, wool batting, 95½ x 91½ in. Hand-quilted in zig-zag pattern, 7 stitches per inch. Descended in the Spink family, Warwick, Rhode Island. URI Historic Textile and Costume Collection (91.09.01). RIQDP #10.

FIG. 98. Photocopied photographs of toile blocks reassembled to show print. RIQDP Archives.

*Down by the Old Mill Stream*

FIG. 99. Copper-plate print from Nantes, France ca. 1788–93. The Metropolitan Museum of Art, Gift of William Sloane Coffin, 1926. (26.265.69).

*A North American Dyestuff*

# Quercitron

JEFFREY A. BUTTERWORTH

FIG. 100. (*Opposite*) Diamond in a Square quilt, 1820s. Cotton top and back, 81 x 67¼ in. Hand-pieced and hand-quilted, 7 stitches per inch. Maker unknown; possibly made in Seekonk or Rehoboth, Massachusetts. Collection of Elizabeth Ramsden. RIQDP #418.

THE QUILT IS PIECED WITH TWO TYPES OF BLOCK-PRINTED FABRICS AND a plain white cotton. The printed fabrics are probably English furnishing textiles, originally glazed, from the first quarter of the nineteenth century. The backing material is a block-printed, floral calico.

The colorful fabrics in this quilt represent the art of the printer. The search for bright and permanent textile dyes has long been a concern for textile colorists. In 1795, Dr. Edward Bancroft, born in Westfield, Massachusetts, in 1744, commercialized quercitron, a fast yellow color derived from the bark of the American oak tree. Quercitron was used with various mordants to make bright, permanent yellows, browns, and greens, when overdyed or overprinted on indigo. The colors in this quilt are typical quercitron colors. Dr. Bancroft tightly controlled quercitron technology until around 1810.[1] He was also a double agent during the Revolutionary War, working for both Benjamin Franklin and England.[2]

This quilt was given to Lydia Belle Miller Kay of East Providence prior to the 1930s by someone whose identity is now lost. It possibly was made in the nearby Massachusetts towns of Seekonk or Rehoboth where Belle and her sister took care of elderly ladies who sometimes gave them gifts.

*Notes*

1. James G. Wilson and John Fiske, eds., *Appleton's Cyclopaedia of American Biography* (New York: D. Appleton & Co., 1887), 1:154.

2. Charles Van Doren, *Webster's American Biographies* (Springfield, Mass.: G. & C. Merriam Co., 1974), 60. Bancroft is further discussed in Martin Bide's essay, "Secrets of the Printer's Palette," in this volume.

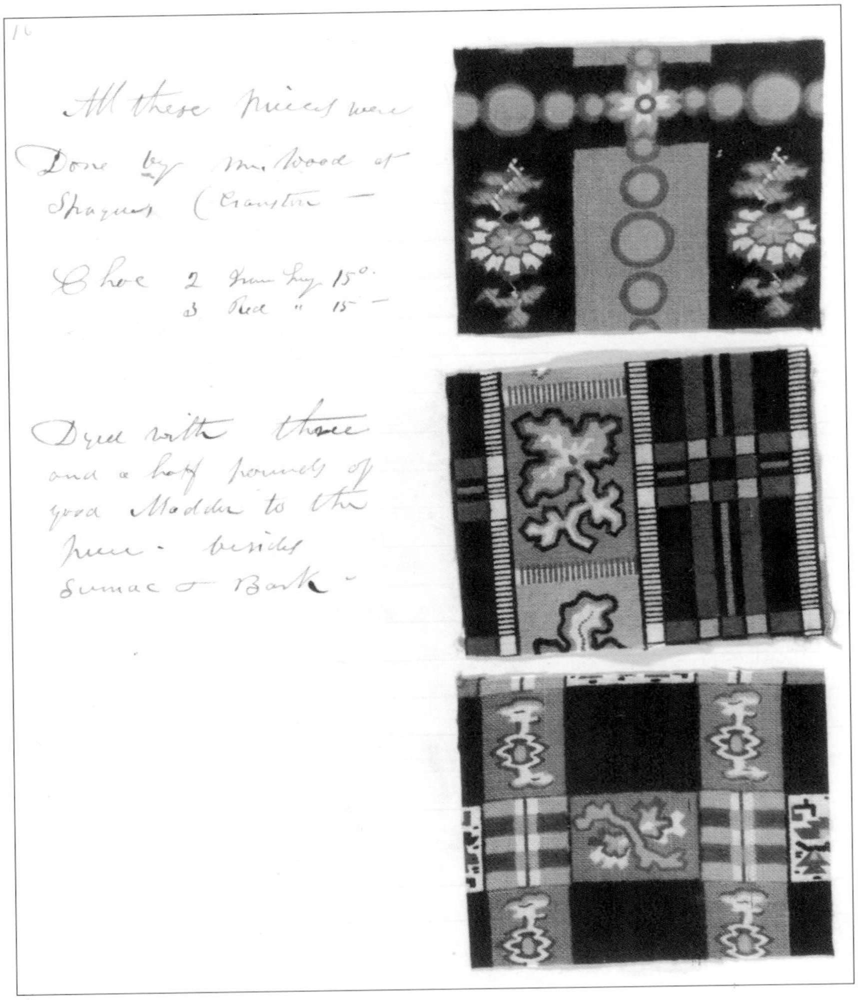

FIG. 101. These madder-style prints from Samuel Dunster's *Print Dyes*, vol. 6 (Clay Print Works, Johnston, R.I.), the work of a printer at Sprague's in Cranston, used madder, sumac, and bark. Bark always meant quercitron. Rhode Island Historical Society Library.

# A Petticoat Quilt

LINDA WELTERS

THE CENTRAL PART OF THIS QUILT IS AN EIGHTEENTH-CENTURY PETTI-
coat that is much older than the quilt itself. Quilted petticoats, worn under
open-fronted gowns, were popular in both England and America from 1710
to 1780.[1] By the end of the eighteenth century, fashions had changed, and
such petticoats were either packed away in trunks or recycled into bed quilts.
Two other petticoat quilts are in the collections of the Rhode Island Historical Society; one of them belonged to the wealthy John Brown family of
Providence.[2]

Family tradition says that this was the wedding quilt of Almira Hall Sowle.
Almira Hall married George W. Sowle (1800–1854) at the First Baptist Church
in Newport on December 26, 1827. The Reverend Michael Eddy officiated.
George Sowle was a whaler, sailing with Captain Whitten on the ship *John
Howland* out of New Bedford, Massachusetts. George died in 1854 in Islay,
Peru. Almira died in 1888 and was buried in the Portsmouth Friends Cem-
etery.

Almira came from a well-to-do Quaker family whose ancestors arrived
in New England on the *Mayflower* and were among the first settlers of Portsmouth, Rhode Island. Almira's father, Parker Hall, was a judge in Portsmouth. Her mother, Hannah Thomas Hall, was accomplished with both
needle and pen as evidenced by the diary she kept from 1859 to 1861. After
Hannah's husband died, she moved from household to household for extended visits with her children. Her diary mentions frequent visits to Almira in New Bedford.

Perhaps it was Hannah who picked apart the sumptuous petticoat and
made it into a quilt for Almira and George's four-poster bed. The original
petticoat probably belonged to Hannah's mother as it would already have

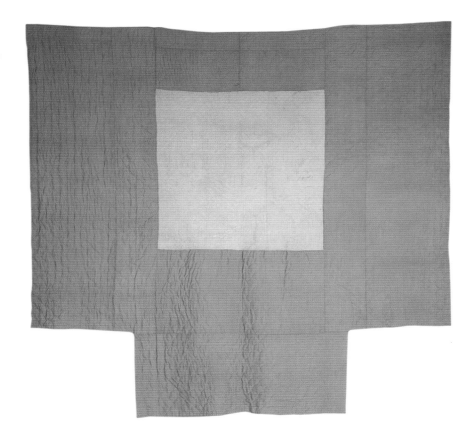

FIG. 102. Petticoat quilt, 1827. Silk, wool border and backing, cotton batting, 100 x 93 in. Hand-quilted, 13–29 stitches per inch in petticoat and 7 stitches per inch in border. Made for Almira Hall Sowle (1810–1888), Portsmouth, Rhode Island. Private collection. RIQDP #92.

FIG. 103. (*Opposite*) Detail of the reverse side of an eighteenth-century petticoat made into a wedding quilt. RIQDP Archives.

been out of fashion by the time Hannah was a young woman in 1800. Quakers like the Halls of Portsmouth wore gowns of plain, solid-colored fabrics; calico was seen as indicating pride and worldliness.[3]

The original petticoat is pale blue green silk. The newer border is a dark blue green worsted wool. The backing of the petticoat is navy blue worsted wool and shows the design motifs more clearly than the front. The quilter(s) used both running stitches and back stitches. The back stitch makes the design stand out in relief although it required more quilting thread. The newer part of the quilt is stitched in a clamshell pattern with fewer stitches per inch than those found in the silk petticoat.

The designs consist of motifs familiar in such petticoats: birds, flowers, trees, deer, lions and a mythical being. This quilt is remarkable for its incorporation of unusual motifs: confronted squirrels, an owl, a horse-drawn chariot, and a figure seated on a throne. Those who have studied such petticoats surmise that the design inspiration might have come from printed sources, earlier textiles, and metal work.[4] Some of the motifs in this quilt have origins in Middle Eastern art, particularly Sassanian silks and Assyrian bas reliefs.

1. Tandy Hersh, "18th Century Quilted Silk Petticoats Worn in America," in *Uncoverings 1984*, Sally Garoutte, ed. (San Francisco: American Quilt Study Group, 1985), 84–85. One of the earliest New England examples is a rose-colored quilted silk petticoat worn by Mary Leverett at her wedding to Major John Dennison of Ipswich, Massachusetts, in 1719 (Essex Institute 108, 486).

2. RIQDP #505 (RIHS #1982.86.1) and #509 (RIHS #1990.36.42). Both petticoats have been assigned mid-eighteenth-century dates. RIQDP #505 is made of pink silk; the provenance is unknown. RIQDP #509 is rose-colored calimanco and belonged to the John Brown family.

3. The Quaker attitude toward fashionable calico is expressed in the diary of young Hannah Fisher of Newport. As a sixteen-year-old, she had succumbed to the lure of a calico gown only to suffer from a guilty conscience afterward. Later, after attending a meeting at North Meeting House on Nantucket, she wrote, "Recommending the example of our blessed Lord and Saviour, that we might obey, and follow *Him* in meekness, in regard to apparel, furniture, & conduct—particularly advising against *silk gowns* and *spotted* calicos." (Diaries of Hannah Fisher, July 3, 1793, Newport Historical Society, Newport, R.I.)

4. Hersh, "18th Century Quilted Silk Petticoats Worn in America," 90.

# An African American Story

LINDA WELTERS

THIS QUILT DESCENDED THROUGH SEVERAL AFRICAN AMERICAN FAMILIES. The current owner inherited it from her godmother, Babe McCastor. The quilt probably was acquired by Babe's father, Samuel Brown (1851–1932).

Samuel was born in Virginia in 1851. While still a boy after the Civil War, he came north. He tried to get work at American Thread in Willimantic, Connecticut, but the company did not hire blacks.[1] He moved on to Newport, where he was taken in by a free black couple, Peter and Sarah Wheelbanks. In Newport city directories, Peter's occupation is listed as "steward."[2] Sam eventually established an express business, transporting people and their belongings around Newport. He was a familiar figure in Washington Square where he had a stand. Sam belonged to the Mt. Zion African Methodist Episcopal Church and served on its Board. In 1878 Sam married Mary Shepherd (1849–1929) of Philadelphia. They had one natural child, a daughter named Julia, and adopted Mary's orphaned nieces, Babe and Mary.[3]

The pattern and fabrics date this quilt to the 1830s.[4] The Sunflower pattern is similar to Mariner's Compass and Sunburst. Such radial patterns appeared in the early nineteenth century.[5] This quilt incorporates a variety of fabrics from the 1820s and 1830s plus a bird print possibly recycled from old bed hangings. Peacocks and game birds, popular motifs for furnishing textiles in the first quarter of the nineteenth century, often were copied from earlier English and French designs. This bird design was first printed by George Swainson at Bannister Hall, England, in 1815.[6] The University of Rhode Island's Historic Textile and Costume Collection has two examples of the fabric in a different colorway. Many other examples survive, attesting to the popularity of this design.[7]

How Sam Brown acquired this quilt is a mystery. His descendants recall that customers sometimes gave him things they no longer needed; perhaps this quilt was one of them. Another possibility is that the quilt came with the house on Johnson Court that Sam inherited from the Wheelbanks after Sarah died.[8]

1. The textile industry in New England discriminated against African Americans in their hiring practices. An article describing the typical early textile factory in New England claimed that the workers, of excellent character, "will not associate with colored persons or mere servants." "Manufactures," *New England Farmer*, December 8, 1826, 158.

2. Newport City Directories, 1867, 1874–75. Peter is identified as "colored." In the later directory, a Samuel Wheelbanks is listed as a laborer (202). Probably Samuel Wheelbanks was actually Samuel Brown who used the name of his adopted family until he became an adult.

3. Information courtesy of Arline Seaforth, Windham, Conn.; compiled from the Brown Family Bible and copies of marriage records, death certificates, and obituaries.

4. A similar quilt from Rhinebeck, N.Y., ca. 1835, is illustrated in *Folk Art* (Summer 1994), 3. A signed and dated quilt, "S. S. Larkin 1833," also of this pattern is shown in Lynn Z. Bassett and Jack Larkin, *Northern Comfort: New England's Early Quilts, 1780–1850* (Nashville: Rutledge Hill Press, 1998), 60.

5. Barbara Brackman, "A Chronological Index to Pieced Quilt Patterns, 1775–1825," in *Uncoverings 1983*, Sally Garoutte, ed. (San Francisco: American Quilt Study Group, 1984): 113.

6. Peter Floud, "The Development of Design in English Printed Textiles," *Ciba Review*, no. 1 (1961): 18.

7. Mary Schoeser and Celia Rufey, *English and American Textiles from 1790 to the Present* (New York: Thames and Hudson, 1989), 40.

8. Sarah is listed as the owner of property at Johnson Court in the 1883 Newport plat map. Names of people to whom she rented rooms are given.

*Notes*

FIG. 104. (*Opposite*) Sunflower, 1830s. Cylinder-printed and block-printed cotton top, cotton back and batting, 79½ x 86 in. Hand-pieced and hand-quilted, 6–7 stitches per inch. Maker unknown. Collection of Arline Seaforth. RIQDP #693.

FIG. 105. (*Above*) Fragment of block-printed furnishing fabric, cotton. Bannister Hall, England, 1815–16. Hershey Estate of Providence and Newport. URI Historic Textile and Costume Collection (1952.99.165).

# Quilts for Four-Poster Beds

SUSAN HANDY KIRBY

FOUR-POSTER BEDS, POPULAR FROM 1700 TO 1850, SPANNED THE CHIP-pendale, Hepplewhite, and Sheraton periods. In Rhode Island, whole-cloth and pieced quilts made before 1850 often had cut-out corners to fit four-poster beds. These quilts disappeared around 1870 after the old-fashioned beds were put in the attic in favor of Jenny Lind and Eastlake styles. They reappeared during the 1920s and 1930s with the Colonial Revival. RIQDP documented twenty-four quilts with cut-out corners, including one for a doll's four-poster bed.

In the seventeenth and eighteenth centuries, a "bed" was composed of a bedstead and furnishings and was considered to be the most valuable house-hold possession. Bed furnishings included mattresses, bed hangings, bed covers, pillows, bolsters, bed ruggs, and perhaps even mosquito netting. The furnishings were often worth more than the bedstead itself.

Prior to the War for Independence, Rhode Island was an influential trade and style center for southern New England. Much of this influence emanat-ed from Newport, an important harbor for international trade during the colonial period. Newport furniture makers, particularly the Townsends and Goddards, produced distinctive styles still recognized today for their sim-plicity and beauty. By 1790 the furniture industry moved to the growing city of Providence.

During the American Empire period (1820–1850), all previous styles were commingled with new styles. The Empire period featured spiral reeding and rope turnings; rings, balls and cones; acanthus leaves and pineapples; high, carved headboards; carved foot boards or blanket rolls; and expansive veneered surfaces with cyma curves. All of these motifs evolved from tra-ditional styles. Woods included mahogany, maple, cherry, birch, and pine. Beds were made in several post heights including high, half-high, and low,

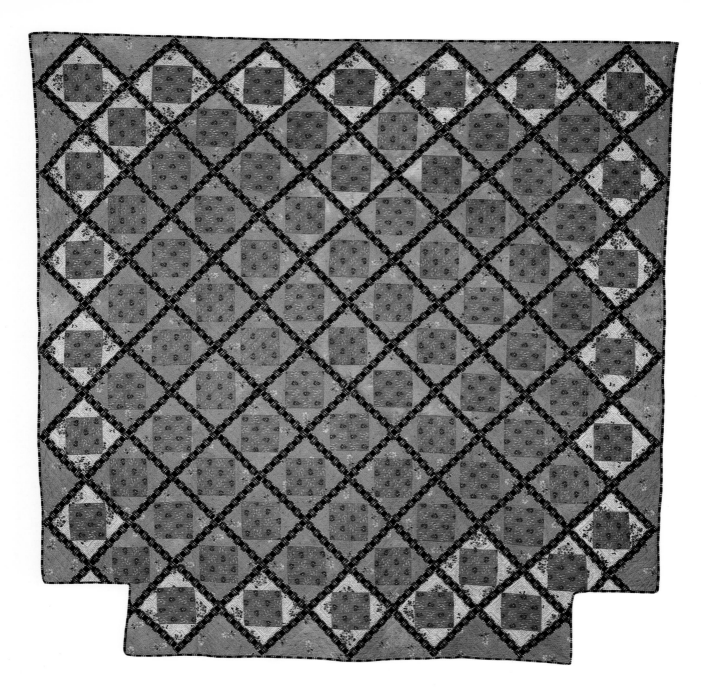

with low posts being the most popular. Between 1820 and 1840, low post beds of cherry or maple graced many a New England home. Four-poster beds gradually lost favor as architects and decorators placed greater emphasis on open space with fewer and lighter furnishings. Simultaneously, bedrooms began to be heated, eliminating the need for bed hangings.

This quilt was donated to the Cranston Historical Society by the late Gladys Brown Brayton, former Curator of the Historical Society, and wife of Robert Brayton. This Dutch Tile quilt was made by "Great Aunt Mary

FIG. 106. Dutch Tile quilt, 1835–45. Cotton top, back, and batting, 93 x 90 in. Hand-pieced and hand-quilted, 7 stitches per inch. Made by Mary Lewis. Cranston Historical Society. RIQDP #539.

FIG. 107. Low-post bedstead, 1820–30.
From Luke Vincent Lockwood, *Colonial Furniture in America* (New York: Charles Scribner's Sons, 1902), 319. RIQDP Archives.

Lewis," Robert Brayton's grandmother's eldest sister. The Brayton family name is a well-established one within the early settlements of Rhode Island, and the original Brayton homestead can still be found on Old Spring Road in Cranston.

# The Ship Quilt

LINDA EPPICH

MARY E. JUDKINS WAS BORN IN DEERFIELD, NEW HAMPSHIRE, IN 1818; Judkins family descendants are still prominent in that area. Mary left Deerfield in 1844 and moved to Providence, Rhode Island, quite an undertaking for a young, single woman. She may have been betrothed and making this move to be wed. She took with her signed muslin squares from friends and relatives, all of which contained well-wishes for her in a new city and new way of life. She was apparently very close to her sisters Celia and Eliza; both are mentioned in squares of her friendship quilt. Typical of remembrances on the quilt are:

> Remember me
> when far away
> > > Your Cousin
> > > S. E. Pulsifor
> > > > Aged 10
> > > Deerfield 1844

> > > Written by C. T. Stowell
> Will you my friend when far away
> Recall the hour you spent with me
> And when at evening far you stray
> Remember one that thinks of thee.
> Remember this and bear in mind
> A constant friend is hard to find.
> And when you find one just and true
> Forget not the old one for the new.

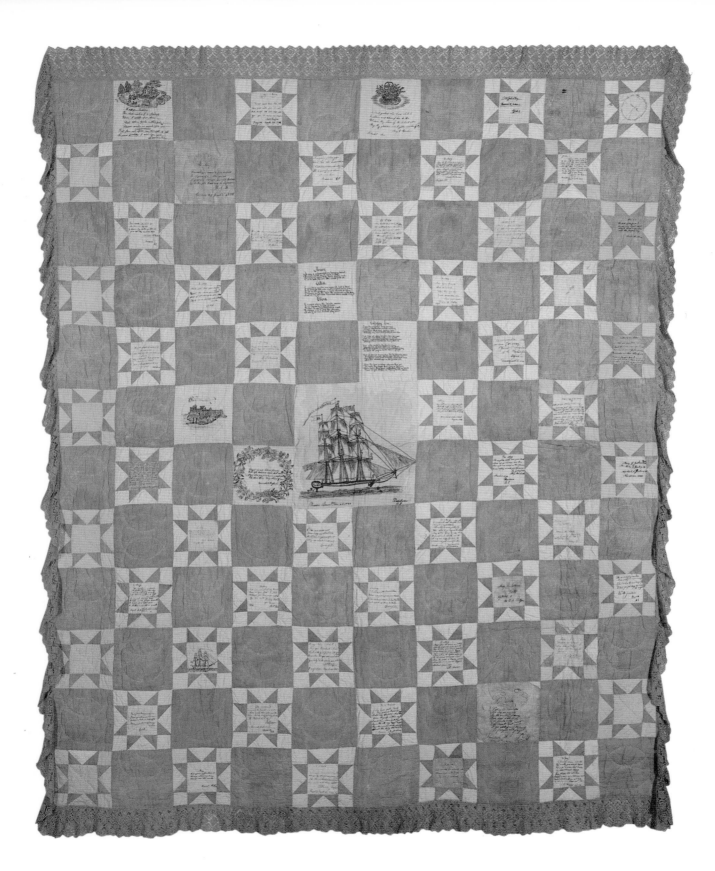

FIG. 108. (*Opposite*) Eight-pointed Star signature quilt, 1844–50. Cotton top, back, and batting, 79 x 63½ in. Hand-pieced and hand-quilted, 5–6 stitches per inch. Made by Mary E. Judkins Rounds (1818–1874). Rhode Island Historical Society (1982.20.1). RIQDP #512.

FIG. 109. Center block of Mary Judkins's quilt depicting the *Laroy*, 1847 (Figure 108). The block is inscribed "Francis Bowen, prov., Dec. 2d, 1847." Rhode Island Historical Society.

Mary probably was forsaking an admirer in New Hampshire, one who professed his "endless constancy" and "love's deep fount o'erflowing." Unfortunately, his lengthy poem is not signed, leaving the reader to wonder who was keeping "my heart still faithful unto thee."

Mary collected more squares with quotations from new friends in Providence and combined them with the New Hampshire ones to make her quilt. She used a simple printed cloth with blue dots on an ecru ground for eight-pointed stars and single blocks. The latest date on a quilt square is 1850, and the quilt probably was assembled after that date. The hand-crocheted fringe indicates a possible date even later than 1850.

In the very center of her quilt, Mary placed a large drawing of a ship named the *Laroy*. That square bears the signature: "Francis Bowen, prov. Dec. 2d, 1847." Francis also writes that he wishes for Mary a life free from sorrow, one of several such mournful wishes in Providence quotations. Research does not show the relationship of Francis to Mary, but possibly he might have known her future husband, James G. Round, as both worked as stonemasons in Providence from 1847 to 1848.

Several other squares from Providence contain quotations and phrases indicating that Mary suffered some terrible loss during the late 1840s:

To Mary

O why is life so short and brief
So full of care and gloom
Why do we go mid tears and grief
Down to the cold dark tomb.

Know thou the cares and woes
Are for wise purpose given
'Tis that the sole by constant
    strife
May train itself for heaven.
    Providence April the 25 1847
        by
    Cordelia C. Rairdon

To Mary

Let us love one another
Not long we may stay
In this world of mourning
Some droop while, this day
The fondest, the purest
The truest that met
Have still found the need
To forgive and forget.

    Providence, RI  JDS
    1848

The mystery of a misfortune suffered during Mary's early years in Providence and any relationship to a sailing vessel remains unsolved.

Mary Judkins and James G. Rounds were married on November 27, 1851, and had three children—Hermione, James F., and Leonidas. James the elder gave up his occupation as a stonemason and opened a grocery store on Friendship Street in Providence. The family's residence was above the store. Mary Judkins Rounds died in 1874, and to date no family diary has been found.

# Patterns in Patches

AUD FJELLBERG ACKERMAN

THE CALICOES IN THIS QUILT ARE TYPICAL OF THOSE PRODUCED BY cylinder printing during the second quarter of the nineteenth century. The triangles are cut from a variety of popular prints with designs such as floral, geometric, fancy machine ground, and Kashmir filling.

Textile designers on both sides of the Atlantic drew inspiration from many sources. In Europe a newly awakened interest in the natural sciences resulted in the publishing of several books that inspired designers. Among them were *The British Herbal* (1770) and Audubon's *Birds of America* (London, 1827–38). In Paris Jean Paul Redouté's *Les Roses* (1830) contributed to a highly naturalistic rendition of floral prints.

The floral stripe used for the strips, cut from an English cylinder-printed chintz, illustrates this botanical influence. The perennials depicted were plants

FIG. 110. Detail, back of whole-cloth quilt, ca. 1835. The fabric is English, ca. 1830. The Metropolitan Museum of Art, Gift of Mr. and Mrs. Harcourt Amory, 1963 (Inst.63.7.10). Photograph by John Bigelow Taylor. Photograph © 1989 The Metropolitan Museum of Art.

FIG. 111. Flying Geese quilt, ca. 1845. Cotton top, back, and batting, 88 x 99½ in. Quilted in crosshatch and chevron patterns, 6 stitches per inch. Probably made by a member of the Saunders family, Westerly, Rhode Island. Private collection. RIQDP #685.

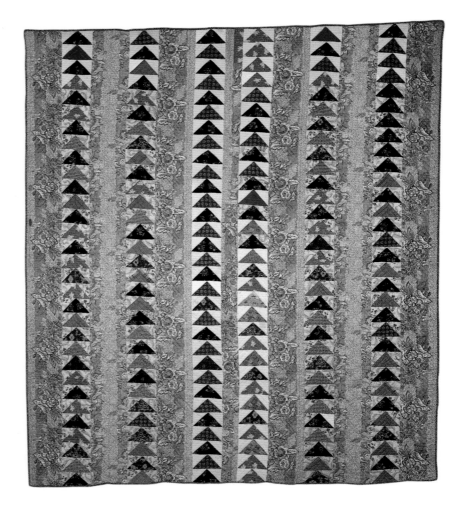

popular in nineteenth-century English gardens: tiger lilies, poppies, roses, geraniums and passionflowers. An identical glazed chintz on the back of a quilt in the Metropolitan Museum of Art in New York has been dated to ca. 1830.[1]

*Note*

1. Amelia Peck, *American Quilts & Coverlets in The Metropolitan Museum of Art* (New York: Metropolitan Museum of Art and Dutton Studio Books, 1990), 113.

# A Signature Quilt from Little Compton

DIANE JOYCE MONTENEGRO

SIGNATURE QUILTS BEGAN TO APPEAR IN THE EARLY 1840S IN THE MID-dle Atlantic states, spreading rapidly south to Virginia, west to Ohio, and north to New England. They were influenced by and related to nineteenth-century sentimental and romantic notions of friendship. The popular *Godey's Lady's Book* presented "friendship" as a theme for verse and music and introduced the autograph album in 1830. Album quilts might have been influenced by a countrywide religious fervor and the large migration west-ward during the 1840s and 1850s, causing separations that often were per-manent.[1]

Improved indelible inks came on the market at the same time, allowing quilters to apply handwritten or stenciled names, secular and religious quo-tations, and intricate drawings to quilts without fear of fading.[2] Most states had instituted primary education programs in which the florid Spencerian handwriting found on many nineteenth-century quilts was part of the cur-riculum.

The apogee of signed quilt production was the 1840s and 1850s, the pe-riod of manufacture for this signed, hand-sewn single-block quilt from Little Compton, Rhode Island. The pattern, Star of the East or Evening Star, is one frequently used for signature quilts. The Little Compton quilt is un-usual in that individual names are located between two points of each of the sixty-one full stars and the twenty-four half stars on the border, rather than within a solid color area inside the star. The writing appears to have been done by two people, except for a unique signature in a third hand.

The eighty-five names, corresponding to the eighty-five stars, include twenty-six surnames of many of the early English settlers of Little Compton.

Genealogical research on over half the names presents a complex pattern of intermarriage among sixth, seventh, and eighth generations of these families. The birth and death dates of the identified names span the latter part of the eighteenth century and the early part of the twentieth. Twenty-eight names belong to the Church family and include all members of one family branch alive between 1847 and 1851.

Research to date has not indicated why, by whom, or for whom the quilt was made. The quilt may have been a record of friendships within the town or produced for a significant event such as an engagement, a marriage, a new minister, a child's birth, or even a death. One of the signatures is that of Arethusa H. Briggs (1821–1886), an active member of the Little Compton United Congregational Church. The Ladies' Sociable Aid Society, founded in 1846, was affiliated with the church.[3]

This quilt never left Little Compton, the place of its manufacture; some unrecorded person(s) cared enough to donate it to the Little Compton Historical Society, reinforcing its importance as a tangible memento of the town's history. The quilt and its eighty-five names remain evidence of family and community life in a small Rhode Island town in the mid–nineteenth century over two hundred years after it was first settled.

*Notes*

1. Jessica Nicoll, *Quilted for Friends: Delaware Valley Signature Quilts, 1840–1855* (Winterthur, Del.: Francis DuPont Winterthur Museum, 1986), 8; Linda Otto Lipsett, *Remember Me: Women & Their Friendship Quilts* (San Francisco: Quilt Digest Press, 1985), 18–19.

2. Margaret T. Ordoñez, "Ink Damage," in *Uncoverings 1992*, Laurel Horton, ed. (San Francisco: American Quilt Study Group, 1993), 149.

3. Benjamin Franklin Wilbour, *Notes on Little Compton*, Carleton G. Brownell, ed. (Providence, R.I.: College Hill Press, 1970), 176–77.

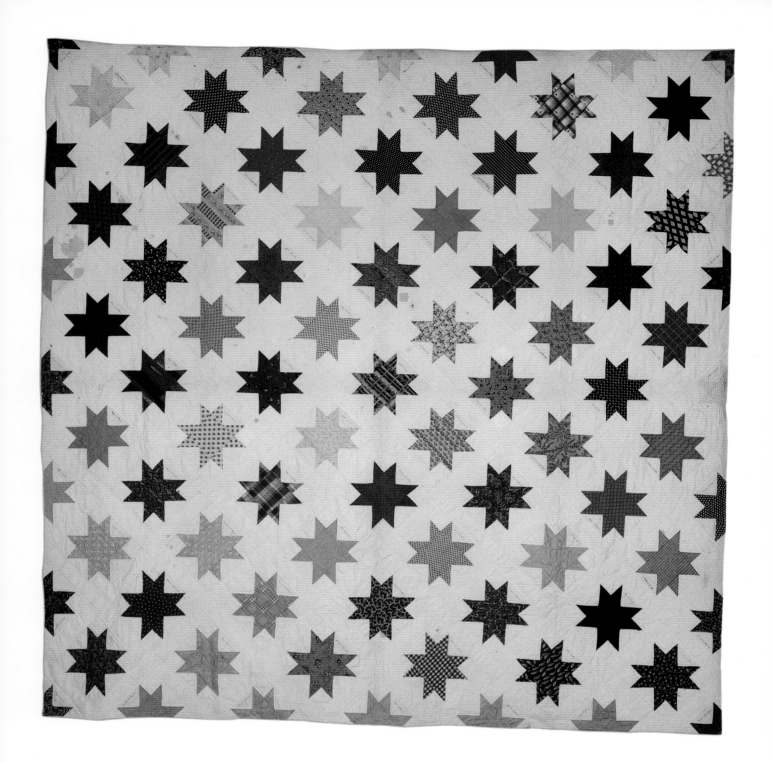

FIG. 113. View at Little Compton
Common, Little Compton, Rhode Island,
1935. Rhode Island Historical Society.

# A Girl's Education

TESS FREDETTE

THE NINE-PATCH, ONE OF THE SIMPLEST QUILTING PATTERNS, HAS BEEN known as the beginner's patch. The piecing of a Nine-Patch taught young girls the essential sewing skills required of nineteenth-century women. They were taught stitching and quilting by completing a "stint," "a specific amount of work to be done each day."[1]

Continuing a European tradition, young girls in America already knew how to stitch by the age of six or seven. Instruction began earlier for Abby Greene of Providence, who was born in 1844. An entry in her mother's diary reveals that Abby, six weeks shy of her third birthday, could stitch before she could thread a needle: "Abby threaded a needle a few days since. She began sewing patch-work a few weeks since and sews very neatly. I shall save her first squares."[2]

Mothers' advice books of the early 1800s encouraged stitching and promoted its virtues, as a skill to be passed on from one generation to the next. Sarah Greene, Abby's mother, expressed delight in her daughter's achievements in the following entry: "Abby studies French and drawing and incidentally writing. She is bright and pliant, and I enjoy teaching her. She knits and sews very well indeed."[3] Sarah Greene started a school after her husband died unexpectedly in 1854. No doubt she taught sewing to her young charges.

Needlework was a primary subject in a girl's education up until the mid-nineteenth century in both private and public school systems. Schools in Newport and Providence advertised "useful" subjects such as plain and fancy needlework as part of their curriculum.[4]

Thankful Nye Pendleton, a contemporary of Abby's who lived in Charlestown, constructed this Nine-Patch quilt as a young girl before her marriage at the age of seventeen. Another of Thankful's quilts, a Four-Patch,

also remains in the family. The design of the glazed chintz of Thankful's quilt is documented as an 1825 English block-printed furnishing fabric in the Victoria & Albert Museum's Textile Collection. The same glazed chintz

has been discovered in two American quilts—one at the De Young Memorial Museum in San Francisco and another at the Shelburne Museum in Vermont.[5]

*Notes*

1. Pat Ferrero, Elaine Hedges, and Julie Silber, *Hearts and Hands: The Influence of Women & Quilts on American Society* (San Francisco: Quilt Digest Press, 1987), 18.

2. Sarah Chace Greene, Diary, 1843–54, October 25, 1847, Manuscripts Collection, Rhode Island Historical Society Library, Providence.

3. Ibid., February 15, 1852.

4. Betty Ring, *Let Virtue Be a Guide to Thee* (Providence: Rhode Island Historical Society, 1983), 110. Advertisements appear throughout the book.

5. Wendy Hefford, *The Victoria & Albert Museum's Textile Collection: Design for Printed Textiles in England from 1750–1850* (New York: Abbeville Press, 1992), 135. The De Young Memorial Museum quilt is illustrated in Patsy Orlofsky and Myron Orlofsky, *Quilts in America* (New York: McGraw-Hill, 1974; reprint, New York: Abbeville Press, 1992), 130.

# "Waste Not, Want Not"

KARIN CONOPASK

THIS STREAK OF LIGHTNING QUILT IS ATTRIBUTED TO EMELINE GALLUP Smith (1816–1886) of Westerly, Rhode Island. Emeline was born in Ledyard, Connecticut, and moved to Westerly in 1848 with her husband Orlando Smith to reside in what is now called the Babcock-Smith House. The quilt was included in Emeline's estate and remained with the house.

The Streak of Lightning pattern is an early patchwork design that had several other names, including Zig-Zag, Rail Fence, and Snake Fence. This pattern is produced by combining alternating light and dark triangles. Pieced quilts often are associated with thrift and economy so important to early New Englanders, who cherished all bits of fabric they made or purchased.

The front of this Streak of Lightning quilt has an over-all color scheme of green and beige, although at the bottom of the quilt fabrics of other colors are substituted. Apparently, from the piecing in the bottom triangles, the maker ran out of green and beige fabric and used brown and red prints to complete the quilt. The green fabric is a printed plaid, a style that became popular in the 1840s and 1850s after Queen Victoria wore the Royal Stuart tartan to Scotland in 1842.[1] Beige calicoes were popular throughout the nineteenth century and continue to be a popular print in quilts today.

The back of the quilt is pieced from an old crewelwork bed cover of off-white linen fabric, with several shades of indigo blue floral embroidery. The needlework is typical of eighteenth-century embroidery in the Connecticut River Valley. Emeline's great aunt, Prudence Geer Punderson, stitched crewelwork hangings and bed covers housed in the collections of the Connecticut Historical Society.[2] Prudence lived in Preston, Connecticut. She was buried in a section of Preston called Poquetamuck.[3]

What makes this quilt unique is the use of the crewel embroidery bed cover for the backing. Although such bed coverings had declined in popu-

FIG. 116. (*Opposite*) Streak of Lightning quilt, ca. 1850. Cotton top, linen back, 82 x 89 in. Hand-pieced and hand-quilted in diagonal pattern, 6 stitches per inch. Made by Emeline Gallup Smith (1816–1886). Babcock-Smith House, Westerly, R.I. RIQDP #599.

FIG. 117. (*Page 222*) The back of this quilt (Figure 116) displays an eighteenth-century crewelwork linen bed cover.

larity, they would not have been discarded or allowed to lay idle in thrifty households. Textiles, considered valuable and scarce, often were reworked into contemporary quilts.

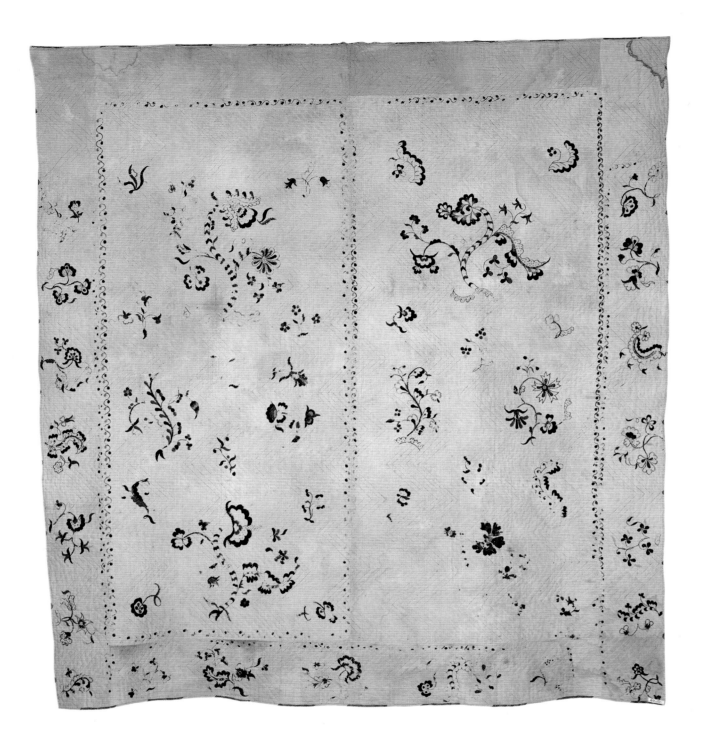

Notes

1. Barbara Brackman, *Clues in the Calico: A Guide to Identifying and Dating Antique Quilts* (McLean, Va.: EPM Publications, 1984), 94.

2. Needlework attributed to Prudence Geer Punderson is illustrated in Carlton L. Safford and Robert Bishop, *America's Quilts and Coverlets* (New York, E. P. Dutton, 1972), 57.

3. Interview with Isaac Smith, Westerly, R.I., February 26, 1995.

# Flour Sacks

LINDA WELTERS

COTTON FLOUR AND SUGAR SACKS PRINTED WITH COMPANY LABELS BEGAN appearing in quilts by the mid–nineteenth century.[1] After removing the stitching and laundering the sacks, women pieced together these recycled fabrics for quilt backings. Early labels, printed with permanent ink, remained visible. Rhode Island textile mills manufactured cotton cloth for flour and sugar sacks in the 1850s as evidenced by a quilt in the Dearborn, Michigan, Historical Museum.[2]

Mary Jane Douglas Holts's quilt, backed with flour sacks, sports eight labels printed in blue or red ink including "Manhattan Family Flour, New York City," "Double Extra Family Flour, J. N. Brown, Stonington," "Extra Superfine Family Flour, A. Holmes, Stonington, Conn.," and directions for "Bread Making."

Mary Jane Stanton was a seventh-generation descendant of Thomas Stanton, who came to New England on the *Mayflower*. The daughter of a sea captain from Stonington, Connecticut, she married Captain Gray Douglas in 1860. He died in 1869, and in 1873 she married Charles Holts. Having no children, Mary gave this quilt along with another Nine-Patch to her brother, who resided in Carolina, Rhode Island. The quilts have stayed in the family, moving first to Westerly, then to Pawtucket, and finally to Seekonk, Massachusetts.

1. Pat L. Nickols, "The Use of Cotton Sacks in Quiltmaking," in *Uncoverings 1988*, Sally Garoutte, ed. (San Francisco: American Quilt Study Group, 1989), 69; Barbara Brackman, *Clues in the Calico*, (McClean, Va.: EMS Publications, 1989), 130; Patsy Orlofsky and Myron Orlofsky, *Quilts in America* (New York: McGraw-Hill, 1974), 103.

2. The name "B. B. & R. Knight, Providence, RI" is visible on one of the sacks backing the quilt. Margaret Malanyn, "Fifteen Dearborn Quilts," in *Uncoverings 1982*, Sally Garoutte, ed. (San Francisco: American Quilt Study Group, 1983), 90.

*Notes*

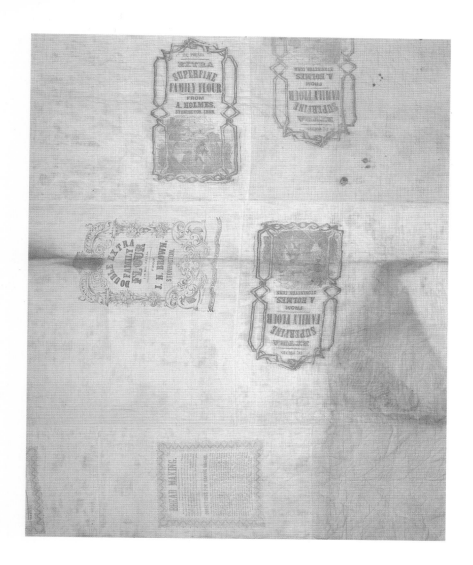

FIG. 118. (*Opposite*) Nine-Patch quilt with flour-sack backing, 1850–70. Plain and printed cottons, 81 x 65 in. Hand-pieced and hand-quilted, 5 stitches per inch. Made by Mary Jane Stanton Douglas Holts (1840–?). Collection of Craig Healy and Linda Hull. RIQDP #294.

FIG. 119. Back of a quilt pieced from flour sacks (Figure 118).

# Esther Slater & Her Falling Blocks Quilt

GAIL FOWLER MOHANTY

AS IS TRUE OF MANY WOMEN OF HER PERIOD, WE KNOW ESTHER PARKINSON Slater largely in reference to her husband rather than by her own achievements. The little we do know of her is because of the importance of her second husband, Samuel Slater. In 1790, British immigrant Samuel Slater made himself famous by spinning cotton yarn and thread by water power for the first time in the United States. We can piece together the bits of Esther's life based on surviving evidence in the form of letters, reminiscences, civil records, and pieces of her stitchery. The collections of Slater Mill Historic Site preserve two examples of Esther Slater's stitchery. These artifacts enable us to peek behind the image of Esther as wife and helpmate of a cotton merchant and a textile manufacturer.[1]

On March 15, 1778, Esther Johnson was born in England, probably near London. At age nine, Esther reputedly stitched a sampler in silk on linen measuring 4 inches by 4.75 inches, demonstrating her skill in seed, cross, feather, closed herringbone, trailing, and hem stitches. Esther fashioned rows of numbers and lower- and uppercase letters. Borders separate the alphabetic rows from the central motif including a stylistic floral and vine design perhaps representing mayflowers, a row of double carnations, and three rows of plain-stitch borders. The central motif consists of five trees. Two are the typical conical pine trees while the other three differ. The two exterior trees evidently represent flowering trees, as does the single tree in the center of the sampler. Esther achieved this impression by interspersing green with white stitches or white with lighter green stitches. Neither her name nor a date appears on the sampler, but a single letter "E" follows the

FIG. 120. (*Opposite*) Falling Blocks quilt, 1851. Silk top and back, cotton batting, 35 x 27 in. Hand-pieced. Made by Esther Johnson Parkinson Slater (1778–1859). Slater Mill Historic Site, Pawtucket, R.I. (52.011). RIQDP #662.

row of lowercase letters. The stitched practice piece is representative of British sampler design of the late eighteenth century. Her sampler is probably over two hundred years old, and family remembrance dates the textile to 1787.[2]

Esther married Robert Parkinson, a cotton merchant. After 1807 and prior to 1812, Esther accompanied her first husband to the United States on a business trip. Unfortunately the Embargo Act prevented Parkinson from completing his mission. Parkinson remained in the United States to avoid the potentially life-threatening ocean voyage home during the War of 1812. Parkinson traveled extensively and then settled permanently in Philadelphia, probably because of its importance for both domestic and foreign trade. Shortly after arriving in the United States, Robert Parkinson met fellow immigrant, Samuel Slater, and both business and social relationships grew between the two men. The Parkinsons visited Slater's family in Pawtucket and Webster and grew to enjoy the family with its six boys. In October of 1812, Hannah Slater, Samuel Slater's first wife and inventor of water-power spun-cotton sewing thread, died following childbirth. Four years later, Robert Parkinson died of "dropsy of the brain." After Parkinson's death, Esther returned to London, intending to stay there. Unfortunately, she had not settled her husband's Philadelphia estate prior to making her voyage home. She returned to Philadelphia in 1817.[3]

By 1817, Samuel Slater had been a widower for almost as long as he had known Esther Parkinson. He wrote to her concerning their similar circumstance.

Dear Madam—As the wise disposer of all events has seen fit in his wisdom to place you and me in a single state—notwithstanding, I presume none of his decrees have gone forth which compels either of us to remain in a state of widowhood. Therefore under these and other circumstances, I now take the liberty to address you on a momentous subject. I have been inclined for some time past to change my situation in life, and have at times named you to my brother and sister for a partner, who have invariably recommended you as suitable, and have fully acquiesced with my ideas on the subject. Now if you are under no obligation to any one, and on weighing the subject fully, you should think that you can spend the remainder of your days with me, I hope you will not feel reluctant, in writing me soon to that effect. . . . I consider myself a plain candid Englishman, and hope and trust, you will be candid enough to write me a short answer, at least whether it be in the affirmative or negative; and should it be in the negative, I stand ready and willing to render you all the advice and assistance in my power relative to settling your worldly matters.[4]

Although Esther Parkinson's reply does not survive, the letter did receive a positive response. On November 21, 1817, the two were married in Saint Paul's Church in Philadelphia. Prior to binding themselves to each other in marriage, the two executed a prenuptial agreement that separated Parkinson's estate from Slater's and ensured that Esther would not bear claim on any of Slater's if he predeceased her. The document also appointed a new administrator for the Parkinson estate. After Samuel Slater had died, Esther Parkinson confessed to her live-in companion Mrs. Francis Conlon, that she married Slater because she thought she might be a good stepmother for his motherless sons. The boys rewarded Esther for her efforts with love and high esteem. Samuel Slater is quoted as saying that she had "stolen the love" of his children from him.[5]

Slater's will left Esther the interest of $10,000, which amounted to $600 annually. In addition, Esther received the income from the Parkinson estate. Esther's affection for Slater grew during their eighteen-year marriage. In honor of her husband, who was buried in Webster, Massachusetts, she saw to it that a memorial was erected in St. Paul's Church in Pawtucket.[6] In 1836 Esther, once again, traveled to London. Her stepson, H. N. Slater, saw to it that she was happy and comfortable during her trip. In one letter to him, she requested that he bring to England six pairs of gloves, dark slate silk, and "some that will suit Ellen."[7] Clearly, her ties with the Slaters were stronger than those to her relatives and friends in England, and she soon returned to the United States, building the house at 69 East Avenue in Pawtucket where she resided until her death in 1859.

If the embroidery sampler represents Esther's sewing alpha then the Falling Blocks infant quilt stitched in 1851 only eight years before she died represents the omega. The silk and velvet piecework design consists of diamonds, 1.25 inches by 1.25 inches. The diamonds are hand-stitched together using an overcasting stitch of cotton thread. The falling block pattern was popular between 1840 and 1877 as were other silk template designs. *Godey's Lady's Book* (1830–98), *Peterson's Magazine* (1842–98), and other ladies' publications often included patterns for silk template quilts.[8] Women cut their templates from used paper as is the case with a falling block quilt top also in Slater Mill Historic Site's collection. Each diamond was stitched around a piece of newsprint or writing paper. Although Esther probably constructed her quilt in the same manner, no paper templates remain behind the diamonds. A thin sheet of cotton batting separates the quilt front from the silk back. The back folds over the front for one-fourth inch to finish the edge. Esther Slater fashioned her quilt for Anna Russell Whitney, the baby daughter of Mrs. J. O. Whitney. Dr. James Orrin Whitney might have been Esther's physician; he had an office on High Street in Pawtucket.

When Esther recognized that her time left on earth was short, she began to look to the disposition of her personal property. Only one of her stepsons survived her, and she had not had any children of her own. Slater's bequest to her became Slater's surviving son's upon her death. In October of 1857, she wrote a will disposing of some of her clothing.

> I, Esther Slater, give and bequeath to Ellen Read, my black velvet mantua, and my best black satin dress and my best satin cloak and the rings on my fingers. And give to Mrs. Sarah Durfee, my best crepe shawl. And I give to Mrs. Francis Conlon, my white cashmere shawl and best muslin delaine dress and my black lace shawl. I give Margaret Black the cot bed she sleeps on with all the cloths that belong to it and my old black satin cloak and whatever is not disposed of she may take if here at my death.[9]

Ellen Read was Esther's niece, the former Ellen Slater, who married Orrin Albee Read of Providence in 1840. This is also probably the Ellen mentioned in Esther's letter to H. N. Slater in 1836. Ellen was presented to the king in the royal court during the trip. Sarah Durfee refers to another of Esther's nieces, Sarah Jane, daughter of John Slater; Sarah married Thomas Durfee on October 29, 1857. Both Francis Conlon and Margaret Black were employed in Mrs. Slater's household. Esther Slater evidently sought to reward those closest to her with her personal belongings upon her death. Esther Slater, who had thought of herself as consumptive in 1836, survived her husband by twenty-three years, dying on December 23, 1859. Esther Johnson Parkinson Slater lies buried beside Hannah Wilkinson Slater in Mineral Spring Avenue Cemetery in Pawtucket, Rhode Island.

*Notes*

1. For more information about Samuel Slater's significant role in the industrialization of the textile industry in the United States, see George S. White, *Memoir of Samuel Slater, the Father of American Manufacures* (Philadelphia: 1836); Paul Rivard, *Samuel Slater, Father of American Manufactures* (Pawtucket: Slater Mill Historic Site, 1973). Information about Esther Slater is from H. N. Slater Papers, Slater Mill Historic Site, Pawtucket, R.I.; Frederick Lewton Papers, Slater Mill Historic Site; E. H. Cameron Papers, Slater Mill Historic Site; E. H. Cameron, *Samuel Slater: Father of American Manufactures* (Portland, Maine: Bond Wheelwright, 1960); Marion Slater Stone, Letter, 1953, Slater Mill Historic Site.

2. *Anchor Manual of Needlework* (Loveland, Co.: Interweave Press, 1990), 49–72; 107–16; Sample 64.011, Slater Mill Historic Site; Sarah Don, *Traditional Samplers* (New York: Viking, 1986); Betty Ring, *Let Virtue Be a Guide to Thee* (Providence: Rhode Island Historical Society, 1983), 1–40; Pauline Brown, *The Encyclopedia of Embroidery Techniques* (New York: Penguin Studio, 1994), 14–37; Georgiana Brown Harbeson, *American Needlework: The History of Decorative Stitchery and Embroidery from the Late 16th to the 20th Century* (1938; reprint, New York: Bonanza Books, 1992), 43–51; and Judith Reiter Weissman and Wendy Lavitt, *Labors of Love: America's Textiles and Needlework 1650–1930* (New York: Wingsbooks, 1987), 119–31.

3. Cameron, *Samuel Slater*, 68, 123–26; Grace Rogers Cooper, "History of Sewing Thread," in *The Sewing Machine: Its Invention and Development* (Washington, D.C.: Smithsonian Institution, 1985), 216; Cameron Papers, Slater Mill Historic Site; and H. N. Slater Collections, Slater Mill Historic Site.

4. Cameron, *Samuel Slater*, 123–24.

5. Esther Parkinson and Samuel Slater Prenuptial Agreement, H. N. Slater Collection, Slater Mill Historic Site.

6. Cameron Papers, Slater Mill Historic Site.

7. Esther Slater to H. N. Slater, May 18, 1836, H. N. Slater Collection, Slater Mill Historic Site.

8. Weissman and Lavitt, *Labors of Love*, 64.

9. Esther Slater Papers, H. N. Slater Collection, Slater Mill Historic Site.

# Grandmother's Quilt

NANCY ANGELINE POTTER

MY GRANDMOTHER, ANGELINE WHITFORD, WAS BORN ON NOVEMBER 15, 1834, the daughter of Almond and Olive Whitford in Coventry, Rhode Island, in the Hopkins Hollow area, halfway between the towns of Greene and Summit. In the early eighteenth century, the Whitfords had pushed westward from coastal settlements into what were then called the "hinterlands" of Rhode Island, now the towns of Coventry, Exeter, and West Greenwich. They had followed cart paths and Indian trails and settled near brooks and ponds, trying to make a living on small farms with inhospitable soil that became increasingly unprofitable. Angeline learned all the small skills of farm life, helped with the garden and livestock, became a good cook and seamstress, and attended the one-room school in Hopkins Hollow. Although she received an Award of Merit, further education was evidently impractical and too expensive.

Fortunately, thanks to the Plainfield and Greenwich Turnpikes, access to the area improved. In 1845 a railroad line opened (Providence to Plainfield), and John Whitford, Angeline's brother, soon had a job as a conductor and bought himself a house in Providence. Angeline left the farm and supported herself by needlework and in shops that various family members owned. She made this appliqué quilt around 1860 before her marriage on March 6, 1862, to a young farmer, David Douglass. Soon after their wedding, he joined the Twenty-first Connecticut Regimental Infantry and died in Virginia on January 10, 1863. She hitched up a team of horses, brought his coffin home from the railroad station, and buried him.

According to the family story, she was scrimping along on her war widow's pension and trying to support herself by working in a bonnet shop in Providence when my grandfather, Elisha Potter—a distant cousin, already twice a widower, and almost thirty-five years older—appeared in the shop

232

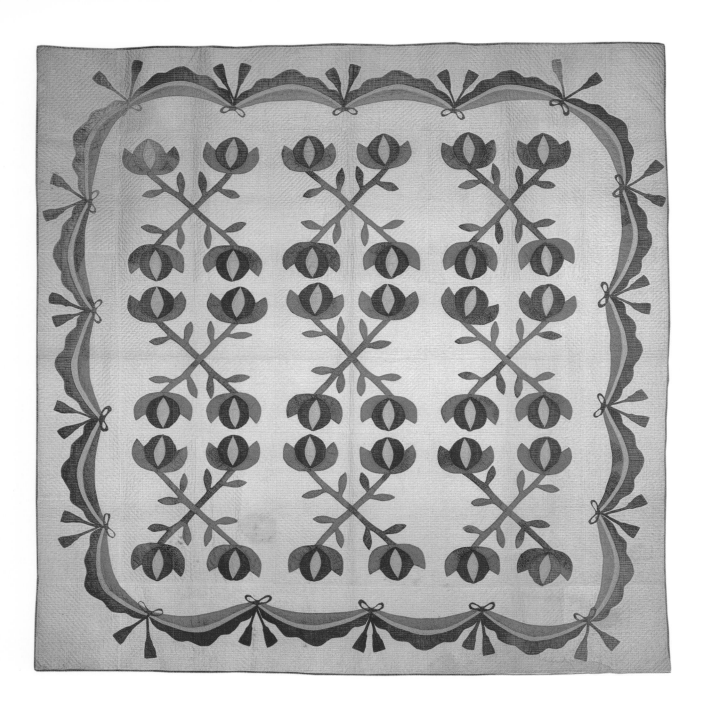

and proposed marriage. She accepted immediately and remained permanently grateful to him. She used her domestic skills on a more prosperous farm, became involved in church and charity organizations, traveled freely, and bought books of all kinds. Although she owned sets of Shakespeare, Dickens, and Byron, she also enjoyed pious verse, sentimental annuals, novels by Alcott and Stowe, and the complete works of Marietta Holley, who wrote satire and humor under the pen name of Josiah Allen's Wife. She subscribed

FIG. 122. Appliqué quilt, ca. 1860. Cotton top and back, 86 x 85 in. Hand-sewn and hand-quilted, 7 stitches per inch. Made by Angeline Whitford Potter (1830–1898). URI Historic Textile and Costume Collection (1993.11.01). RIQDP #199.

FIG. 123. Angeline Whitford Potter (1830–1898). RIQDP Archives.

to *Godey's*, *Peterson's*, *Harper's Illustrated*, and *Frank Leslie's Monthly* and then had issues bound in half-leather for later rereading and for the patterns. One anecdote may illustrate her contradictory impulses toward economy and enthusiasm for books. By the late 1880s she had saved a few hundred dollars and sent my father to buy a set of Audubon bird prints in a Boston bookstore. She was disappointed but forgiving when he arrived home with most of the money and an inexpensive book of black and white engravings. He had learned frugality without the courage to make what would have been a brilliant investment.

She took a great interest in her husband's political career; he was an enthusiastic Jeffersonian Democrat. About women's suffrage, she remained hopeful, believing that it was offensive that she could buy and sell land, plow fields and bring in a crop, even work in a store, but not vote. About twenty years after her death, my father made his first speech in the Connecticut Legislature in 1915 supporting the Suffrage Bill. The last paragraph of his widely reported speech concluded with the quotation, "Can you go home to your mother and look her in the face and say 'Mother, I don't dare to let you vote?'" Despite his impassioned rhetoric, the bill was defeated, 124 to 106.

In addition to the stories of her kindness and quiet competence, Angeline's greatest legacy was her enduring belief in the power of education. Like many farm women, she had a lifelong suspicion of factories for their general atmosphere of exploitation. She was pleased when her husband, Elisha Potter, then a schoolmaster, raided a textile mill and removed the ten- and twelve-year-old bobbin boys to his schoolroom, but less pleased when they escaped back to the mill. She insisted that her son be sent to New Hampton Academy and Yale and wrote him encouraging weekly letters that he kept for the rest of his life. After her death (on October 2, 1898), her will established a small trust fund for the education of any of her grandchildren who might be born. Almost fifty years after her death, that fund sent me to college.

# Homespun Folk Art

LINDA WELTERS

ABIGAIL REYNOLDS GREENE'S QUILT IS RELATIVELY UNIQUE IN THE history of American quilts. Made of appliquéd and embroidered wool blocks, its inscribed 1860 date seems late for both the style and the fabrics. Patsy and Myron Orlofsky illustrated a similar child's bed quilt dated 1810–40 in *Quilts in America*.[1] Yet on this quilt Abigail embroidered the date on two different blocks: "A G 1860 to Abby G. Fry" and "A G 1860." Was the quilt made in 1860 of recycled fabrics, or was it assembled partially or wholly at an earlier date only to be signed and dated in 1860?

An earlier date of manufacture is supported on three counts. First, the One-Patch block set on point without borders is stylistically consistent with other Rhode Island pieced quilts made before 1850. Second, the flowers, birds, and hearts embellishing the squares resemble other American "folk art" that was popular in the second quarter of the nineteenth century, particularly sewn table rugs.[2] Third, fiber analysis reveals that the wool fiber in the backing fabric came from an early breed of sheep.

Quiltmaker Abigail Reynolds Greene gave the quilt to her granddaughter Abby Greene Fry in 1860. Abby was only seventeen at the time, but unfortunately she died that same year of appendicitis. The embroidery thread used for the inscription resembles the thread holding the various appliqué pieces in place. The quilting thread is cotton.

Abigail Reynolds Greene's English ancestors immigrated to Rhode Island in the seventeenth century. Abigail was born to Mary Hall and John Reynolds in 1794 and grew up on the family farm in Warwick. In 1811, at the age of seventeen, she married William Greene of East Greenwich, also a farmer. Family account books reveal that a family relative, Thomas Fry, bartered sheep's wool from his flock for factory-made cloth at Ezra and

FIG. 124. (*Opposite*) One-Patch appliquéd and embroidered quilt, inscribed "A G 1860 to Abby G. Fry." Wool top and back, 81½ x 94 in. Hand-pieced and hand-quilted, 4–5 stitches per inch. Made by Abigail Reynolds Greene (1794–1889). Private collection. RIQDP #562.

236

Jeffrey Davis's carding and spinning mill in nearby Davisville in the years 1815–19.[3] Known to have spun and woven as a girl, Abigail may have used some of her own homespun for the quilt's backing. Another of Abigail's wool homespun quilts survives; its backing dates from before 1811 (see Fig. 33).

1. Patsy and Myron Orlofsky, *Quilts in America* (New York: McGraw-Hill, 1974), Plate 43. The Winterthur Museum currently dates the quilt to 1830–40; child's Bed Quilt, 69.562, Henry Francis du Pont Winterthur Museum, Winterthur, Del.

2. Appliquéd woolen table rugs worked in identical fashion are illustrated in Joel and Kate Kopp, *American Hooked and Sewn Rugs: Folk Art Underfoot* (New York: E. P. Dutton, 1985), 125–27. These table rugs consist of wool hearts, stars, fruit, flowers, and animals,

*Notes*

FIG. 125. Abigail Reynolds Greene (1794–1889). RIQDP Archives.

embroidered and appliquéd on woolen squares of fabric which are then pieced to form table covers. Figures 218 and 221 are dated ca. 1845, probably because of their similarity to a third signed and dated example from Maine (Fig. 222).

    3. Thomas Fry, Account Book, 1815–22, Private Collection, East Greenwich, R.I.

# Family Remembrances

LINDA WELTERS

LUCY LARCOM, WHEN REMINISCING ABOUT GROWING UP IN NEW ENGLAND, wrote of her experiences learning to sew patchwork: "I liked assorting those little figured bits of cotton cloth, for they were scraps of gowns I had seen worn, and they reminded me of the persons who wore them. One fragment, in particular, was like a picture to me. It was a delicate pink and brown sea-moss pattern, on a white ground, a piece of a dress belonging to my married sister, who was to me bride and angel in one."[1]

Mary J. Andrews incorporated this same nostalgic spirit into a small quilt, possibly made for a grandchild. She ensured that the recipient would remember those who had once used the calicoes from which it was made by sewing paper notes to the pieces of cloth. Each piece of paper is inscribed with the name of the original wearer or a comment about the origins of the cloth in the unsteady penmanship one associates with the elderly. Three notes are visible on the top; the remainder are tacked with thread on the back to each of the calicoes in the binding.

The quilt incorporates parts of two earlier quilts. A note attached to a strip containing the pink and blue triangles from one of the quilts states, "These two kinds were your great grandmother Bradley's dresses when she was a young lady—was married in 1805 made the quilt before my rememberance they were fifty cents a yard." A note sewn to a stippled brown and white calico, once part of an Eight-Pointed Star quilt, says, "This was new cloth and the white was new." The brown rainbow print in the corner was from a dress Mary wore as a girl. The fabrics in the top date from 1805 to 1840.

Twenty-five different calicoes, mostly from the second half of the nineteenth century, comprise the binding. Each one has an identifying note attached. Ten of the fabrics came from dresses worn by Cornelia B. Andrews,

perhaps Mary's daughter-in-law. Another three pieces were once dresses belonging to Mary herself. The lengthiest note recalls another Bradley ancestor: "This a piece of your great-great-great aunt Amelia Bradley dress which she made before I can remember. French calico she was a lovely Christian lady. Fifty cents per yd."

Mary's memories of the cost of calicoes illustrates how expensive they were in the early years of the nineteenth century. After the introduction of power looms and cylinder printing, calico prices dropped 60 percent in the space of twenty-five years.[2]

1. Lucy Larcom, *A New England Girlhood* (Cambridge, Mass.: Riverside Press, 1889), 122–23.

2. Merrimack Co. prints sold at auction for 23.07 cents per yard in 1825, two years after the company began printing calico in Lowell, Massachusetts. In 1850 the price had dropped to 9.24 cents per yard. Nathan Appleton, *Introduction of the Power Loom and Origin of Lowell* (Lowell, Mass: B. H. Penhallow, 1858), 4.

FIG. 126. (*Opposite*) Pieced child's quilt, ca. 1870. Cotton top and back. 58½ x 33 in. Hand-pieced and hand-quilted, 5–7 stitches per inch. Made by Mary J. Andrews, possibly for a grandchild. Watson House, University of Rhode Island. RIQDP #717.

*Notes*

# A Story of Love & Patience

MARGARET T. ORDOÑEZ

MAKERS OF PIECED QUILTS OBVIOUSLY ARE PEOPLE WITH PATIENCE AND persistence. With these virtues they are able to cut endless numbers of little pieces of fabric, stitch seam after seam joining points just so, quilt through three layers that resist being combined into one, and stitch even more to finish the edges. Hannah Palmer Burdick was a patient and persistent woman, and because of this she not only produced beautiful quilts, she married the man she loved.

Hannah Palmer grew up in Hopkinton in western Rhode Island. She fell in love with John Burdick, but her parents did not approve of this man. Religious affiliation does not seem to be the reason for their reservations, because they both were Seventh Day Baptists.[1] Ultimately, John married another woman, and Hannah remained single. Her fate was not to pine away and die as did heroines in the literature of the day, but to teach school and make numerous quilts. She and John each had sad times when her parents and his wife died, but after a period of time, John wooed Hannah again. This time she could say, "Yes."

Hannah moved to Pawcatuck, Connecticut, the twin city to Westerly, Rhode Island, where John was an engraver for C. B. Cottrell, an area printer of paper goods. They had four children, so she probably needed the quilts she had made. This quilt, made in the Four Ts or Maltese Cross pattern, incorporates two popular Turkey red calicoes. By this time, Rhode Island firms were producing bright red prints with synthetic alizarin in place of natural madder which required the special Turkey red treatment to be a bright, intensive color.[2] The Clyde Bleachery and Print Works in River Point, Rhode Island, was well known for its Turkey red prints.[3] Examples of their products exist in the collections of the American Textile History Museum in Lowell, Massachusetts.

FIG. 127. (*Opposite*) Four Ts quilt, 1870–80. Cotton top and back, 89 x 76½ in. Hand-pieced and hand-quilted, 6–8 stitches per inch. Made by Hannah Palmer Burdick (1856–1926). Collection of Joan Maxson Grinnell. RIQDP #192.

1. The Seventh Day Baptist Church in America was established in 1671 in Newport. Some of the early "Sabbath keepers" had trouble with other Connecticut colonists for worshiping on the seventh day, Saturday, and working on the first, Sunday. Some of the

*A Selection of Rhode Island Quilts*

FIG. 128. Hannah Palmer Burdick (1856–1926). RIQDP Archives.

FIG. 129. John Burdick. RIQDP Archives.

largest congregations of Seventh Day Baptists in Rhode Island had churches in Westerly, Hopkinton, Woodville, and Green Hill. Karl G. Stillman, *Seventh Day Baptists in New England, 1671–1971: Historical Notes* (N.p.: n.p., 1971).

2. Pettit cites 1868 for the synthesis of alizarin, a natural component of madder. Florence H. Pettit, *America's Printed and Painted Fabrics, 1600–1900* (New York: Hastings House, 1970), 241.

3. Diane L. Fagan Affleck, *Just New From the Mills: Printed Cotton in America* (North Andover, Mass.: Museum of American Textile History, 1987), 82–83.

# Gifts from the Sea

ROBERTA NULL-HAIR

THE OCEAN WAVES PATTERN IS AN APPROPRIATE ONE FOR A BLOCK Island quilter. This particular island had an unusual relationship with cargo brought to its shores on ocean waves. Over the years, powerful, unpredictable currents have caused frequent problems for ships traveling in this area. Countless numbers of ships have discovered that running aground on Block Island was certain doom for ship, cargo, and crew. Twice in recorded history six vessels came ashore on Block Island in a single day, and during one week in the summer of 1880 eleven ships ran aground. The loss of property from this week of wrecks amounted to millions of dollars.[1]

The passage between Block Island and Point Judith on the mainland is almost seven miles in width; however, a number of ships have mistaken the light at the northern tip of Block Island, Sandy Point, for the light at Point Judith, resulting in ships running aground on the island. Ships carrying cargoes of coal were especially prone to wreck on the shores of Block Island, and the islanders were seldom without coal to heat their homes.[2]

"Moon Cussers" and "Wrackers" were names given to people who by various means sought to lure ships ashore so they could be looted. These practices presumably took place along Cape Cod and on Block Island. Evidence of Moon Cussers being on Block Island is only heresay; however, the islanders were extremely thrifty and converted to their own use anything cast up on their shores.

Once a ship wrecked on the shores of Sandy Point carrying a cargo of calicoes and chintzes. The islanders salvaged the fabric and spread the yardage out to dry on a hill located a little beyond the Old Harbor. This hill became known as Calico Hill. The ship could have been the large two-masted schooner *Warrior*, driven ashore on Sandy Point during a heavy gale in March or April of 1831. This salvaged calico was referred to as "wrecking cloth"

FIG. 130. (*Opposite*) Ocean Waves quilt, 1875–90. Cotton top, backing, and batting, 65½ x 82½ in. Hand-pieced and hand-quilted in outline pattern, 7 stitches per inch. Descended in the Willis family on Block Island. Collection of Robert R. Willis. RIQDP #494.

FIG. 131. Wreck of the *Barque*, west shore of Block Island, August 1890. Rhode Island Historical Society.

by the islanders. The pattern of a small red-brown print alternating with plain brown stripes was called "Mincemeat" by the islanders. This pattern made its way into many Island bed quilts. Calicoes were scarce on the island even among the wealthy during this time period; the islanders would have considered them a precious gift from the sea.[3]

This Ocean Waves quilt was inherited from Rubie Willis Clark (1890–1974), who died childless. Rubie did not quilt, and she left no histories for any of the quilts she owned.[4] When Rubie died, her heirs divided the many quilts in her estate among themselves.

*Notes*

1. Edward E. Peltee, *Block Island, Rhode Island* (Boston: Press of Deland and Barta, 1884), 74–75.

2. Thomas Fielders, *Block Island: Fact and Fancy* (no date), 25.

3. Ethel Colt Ritchie, *Block Island Lore and Legends* (West Orange, N.J.: Midland Press, 1955), 26–27.

4. Two of the quilts were stamped with the name of Amanda Dodge (1852–1906), to whom Rubie's parents were related by marriage. Amanda was a seventh-generation descendant of Tristam Dodge (1607–1683), one of Block Island's early settlers.

# Quilting with Friends

MARGARET T. ORDOÑEZ

IN THE SOUTHWEST CORNER OF RHODE ISLAND LIES AN AREA THAT HAS a long history of textile production and quilting. The largest town there is Westerly, a twin city with Pawcatuck, Connecticut, where the textile industry is still a viable part of the local economy. Quilters have been active in the region since before 1850 with a number of extant quilts indicative of their work.

Mary Elizabeth Babcock Cundall of nearby Ashaway contributed significantly to the quilting history of the area. Neighbors plus quilters from Westerly and Pawcatuck regularly went to her house at the corner of High and West Street to quilt. Built in 1875, the house has a large bow window that provided good light for quilters working in the large living room. Her granddaughter, Frances Babcock Cundall (Fanny) still lives there.

Edward Cundall, Mary's husband, was sheriff of Washington County. His family had a long history of involvement in textile production in the state. His great-grandfather, Joseph Cundall, erected a fulling mill on his property in Portsmouth in 1746. The mill remained in the family, serving the surrounding neighborhood, for three generations. Edward's father, Isaac, founded one of the first woolen mills in Ashaway in 1816 as wool cloth production began to move out of the home and into factories. Mary also became involved in the industry; she worked in two Ashaway textile mills during the early 1860s while Edward was away during the Civil War. Some of her letters to him survive, along with a piece of calico that she made into a dress during his absence. In her letter she told him, "I am going to send you a piece of calico dress." She ends the letter "Do tell me how you lik [sic] my dress."[1]

In 1884 Mary completed a signature quilt that she had made probably for fellow quilt enthusiast Elizabeth Davis Babcock (1806–1901) of Pawcatuck.

FIG. 132. (*Opposite*) Christian Cross quilt, 1884. Cotton top and back, 111 x 81½ in. Hand- and machine-pieced, hand-quilted, 5–6 stitches per inch. Made by Mary Elizabeth Babcock Cundall (1838–1910). Collection of Audrey Burdick Nowortowski. RIQDP #759.

248

Most likely Elizabeth is the person who signed "Mother" on one of the squares; people in the region knew her as "Mother Babcock." A number of her friends' names appear on quilt blocks. Other names are those of Mary's friends, two sisters, sister-in-law, and future daughter-in-law Sarah Emmons, then age three. Years later Sarah gave the quilt to Fanny, who passed

FIG. 133. Mary Cundall in the Ashaway home, where she hosted quilting bees, ca. 1895. RIQDP Archives.

it on to her niece Audrey Nowortowski. Audrey's husband Steve has identified fifty-nine of the seventy-two names on the quilt. Five signers of this quilt also wrote their names on squares in another quilt from the same area thirteen years earlier.[2]

The Christian Cross pattern, also called Chimney Sweep, was the most popular of the three patterns that Rhode Island quilters chose for friendship quilts. Prior to 1860 they placed blocks in friendship quilts on point, but that orientation changed during the sixties. Diane Fagan Affleck formerly of the American Textile History Museum in Lowell identified Cocheco Manufacturing Company in Dover, New Hampshire, as the source of at least three fabrics in this quilt. The products of this company, one of the first successful calico printers in the country, had an excellent reputation.[3]

As in many quilts, one block is different from the others; the one odd block has black corners. The popularity of friendship quilts waned in the eighties, and such valuable documentation of people's associations became less common, a significant loss to those searching for clues to their past.

1. Mary Elizabeth Cundall to Edward Cundall, August 5, 1862, collection of Audrey Burdick Nowortowski.

2. 1871 Christian Cross quilt, RIQDP Archives, University of Rhode Island Library Special Collections, Kingston, R.I., #153.

3. Diane L. Fagan Affleck, *Just New From the Mills: Printed Cottons in America* (North Andover, Mass.: Museum of American Textile History, 1987), 84.

*Notes*

# A Log Cabin in Bristol

LINDA WELTERS

A LOG CABIN QUILT, BECAUSE OF ITS NAME, CONJURES UP IMAGES OF pioneer women on the prairie.[1] This quilt and another, in the Straight Furrow variation, originated in a stately Victorian home at 900 Hope Street in Bristol. The quiltmaker, Eugenia Paull, sewed frequently. In the photograph of the house, Eugenia's sewing room is behind the Palladian window above the portico. Eugenia's husband, lumber merchant Seth Paull, constructed this Second Empire residence from 1879 to 1881.[2]

Bristol, incorporated in 1681 as part of Plymouth Colony, is located at the head of Narragansett Bay. Bristol became part of the colony of Rhode

FIG. 134. Bristol home of Seth and
Eugenia Paull, ca. 1930. RIQDP Archives.

252

Island in 1747. Its maritime economy brought great prosperity during the years after the Revolution; the evidence of this survives in the town's distinguished architecture.[3] Bristol enjoys another distinction: the town has hosted a parade every Fourth of July almost continuously since 1786.[4] Every Independence Day the homes along Hope Street are draped in red, white, and blue bunting for the parade.

The Log Cabin pattern emerged during the Civil War period and became popular nationwide in the 1870s.[5] Using a method where patches are

FIG. 135. Log Cabin quilt, Barn Raising variation, ca. 1880–1900. Cotton top and back, cotton string ties, 93 x 91 in. Handpieced, tied. Made by Eugenia Peckham Paull (1844–1936). Collection of Marion Paull Edwards. RIQDP #279.

sewn to a foundation, "log" strips are built around a central square, often red. This red square is the "chimney" of the cabin. By juxtaposing light and dark colors, numerous variations using log cabin blocks can be obtained, each with its own name: Barn Raising, Straight Furrow, Courthouse Steps, and Windmill Blades.

*Notes*

1. Roderick Kiracofe, *The American Quilt* (New York: Clarkson Potter, 1993), 152. Kiracoffe's section on Log Cabin quilts begins with a quotation from a young wife leaving her log cabin in Missouri to set out for California with her husband and two toddlers.

2. *Historic and Architectural Resources of Bristol, Rhode Island* (Providence: Rhode Island Historical Preservation Commission, 1990), 92.

3. Patrick T. Conley, *An Album of Rhode Island History, 1636–1986* (Norfolk, Va.: Donning, 1986), 267.

4. Ibid., 250.

5. Kiracofe, *The American Quilt*, 152; Barbara Brackman, *Clues in the Calico: A Guide to Identifying and Dating Antique Quilts* (McLean, Va.: EPM Publications, 1989), 144.

# Legacy of a Vampire

CYNTHIA DIMOCK-QUAGLIA

THE BEAR'S PAW PATTERN IS RARE IN NINETEENTH-CENTURY RHODE Island quilts; RIQDP documented only three Bear's Paw quilts. This quilt, made by Mercy Lena Brown of Exeter, Rhode Island, is a reminder of the history of the quiltmaker, her family, and the superstitions of their small town.

Nineteenth-century residents of Exeter and other areas in southern New England held strong superstitious beliefs that went back many generations. In one Exeter legend, a farmer shot a black cat with a silver button as he was passing a "witch's house." Several weeks later, the witch fell down and broke her hip; when a doctor examined her injured hip, he found an embedded silver button. Another folkloric theme for southern Rhode Island was that of the vampire. The best-known vampire story involves the Brown family; townspeople were convinced that Mercy Brown was a vampire who was feeding on her brother, Edwin Atwood Brown.

George T. Brown (1842–1922) lost his wife Mary Eliza in 1883, and a daughter Mary Olive in 1884 to consumption (tuberculosis). His son Edwin, who worked as a store clerk at both G. T. Cranston and Taylor & Davis of Lafayette, also became ill with the dreaded disease. Edwin eventually traveled to a sanitarium in Colorado Springs to recover. When he left home his younger sister Mercy Lena seemed to be in good health. When he returned uncured eighteen months later, he found that on January 17, 1892, Mercy had died of consumption after only a few months of suffering.

Edwin's health rapidly failed after the death of Mercy. Many townspeople suspected that a vampire was sucking the life out of him. People in Exeter believed that consumption was a spiritual disease or visitation, not physical in nature. "As long as the body of a consumptive relative has blood in its heart," this relative "was at work draining the blood of the living into

the heart of the dead [which caused] his rapid decline."[1] According to old southern Rhode Island tradition, to rid the family of the blood-sucking fiend, the bodies of deceased family members had to be exhumed and examined. If blood was found in the heart, that person was a vampire. To save Edwin, the townspeople harassed the reluctant George Brown to exhume the bodies of his wife and two daughters.

Nine weeks after Mercy was buried, the exhumation took place. Of the three women exhumed, Mercy was the only one found to have blood in her heart. According to Dr. Harold Metcalf, the accredited physician in attendance who held degrees from Brown University and Harvard Medical School, Mercy was in the proper stage of decomposition and the blood in her heart was normal.[2] The townspeople did not believe his opinion and ordered Mercy's heart and liver to be burned in the cemetery and the ashes mixed into a drug for Edwin to ingest. According to superstition, the burning of the heart should end the vampire hauntings of all family members; the consuming of the ashes by the victim would guarantee that the evil

FIG. 136. (*Opposite*) Bear's Paw quilt, ca. 1890. Cotton top, back, and batting, 84 x 95 in. Hand-pieced, hand-quilted. Made by Mercy Lena Brown (1872–1892). Collection of Betsey L. Reynolds. RIQDP #51.

FIG. 137. Gravestone of Mercy Brown. RIQDP Archives.

occurrence ended and the victim returned to good health. However, not even these precautions could save Edwin, and he died of consumption on May 2, 1892.

**Notes**

1. George R. Stetson, "The Animistic Vampire in New England," *The American Anthropologist* 9, no. 1 (1896): 3.

2. "The Vampire Theory: That Search for the Spectral Ghoul in the Exeter Graves," *The Providence Journal*, March 21, 1892, 8.

# Sampler Quilt

MARGARET T. ORDOÑEZ

THE VARIETY OF BOLD PATTERNS AND THE TECHNIQUE THAT CONNECTS the pieces make this a unique quilt. The source of the pattern for the blocks and the person who stitched them are mysteries, although we know that it came from a Portsmouth family. The use of sashing with no border is typical of earlier Rhode Island quilts.

The patterns could have come from a number of published sources or from other quilters, but the manner in which they are connected is unique. The quilter embroidered a feather stitch where all the pieces joined, then machine stitched the squares and sashing strips. This person might have made crazy quilts in the previous decade because the feather stitch around the pieces is quite typical of the needlework on those silk quilts. Silk fabrics appear in some of the squares, and so do wool and cotton cloth. The back is a wool plaid.

The pattern name for each of the sixteen squares is embroidered on them. These names in order from left to right and top to bottom are:

| | | | |
|---|---|---|---|
| Letter T | Old Crow | Revolutionary Hero | Basket |
| Windmill | Broken Dishes | Wild Goose | Bears Paw |
| Victory | Garden Path | Red Cross | Grandma's Star |
| Fishermen's Reel | Good Cheer | Signals | Double Tooth |

If a source or sources of the patterns can be found, we can determine if the quilter used names passed on with the patterns. In the late nineteenth century, pattern companies such as the Ladies' Art Company designed hundreds of patterns to which they assigned names.[1] Of course, the quiltmaker might have worked out the patterns and invented the names. This would reflect initiative and imagination, traits that the quilt itself exhibits.

FIG. 138. (*Overleaf*) Sampler quilt, ca. 1890. Wool, cotton, and silk pieces, wool back, 77½ x 74½ in. Hand-sewn squares, machine-sewn sashing. Maker unknown. Private collection. RIQDP #463.

1. The 1889 Ladies' Art Company catalog cited in *Barbara Brackman, Clues in the Calico: A Guide to Identifying and Dating Antique Quilts* (McLean, Va.: EPM Publications, 1989), 150. Also on this page is an 1897 sampler quilt top with names inked in each block.

# A French Canadian Quilt

LINDA WELTERS

THE STORY OF MATHILDA RICHARD AND HER SISTERS JUSTINE, EMMA, Valérie, and Bertha is in some ways typical of other French Canadians whose parents were immigrants to Rhode Island. Mathilda's maternal grandparents were "habitants," farmers who lived in rural Quebec. Their daughter, Alphonsine, embraced emigration as a solution for economic betterment. Alphonsine Racette married Narcisse Richard and moved to Rhode Island, where they raised their five daughters.

From 1860 to 1890, French Canadians were the largest single source of immigrants to the state of Rhode Island.[1] Many came to work in the state's booming textile industry. The largest concentrations of French Canadians were in cities and mill villages along major waterways. Woonsocket, Manville, Albion, Central Falls, and Pawtucket along the Blackstone River became predominantly French enclaves. French Canadians also settled along the Pawtuxet River in West Warwick, notably in the village of Arctic, and on the east side of Narragansett Bay in the city of Warren.

The Richard family settled in Pawtucket. Like other French Canadians, the Richards belonged to a French-speaking Catholic church, St. John the Baptist, and sent their daughters to the parish school. Mathilda, the maker of the quilt, taught briefly in the parish school and sewed altar cloths for the church.

Each daughter was handy with a needle and thread, but Mathilda was the one who excelled in needlework. She was the proud owner of a Wheeler and Wilson sewing machine manufactured in Bridgeport, Connecticut. After the girls married, they remained close. Valérie and Justine lived together after their husbands died. When Valérie passed on, Justine went to live with Emma and her family at 7 School Street in Pawtucket, just opposite Slater Mill. When Mathilda's husband died of throat cancer in 1934, she

moved in with her daughter Geraldine. Her granddaughter, the current owner of the quilt, remembers that her grandmother spoke mostly French.

Mathilda's red and white quilt shows her sewing skills to advantage. She used the sewing machine to piece the quilt top, to join the widths of white cotton for the back, and to attach the binding to the finished quilt. Her granddaughter still has the machine in her home.

The quilt is a variation of the Goose in the Pond pattern. Red and white quilts became popular in the late nineteenth century when azoic dyes came on the market for bright, fast reds. Many red and white quilts made at the end of the nineteenth century survive in good condition. The red and white color combination was also popular in Quebec-made quilts.[2] Another characteristic of French Canadian quilts in Rhode Island is the use of rainbow patterns for the quilting.

*Notes*

1. Patrick T. Conley, *An Album of Rhode Island History, 1636–1986* (Norfolk, Va.: Donning, 1986), 129.

2. Marie Durand, "La Courtepoint Québécoise: Création ou Emprunt?" *Material History Review* 34 (Fall 1991): 30.

# Masonic Pride

ALDA LOUISE GANZE KAYE

THIS COMMEMORATIVE SAWTOOTH PATTERN QUILT, DONE IN THE ME-
dallion style, has an appliquéed Masonic symbol. The Masonic compass and
square with a "G" symbolized dividing time between God, work, and rest.[1]
Craftsmen involved in the brotherhood of Freemasonry revered the Masonic symbols that signified patriotism, religion, morality, and other hon-
orable virtues.[2] Such Masonic symbols have been used for centuries on architecture, furniture, vases, jewelry, and other objects in addition to quilts.

Perhaps the Sawtooth pattern surrounding the central motif on this quilt
was chosen by the maker specifically to symbolize the original owner's trade
as a finish carpenter like his father and three brothers. All were Masons in
Canada. Quilters have used the Sawtooth pattern since about 1800 in both
Canada and the United States.

This quilt was designed and constructed by Clytie Alda Alcorn Benson
for her husband, Lewis Zebulon Benson who was an active Mason from
Bear River, Nova Scotia, Canada. The red and white pieced quilt with its
appliquéed emblem was precious to Lewis Benson. He came to the United
States from Canada about 1922 and became foreman of a lumber company
in Portsmouth, Rhode Island. The quilt probably came south when his wife
and their two young daughters arrived several years later. The quilt was one
of many made by young Clytie whose children remember her quilting frame
being set up in the front parlor for long periods of time. They also recalled
seeing the red and white Masonic design quilt on their parents' bed in those
early years and remembered it being their father's favorite.

Lewis Zebulon Benson, affectionately known as "Zebby" by his wife,
was an avid reader and enjoyed discussing historical events. Of English descent, he often told his grandchildren the story of how their ancestor, Colonel
Christopher Benson, fought with George Washington in a battle in New

FIG. 141. (*Opposite*) Masonic emblem
quilt in medallion style with Sawtooth
border, ca. 1910. Cotton top and back, 72
x 67 in. Hand-pieced and hand-quilted in
diagonal pattern, 7 stitches per inch.
Made by Clytie Alda Alcorn Benson
(1889–1974). Collection of Alda L. Kaye.
RIQDP #454.

York during the Revolutionary War. Colonel Washington, he pointed out, was a Freemason just like Colonel Benson.

Clytie Alcorn Benson, of English and Scottish descent, was the second youngest of six children and had been raised on a large farm in Bear River.

FIG. 142. Lewis Zebulon Benson
(1886–1978).

Her mother was well versed in needle skills and taught all of her four daughters to sew. Appropriately, Clytie honored her husband's craft and great pride of membership in his fraternal organization with this Masonic quilt. Their granddaughter, the present owner, also shares this pride.

*Notes*

1. *Masonic Symbols in American Decorative Art* (Lexington, Ma.: Museum of Our National Heritage, 1976), 31.

2. Ibid., 19–22.

# The Male Role in Quilting

ALDA LOUISE GANZE KAYE

MEN HAVE HAD A ROLE IN QUILTING SINCE THE MIDDLE AGES WHEN THEY wore quilted *pourpoints* to protect the body from plate armour. In recent centuries men developed an appreciation for textiles that extended to collecting mill ends from the textile factories, cigar box bands, old neckties, and other fabrics that ultimately ended up in quilts. Quilts in the RIQDP database indicated that men occasionally designed and/or stitched quilts in their spare time; they also quilted while unemployed during the Great Depression, while recovering from illness, or during retirement.

Mr. William Strange, a retired textile mill worker, enjoyed making quilts, lace, and braided rugs. He was remembered by a former neighbor, Veda Downing, as a skillful artisan who took pleasure in producing goods for his family and friends.[1] He wove fabric on his loom and made many household goods, including pillowcases that he trimmed with hand-knitted lace. In 1929, at the age of seventy-six, Mr. Strange found the time and energy to create a prize-winning silk quilt of 2,000 pieces.

A poem about Mr. Strange and his quilt was written by Mrs. Cora Clark, one of the quilt's former owners. It was published in a local paper with a photograph of Mr. Strange.

*The Spirit of 76*

When a man comes from good old colonial stock,
New England ancestry that no one can mock
And is seventy-six and sound as a rock
    Then—he is a man to be proud of!

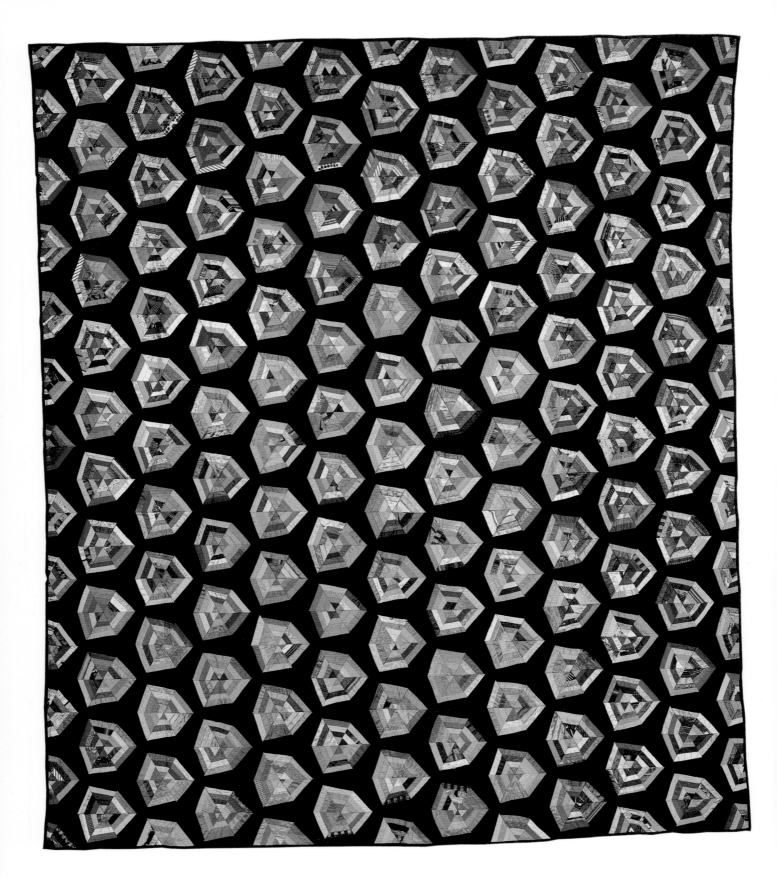

His hair may be white and his name may be Strange
And he is a wonder; all that we cant change
But before everybody I'd like to arrange
    The work he has done to be proud of!

He knits and he weaves in hundreds of ways,
His doilies and laces are worthy of praise,
And rugs that are braided wouls surely amaze'
    You'd know he's a man to be proud of!

He plans his designs, executing with care.
Every stitch is correct, every corner is square.
You feel the perfection, you see it all there
    In the work he has done to be proud of!

And now he comes forth with a new piece of art
A silk cobweb quilt; it would win any heart.
It has taken a year to combine every part
    And it is a quilt to be proud of!

The "cobwebs" are set in a background of black.
It boasts of a colorful crimson-like back
And two thousand pieces. It took quite a knack
    To make up this quilt he is proud of!

FIG. 143. (*Opposite*) Spiderweb or Cobweb quilt, ca. 1929. Silk top, cotton back, 72 x 66 in. Made by William Strange. URI Historic Textile and Costume Collection (1971.15.03). RIQDP #124.

FIG. 144. Newspaper photograph of William Strange, quilt in lap, ca. 1929. Dean Beverly Downing Cusack Donor File. URI Historic Textile and Costume Collection.

It took the first prize when shown at the fair.
It would take the blue ribbon if shown anywhere.
Laid on a four-poster, it's ready for wear.
  Now—WHO gets the quilt to be proud of?[2]

This Spiderweb or Cobweb quilt was originally housed in Voluntown, Connecticut, on the Rhode Island border. It went back and forth between friends and family on both sides of the state line until it was given to the University of Rhode Island in 1952 by Dean Emeritas Beverly Downing Cusack.

Currently the male role in quilting can be observed in the NAMES Project AIDS Memorial Quilt. Many of the memorial panels that make up the gigantic AIDS quilt are made by males in memory of partners, friends, and family members who died of AIDS. The very first quilt panel for this monumental quilt was made by activist Cleve Jones in San Francisco in 1986.[3] This panel was made in memory of a Rhode Island native, Marvin Feldman, who died from the disease.[4] As we approach the twenty-first century, the AIDS quilt continues to grow. The commemorative nature of the quilt's squares harks back to the friendship and fund-raising quilts of earlier periods. Besides its emotional role, the AIDS Memorial Quilt serves to increase public awareness of the need for research and support for those affected.

One of the quilts documented by RIQDP belongs to a man given to him by a friend when the friend was dying of complications from AIDS. This small Victorian Puff quilt made of silk is being carefully preserved by the owner, Len deAngelis, a resident of Newport who serves as a volunteer in the Rhode Island AIDS program.[5]

*Notes*

1. Telephone interview with Arlene Hauck, daughter of Veda Downing, May 18, 1994.
2. Dean Beverly Downing Cusack Donor File, University of Rhode Island Historic Textile and Costume Collection, Kingston, R.I.
3. Cindy Ruskin, *The Quilt: Stories from the NAMES Project* (New York: Pocket Books, 1988), 9.
4. R. E. Reimer, "Quilt is AIDS Comforter," *Newport Daily News*, February 27, 1993.
5. Kathryn F. Sullivan, *Gatherings: America's Quilt Heritage* (Paducah, Ky.: American Quilter's Society, 1995), 136–37.

# Yankee Frugality

LINDA WELTERS

FOR THRIFTY RHODE ISLANDERS, THE SO-CALLED STRING QUILT OFFERED
a method of utilizing fabric scraps too small and narrow for any other purpose. In string piecing, also called pressed work, the quiltmaker sewed
"strings" of fabric to a paper or cloth foundation to form blocks.[1] By arranging the strings diagonally on the foundation, narrow strips of varying
length could be used. When paper formed the foundation, the quilter removed it before adding a filler and backing. A cloth foundation provided a
middle layer of fabric, thereby eliminating the need for a filler.

The technique of piecing scraps of fabric to a foundation appeared in
the second half of the nineteenth century, reaching a crescendo in the last
quarter of the century with the popularity of Log Cabin and crazy quilts.
Easy and economical to make, string quilts persisted through the Depression era. True "utility quilts," they could be created with no-cost materials
like newspapers, cotton sacks, and old clothes.[2]

Despite their humble origins, string quilts have a graphic, painterly quality
about them. Jonathan Holstein and Gail van der Hoof recognized the cur-
rency of their visual appeal by including several string quilts in the landmark exhibition "Abstract Design in American Quilts" at the Whitney
Museum of American Art in 1971.[3]

Mary Matteson Knight used worn-out dresses, blouses, and men's ties to
piece the top for this quilt. Because it contains both rayon and acetate, the
quilt dates after the beginning of the 1920s, when acetate first appeared in
apparel.[4] Mary used a cloth foundation, thus did not add a filler. The quilt is
tied rather than quilted.

Mary's family tree includes such illustrious Rhode Island names as Richard Smith, who owned a trading post in seventeenth-century Wickford,
and Colonial governor Caleb Carr. In 1880 she married Herbert Eugene

FIG. 145. (*Opposite*) String quilt, 1930–36. Printed rayon, acetate, and silk pieces, cotton back, cotton ties, 87 x 68 in. Hand-pieced, tied. Made by Mary Matteson Knight (1859–1936). Collection of Shirley Tibbetts Gulvin. RIQDP #271.

FIG. 146. Mary Matteson Knight (1859–1936).

Knight, who came from another old Rhode Island family. They lived in his parental home on Liberty Church Road in Exeter, where they farmed, and raised four children. Mary and her three daughters, Lurena May (1882–1960), Flora Edith (1884–1961), and Eva Belle (1896–1968) were prolific quilt-makers; a dozen of their quilts survive, including other string quilts. The present owner is the great-granddaughter of Mary Knight.

1. Pat Nickols, "String Quilts," in *Uncoverings 1982*, Sally Garoutte, ed. (San Francisco: American Quilt Study Group, 1983), 53.

*Notes*

Fig. 147. Knight family home on Liberty Church Road in Exeter.

2. Merikay Waldvogel, *Soft Covers for Hard Times: Quiltmaking and the Great Depression* (Nashville, Tenn.: Rutledge Hill Press, 1990), 50–53.

3. Jonathan Holstein, *Abstract Design in American Quilts: A Biography of an Exhibition* (Louisville: The Kentucky Quilt Project, Inc., 1991), 139, 157, 163.

4. Phyllis G. Tortora, "75 Years of Change in Consumer Textiles (1921–1996)," *Textile Chemist and Colorist* 29, no. 5 (May 1997): 19. Both rayon and cellulose acetate were marketed as artificial or art silk until 1924, at which time the Department of Commerce established the name "rayon" for both fibers.

# Block Island's Temperance Quilt

LINDA WELTERS

THE TEMPERANCE MOVEMENT BECAME ONE OF THE COUNTRY S LARGEST women's reform movements. The Woman's Christian Temperance Union (WCTU), founded in 1874, addressed a variety of issues that affected women's lives, chiefly male consumption of alcohol. By joining temperance unions that fought to close saloons, women gained an element of control over the spousal abuse and economic destitution that threatened the American family as a result of excessive drinking. The movement also campaigned for other issues that affected women's lives, namely the eight-hour work day, child care for women workers, prison reform, and women's suffrage.[1]

The Woman's Christian Temperance Union of Rhode Island held its organizational meeting on January 20, 1875, at the First Baptist Church in Providence. It aimed to encourage "political and social progress to correct rampant evils which were mostly drink associated."[2] In time nearly 120 local unions formed. Two Block Island unions are listed in the state organization's records: the Block Island Union organized in 1895 and the Ocean View in 1896.[3]

Textiles became an integral part of the temperance movement in 1878 when a quilt with over 3,000 signatures was presented at the annual national WCTU convention in Baltimore. Known as the Crusade quilt, it symbolized "women's patience in matters of detail."[4] Fund-raising signature quilts like the Crusade quilt aided the temperance cause; each signature represented a cash contribution. At least one quilt pattern, Drunkard's Path, is associated with the temperance movement.

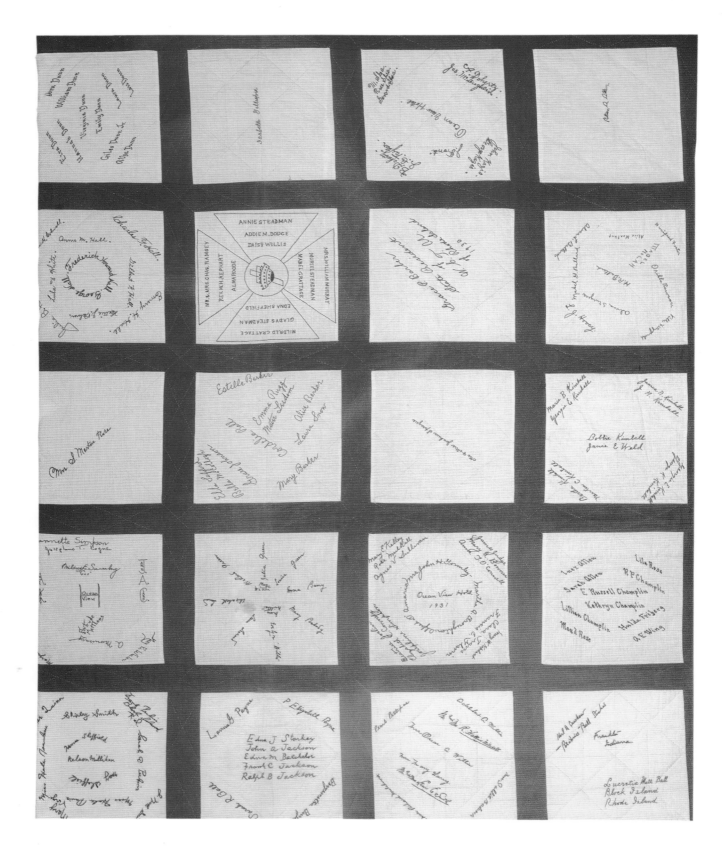

This oversized signature quilt with its sixty-three blocks (plus two on the back) raised money for the national WCTU's "Crusade Crucible" campaign of 1931 to defeat the repeal of the Prohibition Amendment.[5] The quilt's central block is a crucible. The many signatures embroidered on this quilt identify members from national, state, and local chapters. Signatures of Block Island residents include the names Willis, Dodge, Champlin, Mitchell, Babcock, Payre, and Sheffield, plus others. One of the blocks carries the signature of Grace P. Barber, President of the Rhode Island chapter of WCTU in 1930; another contains that of Block Island's Lucretia Mott Ball, founder and president of the Ocean View Union. She also served as vice-president-at-large of the Rhode Island Chapter the year the quilt was made. Lucretia, one of Block Island's most influential women, was married to Cassius Clay Ball, who owned Block Island's largest hotel, the Ocean View.[6] The hotel contributed several squares to the quilt.

Kathryn Champlin Kernan, one of the signers, was thirteen at the time the quilt was made. She recalls that the squares were passed out at school. Kathryn's mother was an active member of the island's WCTU, a group that met regularly for social as well as political reasons. Kathryn and her young friends referred to the WCTU as the "Women Constantly Talking Union."[7]

In 1896, Lucretia Mott Ball's WCTU erected a fountain in the center of New Shoreham with a statue depicting Rebecca. The fountain had three

FIG. 148. (*Opposite*) Detail, temperance signature quilt, 1931. Cotton, red cotton embroidery, 128 x 103 in. Machine-pieced and hand-quilted, 5–7 stitches per inch. Made by members of the Ocean View (Block Island) Chapter of the Woman's Christian Temperance Union. Block Island Historical Society. RIQDP #573.

FIG. 149. Postcard, Ocean View Hotel, Block Island, R.I., ca. 1907. Rhode Island Historical Society.

levels of basins so that dogs, humans, and horses could drink pure, natural water. Although the water no longer flows to quench the thirst of passersby, the statue still stands as a local landmark.[8]

1. Pat Ferrero, Elaine Hedges, and Julie Silber, *Hearts and Hands: The Influence of Women and Quilts on American Society* (San Francisco: Quilt Digest Press, 1987), 82–91.

2. Inventory, Papers of the Woman's Christian Temperance Union of Rhode Island, Mss. 811, Rhode Island Historical Society (hereafter cited as Papers of the WCTU of R.I.)

3. The listing of two unions on Block Island is perplexing as islanders remember only one local WCTU. Perhaps the Block Island Union reorganized as the Ocean View in 1896. List of Unions and Organization Dates, January 20, 1875–May 1947, Papers of the WCTU of R.I.

4. Ferrero, Hedges, and Silber, *Hearts and Hands,* 87.

5. Harry E. Caylor, Press and Community Information, The Seventy-Fifth (Diamond) Anniversary Year of the National WCTU, 1949—The Story of *"The Matchless Machine Manned by Christian Women and Powered by Prayer,"* 1949, Papers of the WCTU of R.I.

6. Robert M. Downie, "'For God and Home and Every Land': Rebecca, a 100-year-old young lady," *Block Island Times,* July 20, 1996, 32.

7. Kathryn Champlin Kernan, telephone interview with author, September 9, 1997.

8. Downie, "Rebecca," 32–33.

# The Cherry Quilt

LINDA WELTERS

THIS QUILT WITH ITS UNUSUAL MOTIF OF RED CIRCLES WITH GREEN STEMS and leaves perplexed volunteers at the Portsmouth Library documentation day. Was it an abstraction of a flower, perhaps a poppy? Was it a fruit? One volunteer suggested that the design might be a lollipop. Everyone had an opinion. Later we learned that the quiltmaker, retired educator Lydia Belle Miller Kay of East Providence, referred to the quilt as "the one with the cherries."

Belle, as she was known, made the quilt as a fund-raiser for her church. She was a charter member of the United Congregational Church of East Providence, founded in 1871, and an active member of its "United Workers." To help reduce the mortgage on the tower and the south wing added to the church's original building in 1931, she created the cherry quilt.[1] Belle's niece offered the quilt for sale to various interior decorating firms on Providence's fashionable East Side, but no one made an offer. Someone suggested she sell chances. The quiltmaker refused on the grounds that a raffle was in essence gambling, an activity incongruent with her membership in the Woman's Christian Temperance Union. Belle packed the quilt in a box where it remained unused.

Lydia Belle Miller was born in Bristol in 1865. She graduated from Rhode Island Normal School, eventually becoming principal of the Williams Street Elementary School.[2] At the age of fifty-five she married John Kay. The quilt's present owner, great-niece Elizabeth Ramsden, was the flower girl at their wedding. Belle lived to the age of eighty-seven. Elizabeth, who graduated from the Rhode Island School of Design in 1939 with a bachelor's degree in Art Education, was given this quilt after Belle's death because of her interest in crafts. Belle left Elizabeth another quilt, an unfinished Dresden Plate pieced from dresses that had belonged to Elizabeth and her sister.

1. The United Congregational Church of East Providence was built in 1888. The church closed in 1951.

2. The Williams Street School, built in 1888, was located just around the corner from the United Congregational Church. It is no longer operating.

FIG. 150. (*Opposite*) Cherry quilt, 1931–32. Cotton top and back, 78½ x 77 in. Hand-quilted and hand-embroidered, 10–12 stitches per inch. Made by Lydia Belle Miller Kay (1865–1952). Collection of Elizabeth Ramsden. RIQDP #417.

FIG. 151. Lydia Belle Miller Kay (1865–1952).

# A Depression-Era Quilt

MARGARET T. ORDOÑEZ

DURING THE 1930S THE WORK RELIEF PROGRAM OF THE WORKS PROGRESS
Administration (WPA) promoted weaving and sewing crafts in an effort to
preserve American handicrafts of the past. Quilting was one of the home
crafts endorsed by the program. In support of this effort, editors published
quilt patterns, often with patriotic themes, in newspapers and farm journals throughout the United States.[1]

An example of the patriotic themes were collections of officially recognized state flowers and birds. In 1933 *The Literary Digest* published lists of
state flowers except one from Pennsylvania where the representative flower
remained undetermined. The cover of their February 4, 1933 edition illustrated a group of eighteen state flowers verified by the governors of those
states. An article titled "All the State Flowers Will Soon Be Budding" provided the key to the cover page along with a review of gardening advice
from an article in *The Country Gentleman*. A footnote promised more offi-
cials flowers the following week.[2]

In these early days of the Depression, state flower designs from quilt-
pattern designer Ruby McKim, appeared weekly in the country's newspapers.[3] Quilters traced the full-scale drawings onto cotton fabric with carbon paper and embroidered outlines of the blossoms in colorful cotton floss.
McKim's designs outlined initials and abbreviations of the state names.

Outline embroidery had been popular since the 1880s when it appeared
on crazy quilts. From 1880 to 1925 red yarn on white cotton dominated until
embroidery threads of many colors became available after World War I.[4]
Susan Rounds Barker, an accomplished needlewoman, obtained McKim's
patterns from the *Providence Evening Bulletin* and worked them in colorful
yarns. Barker worked for E. L. Logee Co. on Chestnut Street and lived at 1

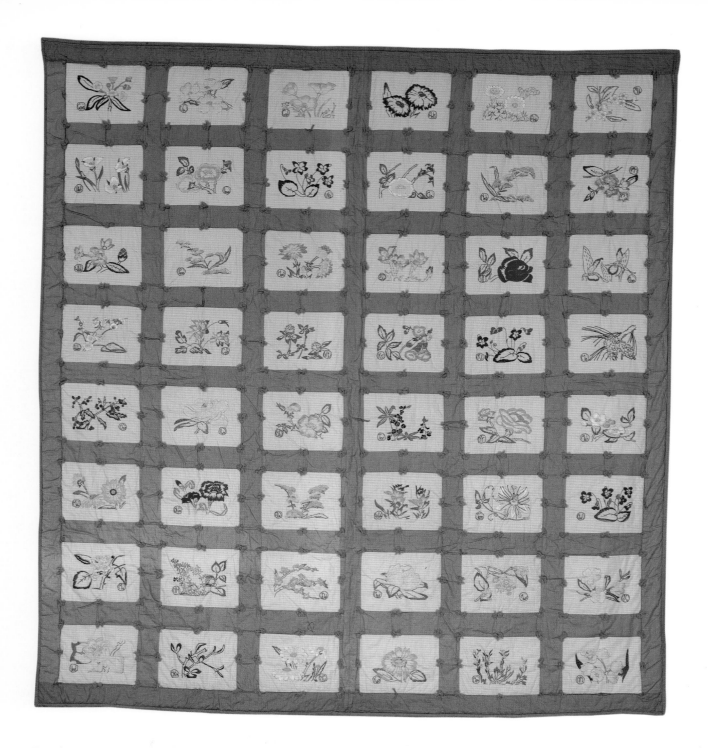

Pontiac Street (now Avenue) in Providence. She set the squares with blue sashing and completed the tied quilt for her young niece, the present owner.

FIG. 152. State Flower quilt, early 1930s. Cotton embroidery thread, cotton fabric, wool ties, 71 x 66 in. Hand-embroidered, machine-sewn, tied. Made by Susan Rounds Barker (1883–1980). Private collection. RIQDP #172.

Notes

1. Patsy Orlofsky and Myron Orlofsky, *Quilts in America* (New York: Abbeville Press, 1974), 80–81.

2. *The Literary Digest* 115, no. 3 (February 4, 1933), cover, 34–35.

3. McKim's designs, like the ones in this quilt, are the basis for a similar quilt pictured in Merikay Waldvogel, *Soft Covers for Hard Times: Quiltmaking and The Great Depression* (Nashville, Tenn.: Rutledge Hill, 1990), 17. Ruby McKim published a well-known book of quilt patterns. Ruby Short McKim, *One Hundred and One Patchwork Patterns* (Independence, Mo.: McKim Studios, 1931).

4. Barbara Brackman, *Clues in the Calico: A Guide to Identifying and Dating Antique Quilts* (McLean, Va.: EPM Publications, 1989), 108.

# Anchors Aweigh

LINDA WELTERS

THE YO-YO TECHNIQUE INVOLVED CUTTING FABRIC CIRCLES, TURNING under the edges with a running stitch, then gathering the fabric into puffs. The fabric disks either could be sewn together to form a lacey fabric or attached to a base. By arranging disks of like colors together, two-dimensional patterns could be created. Since no quilting is involved, "cover" or "spread" is a more accurate term than "quilt" for a bed cover in the yo-yo technique. Yo-yo spreads came into vogue during the 1930s, although the technique originated decades earlier. Women's nineteenth-century periodicals illustrate this technique for Victorian fancywork.[1]

As Catherine Cerny observes in her essay in this volume, the making of quilts sometimes transcended gender to reinforce kinship ties. The making of this yo-yo spread was a father-daughter effort in the Champlin family of Block Island. Robert chose the design and drew it on paper for his sixteen-year-old daughter Kathryn, who executed it. In the Champlin house, built in 1827, the finished spread occasionally decorated a single bed with a dust ruffle. The anchor motif, long associated with the Ocean State, is especially appropriate for this Block Island family.

Robert Paine Champlin, who enjoyed fishing, always owned a boat. At one time he sold lobsters, but mostly he fished for pleasure. Kathryn often accompanied her father on the boat. As his primary occupation, Robert worked the family farm. He raised vegetables to sell to the island's hotels and kept dairy cows. In the summer, he sold milk and cream; in the winter, he made butter.

Robert's father, Edward Peckham Champlin, served as town clerk for forty-eight and one-half years. Upon Edward's death in 1940, Robert assumed the position, which he retained for twenty-four and one-half years. Together, father and son served the town for a total of seventy-three years.

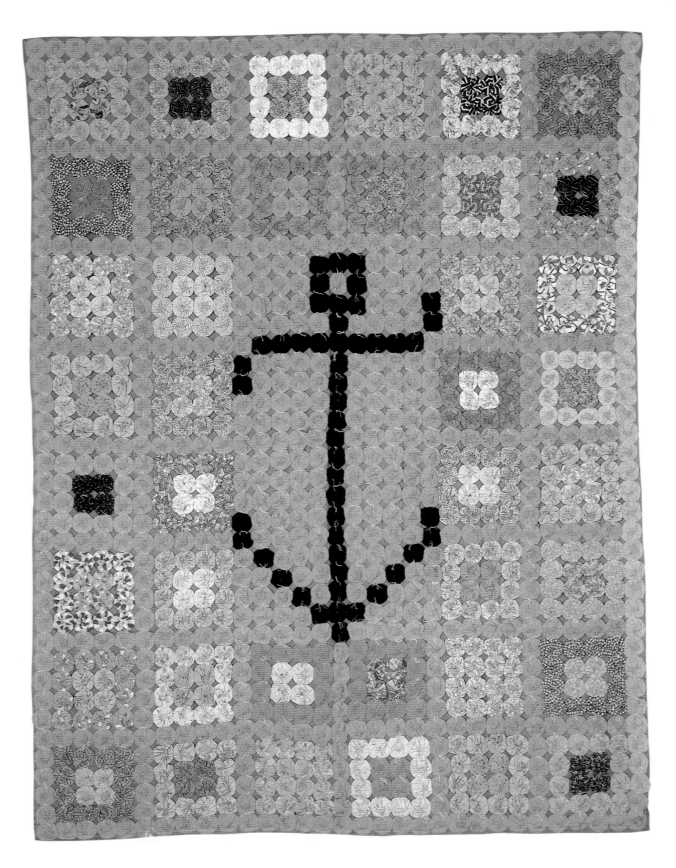

FIG. 154. (*Opposite*) Yo-Yo spread, 1934–35. Plain and printed cotton, 74 x 54 in. Hand-pieced. Designed by Robert Paine Champlin (1889–1972), made by Kathryn Champlin (1918–). Collection of Kathryn Champlin Kernan. RIQDP #576.

FIG. 155. Kathryn Champlin.

1. Virginia Gunn, "Yo-Yo or Bed-of-Roses Quilts: Nineteenth-Century Origins," in *Uncoverings 1987*, Laurel Horton and Sally Garoutte, eds. (San Francisco: American Quilt Study Group, 1988), 136–40.

*Note*

# From Clothes to Bed

LINDA WELTERS

SQUARES ARRANGED IN BLOCKS OF FOUR, NINE, OR SIXTEEN PATCHES are among the earliest and most enduring of Rhode Island quilt patterns. The Four-Patch block ranked fourth most frequent patchwork block in the RIQDP database. Seen in Rhode Island quilts dating from the beginning of the nineteenth century, the pattern continued to be used well into the twentieth century. Easy to piece, Four-Patch quilt designs easily made use of leftover fabrics and are thus emblematic of the thriftiness of Rhode Island quilters.

Caroline Palmer made this Four-Patch in the late 1930s from clothing scraps. The green stripe was left over from a dress ca. 1933, and the blue plaid was fabric remaining from a bathing suit ca. 1935.

The novel fabric in the sashing is a cotton print showing various Native American motifs including teepees, drums, rattles, potters at work, and arrows in a quiver. This print merges the object, also called conversation, print with Art Deco–inspired motifs. Object prints, seen as early as 1840, consist of figurative subject matter other than florals in small-scale, isolated motifs.[1] Textile designers emphasized novelty of motif rather than color, thus the majority of object prints had just one or two colors. The number of colors in object prints increased in the twentieth century. As Caroline Palmer's print illustrates, textile designers of the Art Deco period took inspiration from various sources including American Indian art to create rectilinear motifs for object prints.[2]

Caroline Barber married James Palmer in Peace Dale, Rhode Island in 1892. They were members of the Peace Dale Congregational Church. The couple built a new house on Main Street in Wakefield which is now Booth Contemporary Art.

FIG. 156. (*Opposite*) Four-Patch quilt, after 1935. Cotton, cotton string ties, 77 x 62 in. Machine-pieced, tied. Made by Caroline Barber Palmer (1859–1947). Collection of Patricia A. Barrett. RIQDP #148.

288

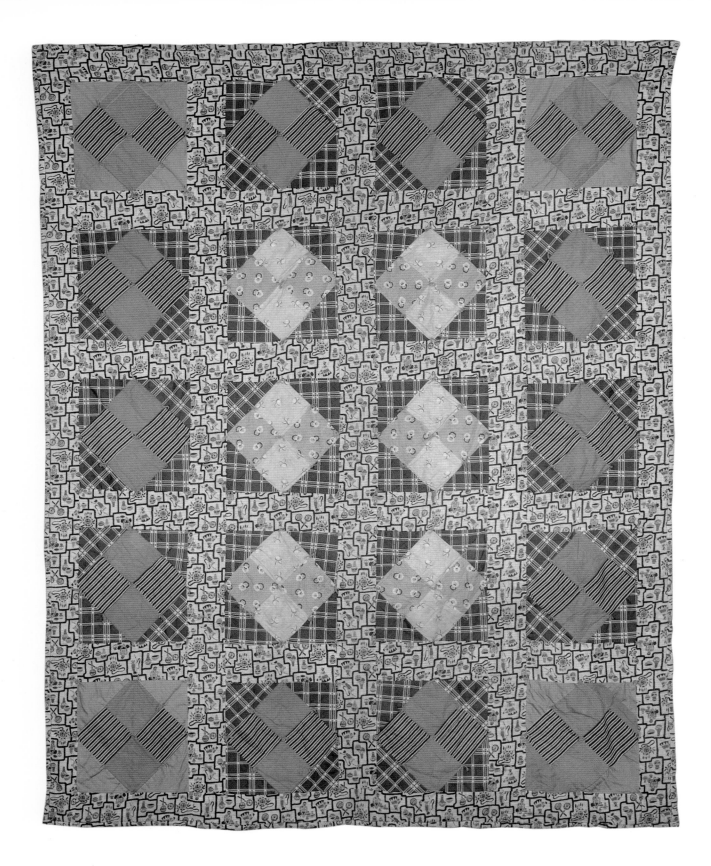

FIG. 157. Caroline Barber Palmer *(center)* with friends.

*Notes*

1. Barbara Brackman, *Clues in the Calico: A Guide to Identifying and Dating Antique Quilts* (McClean, Va.: EMS Publications, 1989), 91–92.

2. Bevis Hillier, *Art Deco* (London: Studio Vista, 1968), 13.

# Glossary

| | |
|---|---|
| ALIZARIN | The principal coloring component of madder (q.v.); synthetically produced after 1870. |
| AZOIC DYES | Synthetic dyes produced directly in the fibers of a cloth by the reaction of their constituent parts; the first ones developed in the 1880s were as bright as Turkey red; also called naphthol dyes or ice colors. |
| BARK | See quercitron. |
| BARONETTE | High-luster silk or cotton satin fabric; can be a mixture of cotton filling and silk warp. |
| BAST FIBERS | Fibers that grow in bundles to provide strength for stems of plants; can be separated to make cloth and cordage; flax, jute, hemp, and ramie. |
| BATTING | Sheets of carded wool or cotton fibers used as middle layer in quilts. |
| BEDTICK | See tick. |
| BINDER | Cement or adhesive used in pigment printing to fix insoluble pigment to fabrics; examples include casein and albumen. |
| BLANKETING | Fabrics used for blankets; plain or twill weave of wool or cotton. |
| BLOCK PRINTING | Use of carved wood blocks cut in relief to transfer print paste to a fabric; a separate block is required for each color in a design; registration is regulated by metal pins at the corners; metal pins and strips inserted into the block produce fine details. |
| BLUE-RESIST PRINT | Technique of creating white patterns on blue ground; involves printing a wax or paste resist on a fabric that is then dipped in an indigo bath until the desired color is achieved; when the resist is removed, the protected area is undyed. |

| | |
|---|---|
| BRODERIE PERSE | Quilt top stitched in the appliquéd chintz style in which old Indian palampores or European calicoes were cut apart and stitched to new white grounds to create quilts and spreads; used on both whole cloth and on blocks. |
| CALENDERING | Finishing process that involves fabric running between rollers that produces a smooth or patterned surface on a fabric; calendering made a smooth finish on glazed calicoes. |
| CALICO | Lightweight, plain weave, painted and printed cotton fabric originally from Calicut, India; describes block, plate, and cylinder printed cottons in England and America. |
| CALIMANCO | A glazed wool fabric, twill weave. |
| CAMBRIC | Plain-weave cotton or linen fabric with a slightly lustrous calendered wax or starched finish. |
| CANDLEWICKING | Tufting technique that imitates use of chenille yarns; loops of heavy yarn create raised, fuzzy patterns on a woven fabric surface. |
| CARONETTE | Possibly meaning caroset, a heavily fulled, twill-weave fabric. |
| CATECHU | Dye extracted from an acacia tree; first used in Europe around 1806, it was available at reasonable cost for use as a dye by 1830; colors include brown, drab, and fawn. |
| CELLULOSIC FIBERS | From plant source; cotton, flax, jute, and hemp. |
| CHAMBRAY | Plain-weave cotton fabric often made with a colored warp and white weft. |
| CHECK, CHECKS | Plain- or twill-woven fabric of dyed and undyed yarns in the warp and filling to produce a square pattern. |
| CHINA BLUE | Indigo printing technique that allows the insoluble indigo to be printed directly on a fabric; the print paste contains finely ground indigo and iron sulfate; the printed fabric is alternately dipped into baths of lime and iron sulfate solutions to dissolve and reduce the indigo so that it dyes the fabric; this technique cannot be used with other styles of dyeing but can produce several shades of blue. |
| CHINTZ | Plain-weave, Indian cotton fabric produced by a combination of mordant printing and indigo resist dyeing; it originally may or may not have had a glazed finish. |
| CHROME YELLOW | Color produced on cloth by a chemical reaction of a lead salt with dichromate; an alkaline treatment can convert the yellow lead chromate to chrome orange; chrome yellow was invented in 1819; chrome orange and chrome green followed. |
| CLEARING | Step in printing process that involves washing the fabric after printing to remove unfixed dye, particularly from white areas of the print. |
| COCHINEAL | A New World scarlet dye from a species of scale louse that lives on cactus plants; merchants made fortunes shipping dried cochineal beetles to Europe where it quickly replaced kermes, also a species of louse, from Mediterranean coasts. |
| COLORWAY | Combination of colors used in a printed fabric; printers used blocks or cylinders to produce fabrics with the same pattern but different colorways. |
| COPPER-PLATE PRINTING | Late-eighteenth- and early-nineteenth-century method that produced very fine lines and precise details in printed designs; the pattern was engraved into flat copper plates; the size of a repeated design typically measured about thirty-six inches in height and often was monochromatic; blocks added additional colors; replaced by cylinder printing. |
| CORDUROY | Weft-pile fabric with pile yarns arranged in vertical bands; pile usually cut short. |

| | |
|---|---|
| COVER AND PAD STYLE | A variation of the madder style using a covering cylinder engraved with a small-detailed design and a padding cylinder engraved with closely spaced fine diagonal lines or dots; a dark-shade mordant printed with covering roller and a light-shade mordant printed with a padding roller produces a dark figure on a solid light-colored ground. |
| COVERLET | A bed cover; a patterned-weave bedcover; usually linen or cotton mixed with dyed wool. |
| CRETONNE | Printed cotton or linen fabric of varying weights, usually unglazed and characterized by large-scale motifs; used for furnishing textiles. |
| CYLINDER PRINTING | Method of printing cloth with engraved or etched copper cylinders; the design is recessed below the surface of the cylinder; a separate cylinder applies each color of a design; the maximum length of a repeat is twenty-two inches; the method was first used in the late eighteenth century; also called roller printing. |
| DELAINE | Also mousseline de laine; a fabric that is a mixture of wool and cotton; dual fiber content limits printing to steam style. |
| DIAPER | Fabric with small diamond-shaped pattern woven in; silk, cotton, or linen. |
| DIE-AND-MILL ENGRAVING | Use of a hardened, patterned die to create a pattern in relief on a mill that imprints the pattern into the surface of a copper cylinder for printing. |
| DIMITY | Cotton fabric woven with grouped yarns in the warp and/or weft that produce stripes or checks; could be printed. |
| DIRECT PRINTING | Applying color directly onto fabric in contrast to methods such as printing mordants or resists and then immersing fabric in a dye bath or discharging a predyed cloth. |
| DISCHARGE STYLE | Printing method using print paste containing a discharge chemical which when applied to a predyed fabric destroys the dye, leaving a white figure; a discharge paste containing a dye that is resistant to the destruction produces a colored or illuminated pattern; method also used to discharge patterns in mordants before dyeing in the madder style. |
| DOUBLE JEAN BACK CORD | A cotton corduroy fabric with a twill-weave foundation; the striped pile of the corduroy is woven as a double cloth (i.e., weft yarns weave through two separate layers of warp yarns, are cut apart with knives, and are brushed to make cut ends stand up). |
| DOUBLE PINKS | Printed pattern with multiple shades of a color produced by printing different concentrations of mordant before dyeing the fabric; often achieved with the cover and pad style (q.v.); also called two reds or three reds, etc.; also produces double purples and double browns. |
| DRUGGET | Eighteenth-century plain- or twill-weave fabric with a worsted warp and woolen filling; an unbalanced plain-weave drugget has a rib. |
| DUNGING | Washing process that followed ageing to continue the fixation of mordants printed on fabrics and to remove thickening material and any unfixed mordant; until the late nineteenth century, dunging was usually performed with cow dung. |
| DYED STYLE | Method of dyeing fabric with a dye that has no substantivity for the fiber in the fabric by using mordants to bind the dye to the fiber; the madder style is a dyed style using madder as a dye. |

DYEING   Application of dye to a fabric by immersion; in contrast to printing, it produces fabric with the same intensity of color on both sides.

ETCHING   Method of creating a design in relief on a copper cylinder; engraver cuts through varnish on a cylinder to expose copper that is eroded when placed in an acid bath; the method improved with the use of a pantograph (pentograph) engraving machine.

FILLING   See weft.

FLANNEL   Plain- or twill-weave fabric of wool or cotton; napped surface.

FULLING   Process involving heat, moisture, and agitation to shrink and felt woven or knitted wool cloth, making a dense, firm fabric.

FUSTIAN   Eighteenth-century term for fabric with a linen warp and cotton filling; sometimes printed.

GARANCINE   Natural madder concentrated by treatment with heat and sulfuric acid; introduced in the 1830s.

GINGHAM   Plain-weave cotton with yarn-dyed warp and filling that form checks or plaids.

IKAT   Patterned fabric with design created by resist dyeing warp and/or weft before weaving.

ILLUMINATED PRINT   Colored design produced when a discharge print paste contains a dye or chemical that is resistant to destruction by the discharge; an illuminated print also can be done in resist style; this method produces a colored design that has uniformly good registration.

INDIENNES   Painted and printed cotton cloth imported from India from the early seventeenth century; the term was later applied to designs with meandering vines, composite blossoms, flowering trees, and exotic birds.

INDIGO   Blue vat dye from plants that is insoluble in its natural state and has no substantivity; it was printed directly on fabric by pencil blue and china blue methods in the eighteenth and nineteenth centuries; finally in 1883 it was successfully direct printed with the glucose process; indigo was often used with resist and discharge styles; a synthetic version of the dye was commercially produced in 1897.

INORGANIC CHEMICALS   Compounds of mineral origin as opposed to carbon-based organic chemicals of vegetable or animal origin.

JEAN   Durable warp-faced, twill-weave fabric of all cotton or cotton warp and woolen weft.

KERMES   Ancient European and North African scarlet dye extracted from the dried bodies of pregnant female plant lice; replaced by cochineal.

KERSEY   Durable napped, fulled wool fabric, twill weave; can have a cotton warp.

LINSEY-WOOLSEY   Coarse cloth of linen or cotton warp and wool filling.

| | |
|---|---|
| MACHINE GROUNDS | Busy ground pattern printed with cover cylinder; die-and-mill engraved patterns on copper cylinders led to busy ground covers instead of plain or solid-colored grounds. |
| MADDER | Principal red dye from the Middle Ages in Europe through most of the nineteenth century; extracted from the roots of the madder plant, it was fast to light and washing. |
| MADDER STYLE | Method of printing one or more mordants or concentrations of mordant on a cloth followed by dyeing the fabric in a madder dye bath; dye is fixed to the mordant in the printed design and washed out of the nonprinted areas; produces different colors with different mordants or mordant mixtures; also called dyed style. |
| MANUFACTURED FIBERS | Rayon and acetate are regenerated from naturally occurring cellulose; nylon, polyester, acrylic, olefin, and others are synthesized. |
| MARSEILLES QUILT | An all-white, whole-cloth, quilted bed cover with a raised pattern; imitated by machine-woven cloths after 1763. |
| MEDALLION QUILT | Piecing pattern with successive borders surrounding center square or rectangle. |
| MINERAL COLORS | Of inorganic origin, mineral colors include Prussian blue, manganese bronze, iron buff, and chrome yellow, orange, and green; they are produced as pigments or created directly on the fiber by a precipitation reaction. |
| MIXTURE | Fabric woven of yarns made of more than one fiber content. |
| MOHAIR | Lustrous fabric made of hair from the Angora goat; fiber also called mohair. |
| MORDANT | Metallic salts, which are printed or painted on cloth and fixed to fibers by ageing and dunging, combine in a dye bath with dyes to fix them on the cloth; iron and aluminum are most common and can be used in varying concentrations or mixed; mordant solutions are named by the color that they will produce, e.g., "red liquor." |
| NANKEEN | Durable, fine-textured cotton twill fabric; may be dyed yellow to imitate original nankeens that were silk and cotton fabrics imported from China; nonwhite because of natural coloring of wild silk or yellow cotton. |
| NATURAL FIBERS | Fibers from animals, plants, or minerals; see cellulosic fibers and protein fibers. |
| NEGRO CLOTH | Low-thread-count cotton fabric made for sale to slaveowners; Peacedale Manufacturing Company was a major Rhode Island supplier of Negro cloth. |
| ON POINT | Orientation of square quilt blocks rotated forty-five degrees from a horizontal position. |
| ORPIMENT | Arsenic trisulfide; orpiment reduces indigo so that it can be brushed (penciled) or printed on cloth; used during eighteenth and nineteenth centuries. |
| PADDING | Method of applying chemicals to fabric by dipping cloth into a solution and then uniformly squeezing it between rollers. |
| PALAMPORE | An Indian painted and printed cotton bed cover, typically with composite flowers and exotic birds on a tree of life growing from a rockery. |
| PENCILING | Brushing dye or pigment onto a fabric; pencil blue refers to penciling with a reduced form of indigo. |
| PERROTINE PRINT | Fabric printed on a continuous printing machine that used three wooden blocks. |

| | |
|---|---|
| PIECED QUILT | Quilted bed cover with a top layer of fabric made of pieces of cloth sewn together to create a pattern; it may or may not have a border; the edges were finished with a binding or with the top or back fabric overlapping the edge. |
| PIGMENT STYLE | Method of printing in which a binder fixes an insoluble pigment to the surface of a fabric. |
| PILLAR PRINT | Pattern of classic columns and large blossoms popular at the beginning of the nineteenth century and revived during the second quarter of the century. |
| PRINT PASTE | A flour- or gum-thickened mixture of dyes and/or chemicals applied to a fabric to produce a colored design. |
| PRINT WORKS | A building, or room in a building, that houses equipment for printing fabrics. |
| PRINTING | Application of colored designs to the surface of a cloth with wood blocks, wood rollers, copper plates, copper cylinders, or screens. |
| PROTEIN FIBERS | Fibers from animal sources; silk and wool. |
| PRUSSIAN BLUE | See mineral colors. |
| QUERCITRON | A fast yellow New World dye from the inner bark of eastern U.S. black oak trees; developed and promoted by Edward Bancroft of Massachusetts in the late eighteenth and early nineteenth centuries; dyers called it "bark." |
| QUILTING | Needlework technique of sewing together two layers of fabric and a middle element such as batting with lines of stitches. |
| RAISED STYLE | Two-step method of coloring a fabric; the first component is printed on the fabric; the color is then "raised" by passing the fabric through a bath containing the second chemical where the two react and produce an insoluble color in the fiber; the method is used chiefly for mineral colors. |
| REGISTRATION | Alignment of pattern components in printing fabrics; also called "fit." |
| RESIST STYLE | Printing method using a substance to prevent penetration or fixation of dye or mordant; the resist style acts by forming a physical barrier or by chemically interfering with the fixation; also known as reserve style. |
| RHEOLOGY | The flow properties of matter; thickeners provide the rheology necessary to allow print paste to flow onto the fabric during printing yet retain a clearly defined edge to the design until drying and fixation occur. |
| ROLLER PRINTING | See cylinder printing. |
| ROVING | A slightly twisted grouping of staple fibers; the stage of yarn production between sliver and yarn. |
| SASHING | Strips of fabric sewn between blocks in a pieced quilt top. |
| SCREEN PRINTING | Method of forcing print paste through a mesh screen that is blocked in the nonprint areas; print paste can be applied by hand or mechanically; flatbed screens were used commercially in the Western world in the early twentieth century; more rapid rotary screens were introduced in the 1960s; screen printing is now a major print technique. |
| SERGE | Even-sided twill fabric of wool, linen, cotton, silk, or a mixture of two of these fibers; often has a two-up and two-down righthand twill construction. |

| | |
|---|---|
| SHEETING | Plain-weave linen or cotton produced in square pieces, often around forty inches or sixty-eight inches square. |
| SPIRIT STYLE | Method of printing dyes directly and developing them by ageing the fabric at room temperature before washing briefly in cold water; this method produced poor fastness so these fabrics were sold on the low-end market. |
| STAPLE | Refers to fibers that are not continuous filaments and that require twisting in a spinning process to make a yarn. |
| STEAM STYLE | Method that combines the dye and mordant in the print paste and uses steam to age fabrics, producing an insoluble complex in the fiber that is reasonably fast to wet treatments; introduced in the 1830s on wool and mixed fabrics, later on cotton cloth. |
| STRIP QUILT | Pieces of fabric organized in strips; unpieced strips may alternate with pieced ones, or printed strips with plain fabric. |
| STYLE | Method used to achieve coloration, rather than a pattern; see Table 6. |
| SUBSTANTIVITY | Physical forces of attraction between a dye and a fiber; a dye with substantivity is attracted from a dye bath to a fiber; necessary for a dye to penetrate a fiber. |
| SURFACE PRINTING | Method using cylindrical wooden rollers carved in relief; the maximum repeat was twenty-two inches; first used in the eighteenth century. |
| SYNTHETIC FIBERS | See manufactured fibers. |
| TAMMY | Plain- or twill-weave fabric of wool or a cotton warp and wool weft with a lustrous calendered finish; also tammie or tammye. |
| TEMPLATE WORK | Technique of basting fabrics onto cardboard or paper patterns to shape pieces for a quilt top; bastings and papers are usually removed after pieces are stitched together, but when newspapers, letters, or boxes are still in place, they can provide valuable historical information; hexagon and diamond patterns were common in English piecing and silk template work. |
| THICKENERS | Materials such as wheat flour or starch with gum provide rheology (q.v.) to print pastes. |
| THROSTLE | Continuous spinning frame for making wool or cotton yarn; has drawing rollers with bobbins and flyers; named because of a birdlike sound emitted when spinning. |
| TICK, TICKING, BED TICK | Strong, tightly woven cotton or linen fabric; can be made of dyed yarns that produce a stripe; plain, twill, or satin weave. |
| TOILE, TOILE DE JOUY | Printed cotton fabric from Oberkampf's factory established in 1760 in Jouy-en-Josas, France; also designs with isolated, monochromatic scenes typical of Oberkampf's toiles. |
| TOW, TOW-CLOTH | Heavy, coarse linen fabric woven of tow, broken fibers less than ten inches long; tow is separated from line, longer fibers, during processing. |
| TURKEY RED | A much-desired, brilliant, clear red-colored cloth produced by the Turks from madder, alum, and oil; eighteenth- and nineteenth-century Western dyers sought to imitate the secret processes, which took at least a month to complete; discharged, illuminated designs in this fabric called Turkey red calico. |
| TWILL | Weave structure in which warp yarns float over two or more wefts in a stepwise progression that produces a right- or lefthand diagonal line. |

| | |
|---|---|
| UNION PRINTING | Method that combined surface printing with wooden rollers and copper cylinders; also called mule printing. |
| VAT | Chemically reducing dye bath; used to dissolve and reduce indigo to a soluble state so that it will dye fabric. |
| VELVET | Warp-pile fabric, usually with the pile cut short; can be any fiber. |
| VELVETEEN | Weft-pile fabric of spun yarns; term might be used for a velvet woven with cotton; velveteen differs from corduroy in that pile is evenly spaced rather than woven in rows. |
| WARP | Vertical set of yarns in a woven fabric lying parallel to the selvage; often stronger and with more twists than weft. |
| WEAVE SHED | Building, or room in a building, containing looms on which fabrics are woven. |
| WEAVERETTE | Fabric with a linen warp and cotton weft; listed in the cloth production books of Almy and Brown. |
| WEFT | Horizontal set of yarns in a woven fabric, lying at right angles to the warp and extending from selvage to selvage; also called filling. |
| WELD | European plant that yields a yellow dye; usually mordanted with alum, weld was one of the most common yellow dyes in England until replaced by quercitron early in the nineteenth century. |
| WHITE WORK | White embroidery on white fabric; raised needlework with cording or stuffing creating a three-dimensional design such as a Marseilles quilt. |
| WHOLE-CLOTH QUILT | Bed cover made of one fabric that is not pieced but is seamed to make the lengths of fabric large enough for the cover. |
| WOAD | Blue dye extracted from a European plant; chemically identical to indigo but not as concentrated; superseded by indigo in the sixteenth century. |
| WOOLEN | Yarn or fabric made of carded wool. |
| WORSTED | Yarn or fabric made of carded and combed wool; more durable than a woolen fabric. |

# Contributors

AUD FJELLBERG ACKERMAN, a native of Norway, studied textile conservation at the University of Rhode Island. Now living in Villanova, Pennsylvania, she is pursuing her current interest in computer graphics.

MARTIN BIDE's background is in the chemistry of dyes and dyeing. He received his Ph.D. from the University of Bradford in England and spent time in the dyemaking industry before crossing the Atlantic to teach at the University of Massachusetts, Dartmouth. Since 1991 he has been at the University of Rhode Island where he teaches textile science and is currently pursuing research in textile pollution prevention and biomedical modifications of textile materials.

JEFFREY BUTTERWORTH received his M.F.A. at the University of Washington. He is an associate professor of English/drama and costume designer/director at the Community College of Rhode Island. He also completed a master's degree in the textiles, fashion merchandising, and design department at the University of Rhode Island.

CATHERINE A. CERNY, who received her Ph.D. from the University of Minnesota, has taught clothing and textiles at the University of Rhode Island and Virginia Polytechnic Institute and State University. Her interest in quilts is directed toward a cultural analysis of contemporary quiltmaking and its significance in American society. She was one of the four-member team steering RIQDP.

KARIN CONOPASK is curator at the Slater Mill Historic Site and develops seasonal exhibits at South County Museum in Narragansett, Rhode Island. She holds a Master's of Science in textiles, fashion merchandising, and design from the University of Rhode Island. She served as Project Intern for "Stitches in Time: Rhode Island Quilts" at the Rhode Island Historical Society.

CYNTHIA DIMOCK-QUAGLIA earned her Bachelor of Science degree in apparel marketing at the University of Massachusetts, Amherst, and her Master of Science degree in textiles, merchandising, and design at the University of Rhode Island. Her thesis involved the conservation and exhibition of Rhode Island Military Uniforms. She is currently employed in product development at Russ Berrie and Company, Inc.

LINDA EPPICH is the chief curator of the Rhode Island Historical Society. She received a Master's of Science degree from Eastern Michigan University in textiles and clothing and did postgraduate work at the University of Minnesota and the University of Rhode Island, studying textile history, conservation, and American history. She researches and installs exhibitions and interprets the Society's diverse collections.

TESS FREDETTE is an assistant conservator at the Textile Conservation Center of the American Textile History Museum in Lowell, Massachusetts. Specializing in tapestry weaving and dyeing, she received a B.F.A. in fibers from the Massachusetts College of Art in 1988 and a Graduate Certificate in museum studies from Tufts University and a Master of Science degree from the University of Rhode Island.

VIRGINIA GUNN, Ph.D., is a professor of clothing, textiles, and interiors at the University of Akron in Ohio. She has published and presented numerous papers on the history of quilts. She served on the board of the American Quilt Study Group for ten years, serving as its president from 1990 to 1993. Since 1994, she has been the editor of *Uncoverings*, the annual volume of quilt research published by AQSG.

ALDA LOUISE GANZE KAYE earned a Master of Science degree from the University of Rhode Island where she was curator of the U.R.I. Historic Textile and Costume Collection from 1972–98. Kaye curated "American Quilts: An Exhibition from the U.R.I. Collection Celebrating Rhode Island's 350th Anniversary" in 1986. During her sabbatical at the University of Hawaii at Manoa, she studied Hawaiian quilts. Kaye was one of the four-member team steering RIQDP.

SUSAN HANDY KIRBY earned her Master of Science degree in 1996 in textiles, fashion merchandising, and design at the University of Rhode Island. Her maternal family manufactured cloth in Blackstone Valley factories and owned textile patent companies in Providence and New York City. Her paternal family owned an antebellum South Carolina plantation. She has worked in a number of textile companies in southern New England.

KATHLEEN A. McAREAVEY received her Bachelor of Arts degree in theater arts from Providence College and studied textile and costume history at the University of Rhode Island. She works in the financial services industry and has a private practice in textile conservation. She cares for the textile and costume collection at the Attleboro Museum, Attleboro, Mass., where she recently curated an exhibition of Panamanian molas, entitled "Mola Magic."

GAIL FOWLER MOHANTY is executive director of Slater Mill Historic Site in Pawtucket, Rhode Island, where she served as curator from 1991 to 1995. She received her Ph.D. from the University of Pennsylvania. The recipient of the first Samuel Eleazer and Rose Tartakow Levinson Prize from the Society for the History of Technology for her article on Rhode Island weaving and weavers, she has written eleven articles and a book-length manuscript.

DIANE JOYCE MONTENEGRO is a master's degree candidate in the textiles, fashion merchandising, and design department at the University of Rhode Island. Her thesis topic is twentieth-century American textiles for commercial and residential interiors and furnishings, particularly those of Dan Cooper. She holds an undergraduate degree in history from Brandeis University.

ROBERTA NULL-HAIR received her Ph.D. from Texas Woman's University in 1986 with a major in clothing, textile design, and construction. She did postgraduate work in textile conservation at the University of Rhode Island in 1993–94. Presently a curatorial technician at Colonial Williamsburg, she is involved in the relocation and restorage of museum objects at the new DeWitt Wallace Collections and Conservation Building.

MARGARET T. ORDOÑEZ received her Ph.D. from Florida State University. An authority on textile conservation, she teaches that subject and the history of textiles and costume at the University of Rhode Island. She is director of the U.R.I. Historic Textile and Costume Collection. Her research interests include archaeological textiles and conservation-related problems. She was one of the four-member team steering RIQDP.

NANCY ANGELINE POTTER is professor of English (emerita) at the University of Rhode Island. She has published two collections of short stories: *We Have Seen the Best of Our Times* and *Legacies.* She has been a Fulbright lecturer on American literature in Argentina, Chile, and New Zealand and now lives in Richmond, R.I.

LINDA WELTERS received her Ph.D. from the University of Minnesota in 1981. She is professor of textiles, fashion merchandising, and design at the University of Rhode Island, where she teaches costume and textile history and chairs the department. She publishes on a variety of topics, particularly European folk dress. In 1998, she assumed the editorship of *Dress,* the journal of the Costume Society of America. She served as director of RIQDP.

# Index